I0014178

Assessing Information Security

Strategies, tactics, logic and framework

Second edition

Assessing Information Security

Strategies, tactics, logic and framework

Second edition

A VLADIMIROV
K GAVRILENKO
A MICHAJLOWSKI

IT Governance Publishing

Every possible effort has been made to ensure that the information contained in this book is accurate at the time of going to press, and the publisher and the author cannot accept responsibility for any errors or omissions, however caused. Any opinions expressed in this book are those of the author, not the publisher. Websites identified are for reference only, not endorsement, and any website visits are at the reader's own risk. No responsibility for loss or damage occasioned to any person acting, or refraining from action, as a result of the material in this publication can be accepted by the publisher or the author.

Apart from any fair dealing for the purposes of research or private study, or criticism or review, as permitted under the Copyright, Designs and Patents Act 1988, this publication may only be reproduced, stored or transmitted, in any form, or by any means, with the prior permission in writing of the publisher or, in the case of reprographic reproduction, in accordance with the terms of licences issued by the Copyright Licensing Agency. Enquiries concerning reproduction outside those terms should be sent to the publisher at the following address:

IT Governance Publishing
IT Governance Limited
Unit 3, Clive Court
Bartholomew's Walk
Cambridgeshire Business Park
Ely, Cambridgeshire
CB7 4EA
United Kingdom

www.itgovernance.co.uk

© Andrew Vladimirov, Konstantin Gavrilenko, Andriej Michajlowski, 2010, 2014

The authors have asserted the rights of the author under the Copyright, Designs and Patents Act, 1988, to be identified as the author of this work.

First published in the United Kingdom in 2010
by IT Governance Publishing: ISBN 978-1-84928-035-8

Second edition published in 2014
ISBN: 978-1-84928-599-5

'He who is willing and able to take the initiative to exploit variety, rapidity, and harmony – as the basis to create as well as adapt to the more indistinct – more irregular – quicker changes of rhythm and pattern, yet shape the focus and direction of effort – survives and dominates.'

Colonel John Boyd

DEDICATION

To Janna, who made this and other works possible.

PREFACE

When a new software version is released, an updated 'changelog' file outlining all changes since the previous version is supplied. It has been five years since the first edition of this book was published: a remarkably long period for the modern information technology milieu, but perhaps not so for its information security shadow or counterpart. This preface is, effectively, a brief changelog for both the book and the environment it applies to in practice.

Strategy-wise, all of the key principles outlined in the first edition stay in place unchallenged. We did not have to change a single epigraph to any section, and remove or replace any quotations forming the book's logical backbone. The schematics that reflect high-level process structures also remained unaltered. In a nutshell, no Black Swans overriding any of the first edition fundamentals have flown by since. Even some of the technical examples (sadly) remained relevant, and we decided to leave them where they belong while providing new examples and reflecting novel technological challenges where necessary. This particularly applies to the areas of application security testing, client-side gaps, and some rather peculiar physical level and wireless risks. If anything, accelerated technological developments such as expansion of cloud networks, application services, business use of BYOD (Bring Your Own Device) and BYOA (Bring Your Own Application), together with all kinds of interconnected mobile devices, have only strengthened the strategies we have elaborated by forcing downstream security tactics to be more aligned with them.

They have made the *information security zone* more fluid, its borders/attack surfaces less certain, *information security anti-patterns* more pronounced, and the roles of the human factor and processes more critical to security organisation.

The common 'combined arms' approach of modern-day cybercrime makes it sometimes difficult to tell where 'technical hacking' ends and 'social engineering' begins. With the dramatic increase in outsourcing, offshore/nearshore out-staffing, and the use of remote freelance contractors, the border between 'insiders' and 'outsiders' is also blurred. Security audits that have been appropriately selected, planned, executed and responded to are becoming indispensable to address the rising information security issues, whether process, technical or human. Even reasonably educated guesswork on behalf of the would-be designers, implementers and maintainers of security controls just won't do the job any more.

Perhaps the most important update of the second edition is that it has become more 'defender-oriented'. We do concentrate more on what the applicable countermeasures and corrective actions should be, and attempt to supply as much information relevant to the auditee side as this book's scope and purpose would allow. Hence, we hope that it has somehow shifted from a targeted treatise on "what a CIO, CTO, CISO, Director of Information Services, or other concerned manager or professional should know about information security assessments" towards a more generic guide to good information security practices, written from both the auditor's and the auditee's perspective. Nevertheless, the auditor's view – or even the attacker's – is still preserved as the predominant, so that the dynamics of this work (and the entire field) are not stalled, and the seeds of the passive check-list attitude are not planted in the readers.

Inevitably, paying more attention to design and implementation of security controls means dedicating more time to the relevant standards and compliance-based frameworks. The most significant compliance change since the first edition of *Assessing Information Security* is the ISO27001:2013 release that has finally superseded the battered 2005 version of this key international information security management standard exactly a year ago. It took us another year to realise the practical significance of this transition by working as both ISO27001:2013 auditors and implementation consultants (for different customers). Describing ISO27001:2013 in detail, or the differences between it and the previous 2005 version of the standard, are not the aims of this work – such publications are already abundant. Where appropriate, however, references to ISO27001:2013 and its Annex A have been added, and overall the second edition of the book is more heavily ISO27001:2013-based. As a side note, we find the following peculiarities introduced in the new version of the Standard worth mentioning in the context of this preface:

- ISO27001:2013 does not mandate the use of PDCA (Plan-Do-Check-Act) cycle anymore. So, for instance, an OODA loop or any combination of nested OODA loops can be applied instead. Nevertheless, we still recommend the hybrid of PDCA and OODA as suggested in the first edition of this book (see *Figure 7*).

- ISO27001:2013 does not explicitly mandate asset-based risk management. So, an 'asset' now could be what we call a "centre of gravity" using the terminology of military strategy. This could provide a very effective approach to both assigning ownership of risks (a requirement of the new Standard!) and prioritising their treatments.

Preface

- Talking about risks, we were pleasantly surprised to see that ISO27001:2013 has adapted a new definition of risk based upon uncertainty, almost as if the standard's authors took to their hearts all that we wrote about 'friction' in the previous edition. Saying that, the more traditional definition remains in use here as more practical for the purpose of quantifying risks.

To summarise, we do hope that this renewed edition of *Assessing Information Security* will become a useful supplementary guidance for ISO27001:2013 auditors and implementers alike. It is not limited to this specific standard, however, and should be helpful in obtaining and maintaining compliance to the PCI DSS (version 3.0 is referenced), SSAE16 SOC1/2, and any other standards or regulations where performing information security assessments, whether third-party or internal, and handling their outcome is a key requirement. Besides, to our knowledge, this book continues to be the only printed source that addresses managing information security audits at all levels and of all types, from physical security checks to social engineering and penetration tests, on both the auditor's and the auditee's sides, regardless of compliance dependencies and adopted frameworks. In fact, it aims to provide a generic strategic principles-based framework, which can always be applied when there is none, and has been proven by many years of practice. It can be consulted when you need an independent security assessment, or want to set up an internal audit team, or review your vendors' or partner companies' levels of security, or even run your own information security services business. Taking into account the possible requirements of government organisations, the real use cases, perhaps, go well outside the original scope we envisioned.

ABOUT THE AUTHORS

Dr. Andrew A. Vladimirov, CCNP, CCDP, CISSP, CWNA, TIA Linux+, is a security researcher with a wide scope of expertise, ranging from network security and applied cryptography, to the relevant aspects of bioinformatics and neural networking. He published his first scientific paper at the age of 13 and is one of the co-founders of Arhont Ltd, one of the leading information security consultancies in the UK. Andrew has an extensive background in performing information security assessments, ranging from external and internal penetration tests, to configuration, security policies, processes and procedures reviews. He has also participated in creating and implementing ISMS and secure architecture designs for large companies, assisted corporations with meeting ISO27001, FSA Annex 2 and other compliance demands, and took part in numerous forensic investigations. Andrew has published a variety of security advisories and papers, authored a chapter on wireless security in Network Security: The Complete Reference, McGraw-Hill/Osborne, and is a co-author of Wi-Foo: The Secrets of Wireless Hacking, Addison Wesley (2004) and Hacking Exposed: Cisco Networks, McGraw-Hill/Osborne (2006). On the basis of these publications and his relevant practical experience, he has composed and read tailored public and private training courses on the subjects of internal security audits, information security strategies, and wireless offence and defence. Andrew is supportive of both open source and full disclosure movements. He is a graduate of King's College London and the University of Bristol.

About the Authors

Konstantin V. Gavrilenko (London, UK) has more than 15 years' experience in IT and security, and together with his co-authors, is a co-founder of Arhont Ltd. Konstantin's writing draws primarily from his real-world knowledge and experience in security consultancy and infrastructure hardening, for a vast range of clients. He is open-minded and enthusiastic about research, where his main areas of interest lie in information security in general and, more specifically, in networking and wireless. He is proud to say that he is an active supporter of open source solutions and ideology, public disclosure included. Konstantin has published a variety of advisories uncovering new software vulnerabilities, alongside essays on assessment types and methodologies, articles on other information security-related topics, and is a co-author of the bestselling Wi-Foo: The Secrets of Wireless Hacking, Addison Wesley (2004) and Hacking Exposed: Cisco Networks, McGraw-Hill/Osborne (2006). He holds a first class BSc Honours degree in Management Science from DeMontfort University and an MSc in Management from Lancaster University.

Andriej A. Michajlowski (London, UK) first became enticed by UNIX flavours back in high school times. He cultivated and expanded his knowledge into the networking aspects of information technology, while obtaining his bachelor's degree from the University of Kent at Canterbury. Soon he was engrossed in network security and penetration testing of various wireless and wired devices and systems. On accomplishing his MBA, he co-founded information security company, Arhont Ltd, participated in security research, published articles and advisories, and greatly contributed to the overall success of the Arhont team. Andriej's technical particularities include user and device authentication mechanisms, database and directory services, wireless networking and application security, and systems integration. He has participated in compliance consulting at many financial and legal sector organisations, and has extensive experience in performing internal and external information security assessments. Andriej has also co-authored Wi-Foo: The Secrets of Wireless Hacking, Addison Wesley (2004) and Hacking Exposed: Cisco Networks, McGraw-Hill/Osborne (2006).

CONTENTS

Introduction..1
Chapter 1: Information security auditing and strategy
....19
   The mindsets of ignorance...24
   Defence-in-depth...48
   Compelling adversaries to adapt.................................54
Chapter 2: Security auditing, governance, policies and
compliance 67
   General security policy shortcomings...........................94
   Addressing security audits in policy statements..........100
   The erroneous path to compliance..............................103
   Getting down to earth...106
Chapter 3: Security assessments classification...........115
   Black, grey and white box tests..................................118
   Assessments specialisations and actual scopes..........120
   On technical information security assessments...........124
   Server, client and network-centric tests......................125
   IT security testing levels and target areas...................128
   'Idiosyncratic' technical security tests........................134
   On non-technical information security audits..............138
   Premises and physical security checks 139
   Social engineering tests...149
   Security documentation reviews...................................156
   Assessing security processes..162
Chapter 4: Advanced pre-assessment planning..........169
   The four-stage framework..172
   Selecting the targets of assessment.............................177
   Evaluating what is on offer...184
   Professional certifications and education.....................188
   Publications and tools...192

Contents

The auditor company history and size 195
Dealing with common assessment emergencies 203
Chapter 5: Security audit strategies and tactics 207
Centres of gravity and their types 209
Identifying critical points 214
The strategic exploitation cycle 221
External technical assessment recon 225
Social engineering recon 230
Internal technical assessment recon 237
Technical vulnerability discovery process..................243
A brief on human vulnerabilities 258
The tactical exploitation cycle 261
Front, flank, simple, complex 264
The strategies of creating gaps...................................267
Chapter 6: Synthetic evaluation of risks....................275
Risk, uncertainty and ugly Black Swans....................279
On suitable risk analysis methodologies....................282
On treatment of information security risks 285
Relevant vulnerability categories...............................290
Gauging attacker skill 292
Weighting vulnerability impact 295
Contemplating the vulnerability remedy 301
Defining vulnerability risk level 303
Risks faced by large components.................................309
Compound risks, systempunkts and attacker logic 313
Total risk summary utilisation and dissection 318
Chapter 7: Presenting the outcome and follow-up acts
..323
The report audience and style 324
The report summary...328
The report interpretation chapter 331
The bulk of the report 333
Explaining the overall security state 337

Contents

Elaborating on breakdown of risks 338
Using vulnerability origin investigations......................349
Post-audit assistance and follow-up hurdles 368
Chapter 8: Reviewing security assessment failures and auditor management strategies..375
Bad tactics and poor tests...384
On the assessment team ordnance................................391
Of serpents and eagles 400
ITG Resources..409

INTRODUCTION

'We can't just look at our own personal experiences or use the same mental recipes over and over again; we've got to look at other disciplines and activities and relate or connect them to what we know from our experiences and the strategic world we live in. If we can do this we will be able to surface new repertoires and (hopefully) develop a Fingerspitzengefühl[1] for folding our adversaries back inside themselves, morally-mentally-physically – so that they can neither appreciate nor cope with what's happening – without suffering the same fate ourselves.' – Colonel John Boyd

A thorough treatise dedicated to various aspects of information security auditing – including successfully passing an audit – must cover why and what kind of assessments have to be performed subject to a particular situation. This, in itself, depends on a variety of variables, both external (regulations, litigation, customer requirements) and internal (business strategy, plans, politics, culture). Such a thorough treatise is further expected to elaborate by whom, when, how, and in which specific sequence they should be executed. It ought to address how to present the audit results in the most palatable manner and which corrective actions these findings might trigger. On the auditee side, it must cover justifying controls or their absence, presenting objective evidence to the auditors, executing corrective actions and providing sufficient evidence of their execution. Everything we have just listed,

---

[1] This German term literally means 'fingertip feeling', and is synonymous with the English expression of 'keeping finger on the pulse', while emphasising intuition.

however, is mere technicality. If you concentrate on them too much and without applying a sufficient level of abstraction and generalisation, you risk missing something of a much greater importance: their logical, strategic, and even philosophical backbone.

You will fall into a trap of adhering to rigid, mindlessly executed 'if-then-else' mechanical instructions. These can easily become outdated and flawed, even by a subtle change in the operating environment – not to mention business, organisational, market or regulatory change. A smart opponent can outwit them using non-conventional methods. Until the new, appropriate schemes are generated – usually by someone else and late – you are lost. Any approach without a solid strategy is destined to remain reactive.

Conversely, if you have a firm, holistic grasp of the whole picture and understand what we may rightfully call 'the philosophy of information security', you can easily adjust to any change on the fly, and with minimal expense. Even more, you can shape the change yourself, become its primary engine and source. This means that you will be able to dictate the rules of the game, and it is others that will have to adapt. Or – to put it plainly – submit. The 'bird's-eye view' idiom is misleading: an eagle hovering high in the clouds can spot a tiny mouse lurking in thick grass and nosedive in no time. This is a good analogy to describe what we have alluded to as "a sufficient level of abstraction", coupled with a rapid and precise low-level, 'ground' act.

Unfortunately, when we have scoured for what others have said about 'the philosophy of information security' and its implications towards security assessments in specialised texts, we were strongly disenchanted. We stumbled across multiple security management sources presenting solely managerial perspectives; technical displaying purely technological perspectives; and legal offering exclusively legal perspectives. Numerous works are written on the subject of social engineering, but they are neither produced by expert psychologists nor take into account technological means that enhance social engineering attacks in a sufficient depth. The existing information security standards are presented as some kind of an infallible verity that contains everything a security specialist might need. Adaptation and implementation in every particular case is left solely to the experience of implementer, as if no hints could be provided. There are multiple occasions of transient, specific or narrowly technical statements passed as grand philosophical truths. Tactical discourses are presented as strategic paradigms. Endless arguments about information security being a process, approach, system, a state of mind or even a lifestyle are rampant. Generalisations like "be paranoid", "security through obscurity never works", or "everything is vulnerable" are omnipresent. We are not implying that these are somehow entirely incorrect. They have their time, place, value and significance – but they do not form a coherent integral framework that can be easily adapted to a variety of relevant situations in both theory and practice.

Then we have turned to other disciplines for guidance. For instance, we have looked at modern mathematical chaos and game theories. In fact, we have borrowed from them. These are fine examples of applicable 'coherent integral frameworks' that offer useful insights. It was the philosophy of war and its core principles, however, that truly hit the nail on a head. This is hardly surprising. When writing *Wi-Foo*, we employed numerous quotes from ancient Chinese military masterminds as epigraphs for the majority of chapters. Being highly reusable and appropriate, some of these epigraphs would be repeated in this book. We have left them in place for the second edition, too. At that time, we found the high suitability of statements written more than two thousand years ago to what is still considered a cutting edge technology today at the very least amusing. Besides, they provided a necessary symbolic martial arts link. In this work, however, the assertions, opinions, estimations and judgements of master strategists of all times are not just some fancy spice-up citations and epigraphs to attract certain categories of audience. They form its *fluid backbone*. They are the "Mozart" part of "Mozart and I".

Apart from the noted completeness, coherence, all-around applicability, systematic nature and apt abstraction, we are fond of taking advantage of the philosophy of war for the following reasons:

- Focus on conflict and its polarity – no toying around!

- Realism and utilitarianism (one who does not apply it properly may be doing it for the last time!).

- Simplicity and clarity of statements (often at lack in numerous security policies we came across).

- Clear distinction between strategy and tactics (a flaw more common in ISMS we have observed than one might think).

- Taking into account wide selection of variables (organisational, technical, but – above all – human!).

- Reusable terminology (which is also not technology-specific and can be comprehended at any organisational level).

- Multidisciplinary approach (as is the field of information security itself, ranging from applied cryptography to personnel background checks).

Introduction

As a matter of fact, the contextual replacement of 'war' or its synonyms by 'information security' or 'information security assessment' in many excerpts of military classics naturally produces shrewd observations. Practise this technique on Carl von Clausewitz's infamous saying, *'Everything is very simple in war, but the simplest thing is difficult'*, and see where it might lead your thoughts. Then perform this simple exercise every time you encounter a classic martial citation in this book.

Of course, applying philosophy and strategy of war to other disciplines is not news. In particular, this was extensively (and, perhaps, excessively) done in business management. We have even encountered a linguistic opinion stating that "Sūn Zǐ Bīng Fǎ", traditionally translated as "Sun Tzu's Art of War", actually means "Sun Tzu Competitive Strategies". The Boston Consulting Group book, *Clausewitz on Strategy*, affirms: *'As perplexing as this may appear at first for a work on warfare, Clausewitz speaks loudly and clearly to the modern business executive who is inclined to listen. He does not, of course, speak the language of today's audience. He does better: He speaks the executive's mind.'* This is one of the reasons why we make a sustained heavy use of his thoughts throughout this work. Note that Clausewitz himself did compare business and military conflict: *'It would be better, instead of comparing it with any art, to liken it to business, which is also a conflict of human interests and activities; and it is still more like State policy, which again, on its part, may be looked upon as a kind of business on a great scale.'*

Nonetheless, this approach has met its sharp and objective criticism. The spearhead of critics is that business, after all, is not war. It is more akin to politics and diplomacy. A company is not an army detachment. Its CEO is not a general and is not likely to wield such power. Attempts to do so may actually lead to some of the anti-patterns we warn against later in this book, namely the "stovepipe" and "management by perkele". But perhaps the mightiest blow comes from modern game theory. From its point of view, the majority of situations in business and commerce can be described as 'non-zero-sum games'. That is, at least to an extent they are cooperative. They involve rather complex relationships between different sides with net gain or loss. There is a mutual benefit even from some forms of intercourse with direct competitors. As a security consultancy, we are not at other information security companies' throats. We have met their professionals during numerous industry conferences and informal gatherings. We have exchanged ideas and shared research. We have had many beers together. We may outsource some work to a competitor when specific resources or expertise are scarce. They may outsource it to us under similar conditions. It does not even have to involve commission in all cases. It could be an act of a goodwill to a customer, or birth of a partnership. This is good for business and develops the industry, thus it eventually benefits us all whether we think about it or not. Even the compliance auditors are not enemies no matter how harsh they might be. Years after graduation, many come to realise that the harshest examiners brought the most benefit and, perhaps, were the best.

When it comes to real aims of safeguarding your information and other assets, however, please consider the following suppositions:

- *'At the end of the day, information security is a form of warfare'.*
- *'In essence, it has plentiful similarities with "traditional" counter-intelligence and counter-insurgency efforts'.*

Introduction

- *'Unlike the information security industry, such efforts existed and have evolved for centuries, if not millennia'.*

These are the cornerstone ideas actively elucidated in this book. Note that more than a decade ago RAND researchers John Arquilla and David Ronfeldt coined a term – 'netwar' – to distinguish "an emergent form of low intensity conflict, crime, and activism" waged employing "decentralized and flexible network structures". Now we can observe such never-ending global scale conflict in everyday news. These researchers also proposed the somewhat ill-fated term 'cyberwar', which is constantly abused and misunderstood by media and general public who think it's all about 'hacking'.

Returning to game theory:

- *'Applied information security is a zero-sum or strictly competitive game'.*

Cooperating with a cyber criminal does not make more sense than collaborating with a burglar who broke into your house. The same applies to a disgruntled employee who has decided to sabotage business or sell internal data to a competitor. The reasons for it could vary, and the perpetrator might even have a point. However, the latter is for the court to decide, and in this book we are interested in the end result. One can, and should learn a lot from security incidents, but this is not cooperation. Collaboration with criminals, no matter what the possible justification, is a crime per se. Cooperation with the enemy is treason. According to Clausewitz, *'the principle of polarity is only valid when it can be conceived in one and the same thing, where the positive and its opposite the negative, completely destroy each other. In a battle both sides strive to conquer; that is true polarity, for the victory of the one side destroys that of the other'*. Thus, we conclude that the philosophy and strategy of war is fully applicable to the field of information security in theory and practice, when real security issues are dealt with.

Where does it bring us? Let's formulate some basic founding principles.

- *'Information security is the science and art of protecting data and other assets'*.

It is not merely a system, process, approach, service, set of methods, mindset, and so forth. It is all of those things listed and much more. We will discuss the perceived 'science versus art' dichotomy at the end of the very last chapter of this book.

- *'IT security is the science and art of protecting information in electronic format'*.

IT security is a sub-discipline of general information security. Protecting information in electronic format inevitably includes defending all systems, media and communication channels that carry it one way or another. It will also affect all people that have, or can potentially have access to this data and resources, and physical means of such access.

- *'Information security assessments are a practical way of improving the state of information security'*.

They can and should be about more than evaluating the risks, or verifying compliance to security policies, or finding and consequently eliminating tangible security gaps. This is the main subject of our study.

Further interesting clarifications can be gathered from the so-called teleology of conflict. Anatol Rapoport was a renowned mathematician and a Nobel Prize winner with major contributions to game theory and cybernetics. In his foreword to a (much criticised) Penguin edition of Carl von Clausewitz's opus magnum, *On War*, Prof. Rapoport suggested three main teleological concepts of warfare:

- eschatological
- political
- cataclysmic

In Rapoport's own words, '*metaphorically, in political philosophy war is compared to a game of strategy (like chess); in eschatological philosophy, to a mission or the dénouement of a drama; in cataclysmic philosophy, to a fire or an epidemic.*'

From the information security specialist's standpoint, we find the eschatological approach to be nearly irrelevant. It has played a grand role in the history of mankind, primarily due to its immense propaganda value and power. Examples of classical 'eschatological conflicts' include crusades, jihads, Communist 'final worldwide revolution', Nazi 'domination of the master race' and American 'Manifest Destiny'. The instances which are closer to this particular discourse are the so-called 'war on drugs', 'war on guns' or 'war on knife crime' sometimes declared by law enforcement bodies. Being realists, we understand that in a foreseeable future there will be junkies, dealers, shootings and stabbings unless some unthinkable miracle happens. In a similar manner, you may announce and promote the epic 'war on cyber crime', 'war on SPAM', or 'war on web application insecurities'. It may motivate some people to do something about these issues in your organisation, but that is the best you can hope to achieve by such an act.

Introduction

The political concept of warfare is the one we find to be the most pragmatic, fruitful and efficient. In relation to applied information security, it is advocated throughout this entire work. As such, it can be rightfully dubbed 'Neo-Clausewitzian'. This is particularly evident in the second chapter of the book, which is dedicated to directing and shaping effects that policies, governance and compliance have on information security assessments and their outcomes. Note that the political approach is always heavily at play when security budget and other resource considerations are discussed.

Unfortunately, many security professionals consciously or instinctively adhere to what can amount to a cataclysmic concept of information security. This outlook seems to be common among both management and 'techs', especially those with no security-centric background. It is reflected in viewing security as a mere part of business continuity, disaster recovery and prevention, or even service availability. In application development, security flaws might be viewed on par with other bugs, with no priority given to their elimination. It is often expressed by the essentially defeatist 'c'est la vie' statements, such as "everything can and would be hacked anyway", "we can do our best, but sensitive data will still leak out", or "by providing our information to the Cloud we are losing control over it anyway". It appeals on the grounds of realism, along the line that "the pessimist is a well-informed optimist". *However, we scorn this way of thinking as fundamentally, strategically flawed no matter how correct it **seems** to be.*

Such a cataclysmic approach to information security reduces initiative, decreases morale, and promotes passive defensive, reactive responses, if not paralysis of action. By succumbing to it, one may even start accepting security incidents as something close to a divine wrath that can only be (partially) softened by countermeasures and insured against. *'Experienced security auditors should be able to determine whether the cataclysmic doctrine dominates the company's or organisation's information security paradigm, and deliver appropriate warnings and explanations'.*

Having said all of the above, of course, it does not matter that the company or organisation should not have implemented a quality incident response and business continuity and disaster recovery plans. Information security standards do not include these within the list of controls (such as ISO27001:2013 Annex A 16 and 17) by accident. What we imply is that these are only one line of what should be a multi-layered defence. The last line.

Comparing a natural disaster or unfortunate accident to premeditated malice is senseless. Even if the end effects and even some of the countermeasures appear to be the same, both preventive and reactive responses will have to differ. Assessing the related risks, and predicting their likelihood and impact, will be distinct. To summarise,

- *'There are "passive" and "active" security incidents'.*

Accidentally losing a memory stick or portable computer with sensitive data is a common instance of the former. Deliberate unauthorised access is an example of the latter. This can be compared to non-combat and combat-related losses in the military.

- *'Passive security incidents happen due to error only'.*
- *'Active security incidents happen due to the combination of error and hostile action'.*

Practically every successful attack involves some mistake on the defender's side. Infectious disease happens when virulence of the microbe and lack of immunity of the infected host, augmented by poor hygiene, are superimposed.

- *'Passive security incidents can easily pave the way for their active counterparts'.*

An accidental access control flaw or sensitive information leak are likely be deliberately abused later. It is better to be prepared for the worst and base any impact estimations on it.

- *'Security assessments must evaluate probabilities and potential impacts of both passive and active security incidents'.*

While different in nature, both present significant risks that should be reduced. Besides, see the previous point.

- *'To assess the likelihood of passive security incidents, it is usually sufficient to analyse controls, their implementations and enforcement'.*

In the example of accidental loss of data on a portable carrier, it is generally enough to verify that:

1. correct security policies that prohibit the use of portable storage media in the company or organisation are present.
2. all users are aware of them and have agreed in a written form.
3. the policies are reinforced by appropriate technical means, such as specialised software blocking use of all USB ports on all systems involved.

4. the enforcing software is present on all corporate systems that contain, or may contain, sensitive data (mind BYOD and telecommuter systems!). It is correctly installed, configured, maintained and documented. Users cannot easily disable it, and such action will trigger a policy violation alarm.

Alternatively, the prohibition of use can be substituted by appropriately employing strong cryptography to protect data on portable computers, smartphones and mobile media.

However:

- *'To assess the probability and impact of active security incidents, a more aggressive and all-encompassing path must be taken'.*

In the example above we will have to add the fifth point: verify that our USB port blocking software cannot be circumvented. If this is possible, then it becomes necessary to discover how much effort and skill such a hack would require from a potential attacker. And then the sixth: check whether other mobile storage media that does not rely on USB ports can be and is used to carry information. For instance, can sensitive data be automatically copied to any such media over Wi-Fi, Bluetooth or any other wireless connection? If encryption is employed, strength of ciphers, keys and its actual implementation, key management in particular, must be analysed. Again, one must estimate how much skill, effort and time the attacker has to expend to break it. Are there any publicly available tools or exploits one can simply download and run? In a nutshell, all these additional security auditing means are a form of *penetration testing,* which is always active and highly intrusive intervention.

Introduction

Thus, we have finally arrived to a crucial statement of unequalled, unsurpassed gravity:

- *'Prevention and mitigation of any hostile information security act always involves the clash of human wills'.*

Which is, essentially, a specially adapted version of:

- *'all war supposes human weakness, and against that it is directed'* (Clausewitz)

While this is common sense ("guns don't kill people, people kill people"), in information security it is strongly obscured and obfuscated by technology, bureaucracy and lack of abstraction. Even when you are dealing with a 'purely technical' threat such as viruses, worms and other malware, you are not battling an inanimate piece of code. It is nothing less than your and your allies will against the will of malicious software creators and deliberate users. If you are a technical specialist, just add skill to will. If you are an IT manager or a CISO, that skill is managing or directing the technical team. For some, this may sound unsettling. Still, disgruntled employees, fraudsters, cyber criminals, vandals, industrial spies or political activists are all flesh and bone. Unless your name is John Connor and the year is 2027, you are not engaged in some chimeric stand-off against swarms of hostile intelligent machines.

There are information security consultants that would assume a discussion of social engineering any time 'the human factor' is mentioned. The implications we are looking at in this book are of a much broader scope. In this context, social engineering is one of the highly important technicalities, just like intrusion prevention or antimalware are on the IT side. If Clausewitz meant anything like it when he wrote about war being aimed at human weakness, he would have explicitly written about penetration of enemy ranks by spies. It was the closest equivalent of social engineering at his times. What the master strategist did have in mind is that

- *'the activity in war is never directed solely against matter, it is always at the same time directed against the intelligent force which gives life to this matter, and to separate the two from each other is impossible'*
- *'if we desire to defeat the enemy, we must proportion our efforts to his powers of resistance. This is expressed by the product of two factors which cannot be separated, namely, the sum of available means and the strength of the will'*

Note that the energy in the excerpt is directed at both "matter" and "intelligent force" as they are fully indivisible. The significance of the 'material side' (resources, documentation, technology) is by no means denigrated. Instead, the balance between 'human' and 'material' factors is underlined. *'In the event of any security incident, both will be simultaneously affected because they are inseparable. Therefore, both have to be synchronously implemented, maintained, audited, analysed, measured and improved, so that all available reasonable means of defence are employed, yet you do not overreact'*.

You may still ask what the 19th century military strategist could know about the role and contributory proportions of such things – in particular technologies – in modern times. Collate his words with the following extract from the current US MCDP (Marine Corps Doctrinal Publication) 1 *Warfighting*: *'No degree of technological development or scientific calculation will diminish the human dimension in war. Any doctrine which attempts to reduce warfare to ratios of forces, weapons, and equipment neglects the impact of the human will on the conduct of war and is therefore inherently flawed.'*

Based on multiple observations, we have developed our own little model of the 'clash of wills' in typical information security conflicts. We call it 'the FUD game'. As a reminder, FUD is a common abbreviation standing for Fear, Uncertainty and Doubt. FUD undermines will and leads to paralysis of action.

The rules of the FUD game are simple: the 'attackers' are trying to maximise the FUD of 'defenders' while diminishing their own, and vice versa. Whoever is the first to increase the opponents' FUD above the breakpoint of their will gains the upper hand. A typical defender FUD can be described as:

- *fear* of being successfully compromised (or failing an audit!) and held personally responsible for negligence and blunder.
- *uncertainty* regarding how, where and when the effective blow will occur.
- *doubt* in one's abilities to prevent or mitigate the breach.

A typical attacker FUD encompasses:

- *fear* of being discovered, caught and persecuted.
- *uncertainty* regarding defender preparedness, knowledge, skill and means.
- *doubt* in one's ability to disengage without leaving a give-away trace.

The situation is asymmetric. In the real world, the Uncertainty element tends favour the attacking side. Fear, though, often reinforces competent defenders: in the case of defeat, the (legal) repercussions for attackers are often far more severe. The defending side has another important advantage: there is no actual draw. Repelling the opponents and simply avoiding the breach counts as the defenders' victory. *'The key factors for winning the FUD game appear to be resolve, initiative, good observation and orientation, foresight, cunning and swiftness. Chance always plays its role and cannot be dismissed. Other factors are subordinate, providing that neither side has enormous superiority in technological prowess'.*

With this observation we shall complete this hopefully provocative preamble that sets logical and philosophic grounds for the principal work.

CHAPTER 1: INFORMATION SECURITY AUDITING AND STRATEGY

'We should base our decisions on awareness rather than on mechanical habit. That is, we act on a keen appreciation for the essential factors that make each situation unique instead of from conditioned response.' – MCDP 1 *Warfighting*

Rephrasing Clausewitz, to produce a workable scheme for information security assessments is one of the tasks that are inherently simple, yet the simplest thing is difficult to implement. It is simple because the underlying logic is clear. It can be formulated in a minute. Here it comes from the (independent) auditor's viewpoint:

- Find out about the assessment's goals and conditions.
- Plan the appropriate actions.
- Select the corresponding methodologies and tools.
- Check and test everything you can within the limits of budget, requirements, time and means.
- Ensure that you have collected a sufficient volume of quality objective evidence.
- Analyse it.
- Pull the analysis results together.
- Measure and analyse relevant risks.
- Consider realistic remedies.
- Generate an impressive report.
- Work with the customer on any follow-up acts if needed.

A mirror version of this scheme as seen from the auditee's perspective is also easy to generate and you can try it as an exercise. It will have to be more strategic in nature. To an extent, it is defined in the recent ISO27000 and Annex SL aimed at streamlining various ISO standards. The auditor receives goals and directions, but it is the management of the auditee that formulates and sets them. It must also select suitable auditors for the task and a qualified manager to oversee the process. At the end of the day, for the auditors the assessment is often a separate assignment within a limited timespan of a few days. More often than not, only glimpses of what is really going on in the audited entity are caught. For the auditee it is an element of some larger long-term security program that does not end with passing the assessment. Or, at least, this is how it should be.

Wing Tsun is an effective and increasingly popular Chinese martial art. Bruce Lee derived his Jeet Kune Do from it. There are only eight principles in Wing Tsun. Some even reduce them to four: forward pressure, sticking to the opponent, using the opponent's strength, and centreline control. Reading and comprehending these fundamentals a thousand times will not make you a formidable fighter. That would require many years of intense practice. Still, there is no guarantee that you will win every single fight. Even in very rare cases where the governing principles do not have to be built into a resistant and inert (physical, organisational, corporate) body by dedicated, sustained effort, things are not straightforward. Knowing the major winning strategies will not instantly make you a chess grandmaster. And chess is only an ancient board game with an immutable set of rules.

Unlike chess, in the field of modern information security there are no defined winning strategies accepted by everyone, anywhere, at any time. This leads to two extremes. One is reducing everything to specialised schematics, detailed local standards, checklists and guidelines, and ad-hoc 'technical' countermeasures and safeguards. Correspondingly, the auditors would be asked, or are expected to test and analyse them. When, instead of the expected positive outcome, the auditor uncovers a major program, planning or process non-conformance, it comes as a big surprise. A typical example of such a situation relevant to ISO27001 is paying more attention to Annex A controls than to the body of the standard and thinking "if all Annex A controls are implemented, we will pass". An auditor might also concentrate on Annex A since it provides a comfortable checklist, providing that the requirements of the Standard body appear to be *formally* fulfilled. This approach reduces information security and its assessments to nothing more than craft.

The other extreme tends to be the opposite. Personal experience, judgement and professional intuition are proclaimed as infinitely superior to all other ways, which are usually viewed as too conservative and formal. Detailed planning is often disregarded, and minor non-conformances could be ignored regardless of the real risks they may be associated to. This attitude is common among many security auditors. However, even fine arts have certain rules, and the so-called chaotic systems are mathematically deterministic while looking random at the first sight.

We do not believe that a healthy balance between these extremes cannot be reached. Nor do we think that there are no general strategies, principles and philosophies that can increase the effectiveness of information security audits and streamline them while preserving necessary adaptability, diversity, creativity and initiative. Exactly the same applies to passing the audits from the auditee's side ('the defender') and, on a more general note, to designing and implementing a workable information security management system and its controls. After all, military science does research and has employed such fundamentals for centuries. Is sustaining and assessing information security of a company or organisation of any size more complex than waging a modern interstate combat? Some theoretical groundwork for a potentially productive approach to this issue was already laid in the introduction, and a few broad principles were formulated. But prior to proceeding further with this ambitious exercise, we need to address that annoying 'why' question.

To do or not to do?

> *'Military action is inauspicious – it is only considered important because it is a matter of life and death, and there is the possibility that it may be taken up lightly.'* – Li Quan.

There are many sound theoretical and logical reasons why information security assessments, whether internal or external, must be performed. They come from both managerial and technical perspectives. The majority of these reasons are maintenance-related and can be summarised as 'if things are not regularly verified, analysed and improved by specialists they would go wrong and eventually collapse'. Alas, the 'improvement' part (Section 10 in the body of ISO27001:2013) is frequently understated. More often than not, in the real world these reasons are simply ignored. Companies or organisations that subscribe for professional security auditing usually do it because:

1. compliance and regulations, or customer contracts demand it.

Today, the PCI Security Standards Council seems to be the most successful at that. SSAE16 (usually adapted by service providers), FISMA and HIPAA in the US, and FSA (primarily its chapter on IT Controls) in the UK definitely deserve some credit. ISO27001 is also gaining popularity, at times because large customers demand it and it is easier to certify to the Standard and pass one monitoring assessment per year rather than several assessments from such customers. Failing a customer (second party) assessment could lead to a contract loss. If the profit brought in by such a contract exceeds the costs of formal certification the latter should be opted for without a second thought, not least because of the additional benefits brought in. Quite often, certification to an internationally recognised standard is a market opener, especially for foreign companies that begin operating in the West.

2. a serious security incident has happened.

One that's been caned is worth two that haven't, for sure. At least some of the security audits we have performed in the past were follow-ups to computer forensics. It does take some pain to realise that if no preventative action is taken its reactive counterpart can become a never-ending loop. Besides, at times only security auditing (often external) can help to establish the root cause of an incident.

3. there is someone with high security awareness and understanding amid the executives who lobbies it through.

This usually applies to specialised high-tech companies or government agencies.

4. the company or organisation is a lucrative target for cyber criminals or malcontents and knows it.

This is commonly complemented by points 1 and 2. Aspiring to 3 is warmly recommended.

5. there is an internal security auditing team in the company anyway.

They should be kept busy to justify their salaries.

Other, less common causes can drive such a decision, too. For example, we ran (internal) IT security assessments for companies where the IT management head had just changed. So, the new IT director wanted to clean the house, get a better grasp of what is going on and, no doubt, show the bosses that his predecessor was incompetent. We have also performed independent security reviews of novel pre-production appliances, services and software for their vendors.

The mindsets of ignorance

Overall, it is more educating and informative to analyse the surprisingly persistent reasons explaining why companies and organisations *do not* perform any information security assessments. If they have a turnover of six digits or more, we can safely bet that these reasons are within the managers' skulls no matter what they might say about the budget. There are three most common 'mindsets of ignorance'.

1. *'The "it will never happen to us"/"it always happens to other people" mindset'*

We will not tell hair-raising stories about wily cyber criminals and sly insiders in return. This is constantly done by today's media – just visit any major news site. The hype is such that at times even the report of a not-so-critical and specific technical security issue makes it to the top ten read on BBC News. With his metaphor of knights and dragons, Ira Winkler has already examined the security media hype very well – consult his *Zen and the Art of Information Security* book if interested. What we will note, nonetheless, is that 'it' always befalls those 'it will never happen to' because they are not prepared. Consider it our modest contribution to Murphy's laws. By the way, "but it has never happened to us and we are in business for many years" should be translated as "we don't have an effective monitoring system set up and maintained, and audit trails are not our strongest point". Pick up any company that claims so and verify their incident detection and response processes and controls if you disagree.

Another variety of this tune people frequently whistle to is "our data (systems, networks) are not interesting for any assailants-to-be". First of all, one has to be in the attacker's shoes to know what is intriguing for such a person and what isn't. Then, how would the assailants guess that it is not interesting until they gain access to it? And if it is truly the case, why waste time and effort on gaining this access while it can be used for other amusing things, such as hacking into 'more interesting' systems to hide their tracks and preserve resources at your expense? Or launching DDoS (distributed denial-of-service) attacks, whether commercially or politically motivated. Or sending SPAM. Or distributing 'wares and pr0n'. Or anything else. Nowadays, no sane attackers will ever perform any such activities from systems that can be traced back to them. It even comes to selectively targeting countries with weak cyber crime laws to establish a foothold for further attacks from there. Until a few years ago, Brazil was the favourite. After its legal system was improved the focus shifted to Vietnam. On some days the overall number of attacks launched from (read – 'via') this country could reach a half of all registered attacks in the world. To underline this point, modern cyber crime is a big business, botnets are lucrative, and there are hundreds of things that could be done (ab)using a hijacked system or service. Very few of these have a relation to that system's original purpose. Besides, many attacks are simply opportunistic and indiscriminate, like spraying bullets in the dark.

It has been said that selling information security is akin to selling insurance. However, insurance typically covers what we might call 'passive' incidents. The difference in approach towards the passive and the active has been already reviewed in the preface.

2. 'The "shiny box with flashing lights" mindset'

The "it will never happen to us" is a major overall information security issue. The "shiny box with flashing lights" mindset is more pertinent to information security assessments and preparation for them. It is human nature to associate security with something palpable, like walls, doors, locks, safes and barbed wire. Vendors actively exploit this perception for profit. Buy this appliance and you will become secure. Buy that software and you will become compliant. To stay secure and compliant, however, you need a whole complex of interrelated measures, many of which are not technical or cannot be solved by any technology. Recall the discussion of 'human' and 'matter' factors in the introduction. Guns alone never win wars. Even on a purely technical level, the safeguard must be properly positioned, configured, maintained and usually interconnected with other relevant systems and applications. Adversaries should not be able to bypass it by either a frontal or lateral attack. To ensure that all of this is done right and eliminate inevitable errors, timely IT or physical security audits are a must. Otherwise, there is a good chance that you have simply wasted your cash on that precious intrusion prevention system, content filter or firewall.

Did anything really change from the first edition of this book? Well, the *"shiny box with flashing lights"* mindset has been complemented by its *"shiny SaaS (software-as-a-service) app with colourful buttons"* service equivalent. Subscribing to a third-party service is more economical, and is it not run by the real specialists in the field your company cannot afford? It usually is, but do they really know about your business requirements, organisation, politics, typical user behaviour, environment changes, and so on? Even moving everything to the Cloud may not resolve all of the associated information security problems, rather creating a comfortable and affordable illusion of such a resolution. A new section (A.15) on analysing security (and reliability) of suppliers and supply chains has been added to ISO27001:2013 for a good reason.

3. *The "we are glad to accept this risk" mindset'*

This attitude is typical for people who are able to see through the media and general public hype. As a result, they adopt the "devil is not so black as he is painted" view. However, common sense tells that you cannot reduce, retain or transfer risks without a prior professional, desirably independent risk evaluation. How else could you justify exclusion or inclusion of controls (now mandated by ISO27001:2013 in relation to its Statement of Applicability)? Which brings us back to the topic of security assessments.

Are there any companies or organisations that actually do not need any information security audits at all? At the very minimum, such an entity would have to:

* stay away from personal and other sensitive data, such as customer databases, customer data and trade secrets.

- thoroughly vet and fully trust all its employees, partners and guests.

- be disconnected from the Internet and other untrusted networks.

We have never encountered such a corporate or governmental body in the real world.

On monetary contemplations

'Benefit and harm are interdependent, so the enlightened always consider them.' – Ho Yanxi

The budget is the main restricting factor in performing information security assessments and, in fact, in doing anything involving information security at all. Even during a financial crisis no highly skilled professional auditor or implementer wishes to toil for pennies. At the same time, selling security services is a raw spot of all companies that offer them.

Information security audits are 'intangible'. Many countermeasures and controls are just as intangible: consider what is often referred to as 'the change in corporate security culture'. We have already discussed the "shiny box with flashing lights" mindset, its current state and expected outcome. Even those who understand the need to perform security assessments often purchase 'the shiny box' or subscribe for 'the shiny service' first and only then ask the auditors to test its usability and integration. This is potential financial and man-hour loss. The assessors may or may not recommend getting the 'box/service/app' in the first place. They could advise you to get a somewhat different solution or position it at the bottom of the risk treatment/corrective actions priority list.

They may suggest that a cheaper solution will suffice. In any case, if you have decided to seek professional advice (which is a necessary outcome of any proper security audit), get it first and then put it to good use. Avoid making uninformed guesses, and note that the availability of numerous third-party services to subscribe to, often run by little-known start-ups, makes it all only more confusing for the decision maker.

To make the situation worse, practical end results of information security audits are usually 'negative'. By 'negative' we mean that auspicious security assessments do not make easily recognisable good things happen. They stop the bad ones from unexpectedly popping up. In the words of the ancient Chinese strategist Ho Yanxi, *'when trouble is solved before it forms, who calls that clever?'* We have already stated that subscribing to regular security assessments is somewhat akin to getting an insurance policy, but paying for something not to occur is not even an insurance premium. It is more like charges for in-depth private medical examinations. You do not undergo them to increase your direct income, and the procedures can be rather costly. They are 'a matter of life and death', however, that 'may be taken up lightly' by many.

Thus, from the financial standpoint information security audits (and security in general) are always viewed as necessary evil. Psychologically, everyone wants to save on this evil and convince themselves that it isn't so necessary after all. Information security is traditionally valued only in terms of reducing loss, and practically never as a profit generating factor. To aggravate the issue, a significant part of this loss is, again, intangible. Have a look at the costs of IT failure as stated in the ITILv3 "Service Design". In accordance with this widely accepted set of best practices for IT service management, the tangible costs can include:

- *Lost user productivity*
- *Lost IT stuff productivity*
- *Lost revenue*
- *Overtime payments*
- *Wasted goods and materials*
- *Imposed fines or penalty payments*

The intangible costs can comprise:

- *Loss of customers*
- *Loss of customer goodwill (customer dissatisfaction)*
- *Loss of business opportunity (to sell, gain new customers and revenue, etc.)*
- *Damage to business reputation*
- *Loss of confidence in IT service provider*
- *Damage to staff morale*

Regarding the second category, ITILv3 states that *'it is important not simply to dismiss the intangible costs (and the potential consequences) on the grounds that they may be difficult to measure'*. Indeed, designing any financial metrics on information security remains difficult unless we talk about specific cases of online services' availability and their downtime due to attacks. The majority still sticks to the traditional metrics, such as the number of incidents per period of time, and will continue to do so.

To emphasise, the damages listed above are assumed to result from accidental failure, disaster or seldom lapse. In the case of a directed and planned act of a hostile intelligent force, they would be naturally magnified. Additional legal and investigative expenses are likely to be incurred. External public perception of the events would also be unfavourably different. Everyone is sympathetic to victims of a genuine cataclysm. In our highly competitive world, this is not so when *avoidable* trouble is deliberately caused by fellow humans. Vae victis – "Woe to the vanquished!" There is at least one bank that none of the authors would use because it has suffered far too many security incidents that led to sizeable losses. This is not misfortune: every bank is regularly attacked by cyber criminals and other fraudsters, but the outcome is different. This is negligence.

Examine another curious observation we have made: if the act is deliberate, tangible and intangible losses tend to be more interconnected and amplify each other to a larger extent. According to Clausewitz, *'it is chiefly the moral force which is shaken by defeat, and if the number of trophies reaped by the enemy mounts up to an unusual height, then the lost combat becomes a rout'*. Making things worse, the disclosed security incidents often attract more assailants. The bad guys start viewing the victim company or organisation as a soft target and step in like marauders.

Is it possible to consider information security as a potential source of profit? ITILv3 "Service Strategy" explicitly names security as the essential element of warranty. The other key elements are availability, continuity and capacity. Note that all three are dependent, or at least can be heavily influenced by their security counterpart. Indeed, all three are covered in the corresponding sections of ISO27001:2013 Annex A, and from the security specialist's perspective, availability is the A in the infamous CIA triad. *'Warranties in general'*, continues the ITIL, *'are part of the value proposition that influences customers to buy'.* Nowadays, utility alone would not suffice. What was a differentiator in the past has become the enabler.

This, no doubt, can be effectively exploited in marketing and advertisement. There are a great deal of services and products that come from different vendors yet their utility is essentially the same. As everyone is catching up with the general technological side, the difference in security can provide the margin needed to overcome competition. This is especially true in the areas where trust is the key, as when the customer entrust their key business processes, commercial secrets or employees' personal data to a third-party service or product. At the same time, such a difference may not be very difficult to achieve. We have effectively partnered and regularly worked with IT integration and maintenance companies. Our assistance has allowed them to offer customers discounted security audits and mitigation and implementation services as parts of a complete service package.

Of course, using information security as a selling point to achieve service or product warranty superior to that of your competitors carries its share of risks. It must be done with caution, since the detrimental effects of any security blunder in a commercial proposition of this sort would be magnified. The balance of expenditure on the security element of the offer, which can easily grow to an unacceptable level, must be constantly checked against the additional profits gained. This approach is by no means impossible, however. It only takes some initiative, confidence and solid skills:

- *'Therefore armed struggle is considered profitable, and armed struggle is considered dangerous.' (Sun Tzu)*

- *'For the skilled it is profitable, for the unskilled it is dangerous.' (Cao Cao)*

Thus we conclude this brief discussion of 'why's' in respect to finance and choice and can safely turn back to more 'philosophical' strategic matters.

The fundamentals

'War is only a part of political intercourse, therefore by no means an independent thing in itself. **It has certainly a grammar of its own, but its logic is not peculiar to itself.**' – Carl von Clausewitz

By definition, this is the most vital section of this book. Comprehending and putting the rest of the material to good practice depends on gaining firm understanding of the fundamental principles. A lot of them are pure logic and common sense, and are applicable for the auditor and auditee alike. Nevertheless, until the maxim is clearly formulated, its meaning and use will remain beneath the surface. That is, in the realm of intuition.

We have already expressed some of the basic postulates in the introduction. To recap the most relevant ones:

- *'Information security is the science and art of protecting data and other assets'.*
- *'IT security is the science and art of protecting information in electronic format'.*
- *'Information security assessments are a practical way of improving the state of information security'.*
- *'Security assessments must evaluate probabilities and potential impacts of both 'passive' and 'active' security incidents'.*

- *'To assess the likelihood of passive security incidents, it is usually sufficient to analyse controls, their implementations and enforcement'.*

- *'To assess the probability and impact of active security incidents, a more aggressive and all-encompassing path must be taken'.*

- *'"Human" and "material" information security elements have to be synchronously planned, designed, implemented, audited, analysed, measured and improved'.*

Like the scheme in the beginning of this chapter, these principles are sufficiently general to be applied to any security assessment (and preparation for it) in any given situation. When we have looked at information security auditing from the bird's-eye perspective trying to dissociate ourselves from narrow technological and procedural aspects, twenty such principles have surfaced. Let us list and analyse them in brief.

1. *'Information security assessment is an act of corporate or organisational politics'.*

This is a pure Clausewitzian statement that goes well with his infamous statement that *'war is not merely a political act, but also a real political instrument, a continuation of political commerce, a carrying out of the same by other means'.* At the end of the day, it is the politics and business goals of a company or organisation that leastwise determine:

- whether an audit will be undertaken.
- when and by whom it is going to be done.
- its overall scope, depth and type.
- how it will be managed from the auditee side.

- how the audit results will be interpreted.
- which actual follow-up reactions will be performed, the next 'monitoring' audit included.

This reflects the planning of large scale security programs by the auditee's management, of which security assessments should be the integral parts.

2. *'Information security assessment is always shaped by political, administrative, technical and human "terrain"'.*

Having strategic and political aims at its roots, the character and performance of information security assessments will be inevitably influenced by the auditee's policies, operations and procedures, technology, corporate culture, relationships and personal traits of the people involved, and so on. This is similar to the effects terrain, environmental conditions, channels of communication, quality and quantity of troops and their armaments have on any battle. Assessments of a bank and a high-tech Californian start-up will be very different, even if done to the same standard, using the same methodologies and tools, and by the same auditor team. Thinking otherwise – as in "the standard <insert the standard name here> is the same for everyone" – is a fallacy.

3. *'Information security assessment must shape information security systems of its target'.*

Any action is reciprocal and triggers reaction. The absence of a tangible response is a type of reaction, too. Even if the security assessment did not identify any gaps, it should still trigger (or prevent) change.

4. *'Information security assessment is never complete'.*

This can be compared with *'the result in war is never absolute'* (Clausewitz). Neither, in accordance with the strategy classic, it has to be: '*but this object of war in the abstract, this final means of attaining the political object in which all others are combined, the disarming the enemy, is by no means general in reality, is not a condition necessary to peace, and therefore can in no wise be set up in theory as a law*'. There is always something else to check, test, verify and analyse. A typical security auditor or audit team only has a few days to collect and analyse sample evidence, which is hopefully representative. A typical penetration test against an infrastructure comprised of thousands of hosts will only encompass a small selection of them, usually defined as standard builds. But are all such builds up to the standard? You cannot discover all the existing flaws. You cannot "disarm the enemy" by foreseeing and preventing every opportunity for hostile acts. Some security auditors are devoted perfectionists, but this perfectionism must be carefully controlled to bear fruit. The approach based on prioritisation of (potential) risks is the key. Some actions can be placed at the bottom of the priority list and postponed for later. Which brings us to the commonly repeated maxim that:

5. '*Information security assessment must be a part of a continuous process*'.

The environment changes. What was secure yesterday is not so today. What was sufficient to become compliant a month ago may be unsatisfactory now. Standards alter. Technology constantly moves forward and can introduce significant correctives – adoption of the Cloud and 'bring your own application' provide good examples. The audit methods evolve. Besides, as stated when examining the previous principle, the next audit can accomplish what the previous did not. In any case, it is clearly required to verify both completeness and correctness of any follow-up reaction to its predecessor. Information security auditing is a powerful *way of monitoring the state of information security*. A stand-alone assessment completely misses this point.

6. *'Information security assessment should maintain proper balance between tempo and depth'.*

As often, the art is in doing as much as you can in as little time as you have. Those days 'for the budget one can get' became a critical addition. Because the conditions change, a protracted audit can end up with findings of its beginning becoming obsolete or irrelevant when the end is reached. All critical vulnerabilities and gaps should be promptly analysed and reported with emergency warnings issued without waiting for the assessment to end – *'each minute ahead of the enemy is an advantage'* (Gen. Blumentritt). Hurrying up and reporting false positives while missing important discoveries, however, is another highly unpleasant extreme.

7. *'Information security assessment must always exceed its **perceived** scope'.*

This principle can be easily misunderstood. It does not mean that you have to go after more targets than were assigned by the audit agreement. What it implies is that the information security of a company or organisation is a complex interconnected system. You cannot analyse a single component of this system without somehow contemplating the rest. Recall the introductory fundamental on material and human factors being simultaneously attacked or evaluated. For instance, the *perceived* scope of an external penetration test is verifying the security state of a network perimeter. At first glance, this task is purely technical, being concentrated on any exposed services and perimeter safeguards. Nevertheless, in the process of testing all related policies and procedures, as well as management, qualifications and skills of the responsible personnel are inevitably checked. This must be accounted for when synthesising and analysing the test results. Another example we have already discussed is the interrelation between security, capacity, resilience and availability. Indeed, *'war is never an isolated act.'* (Clausewitz)

8. *'Information security assessment always targets corporate or organisational ISMS'.*

The ISMS is the glue that ties and holds together different components of the entity's information security. It doesn't matter which particular technical, operational, policy or human elements are assessed, the auditors should always encounter and hit that glue. If at some point they don't, it should be counted as a discovered security gap.

9. *'Information security assessment should aspire to establish the roots of all discovered vulnerabilities, weaknesses and gaps'.*

Security flaws do not condense from utter nothingness. If their root causes are not properly addressed, the flaws reappear and proliferate no matter how hard you are trying to remove them one-by-one. Close one gap and another gap opens. Finding the real source of a problem is an abstract *analytic and synthetic* task that requires both experience and holistic judgement. It can lurk anywhere, at any level. The true cause of what appears to be a solely technical issue could be organisational, procedural or human. In the case of, for example, miscommunication the 'why' of a perceivably human-centric vulnerability can be technical. A gap in security policies can be the origin of any related downstream shortcomings, from faulty processes to misconfigured applications. One issue can have multiple roots. One source can create numerous issues.

10. *'Information security assessment should aspire to discover strategic problems through tactical means'.*

Strategic (planning, program, organisation, policy) blunders are the worst. They have the highest negative impact and usually require tremendous corrective efforts. Yet they are commonly obscured by a cloud of details on lower, 'tactical' planes. When searching for the real source of uncovered problems, try to look as high and as broadly as you can. Metaphorically speaking, an astute security auditor should strive to be able to look at one drop of water and understand the ocean. For example, major shortfalls in high-level information security management and yawning gaps in security policies can sometimes be revealed by scanning networks and systems, or performing configuration reviews and social engineering tests.

11. *'Information security assessment must be endorsed, controlled and debriefed at the top'.*

This is an extension of the much discussed 'top-down' approach in information security management. While it is mandated by ISO27001 (and the latest version of this standard explicitly mandates senior management review, while senior management representatives are expected to take part in the opening and closing meetings of the audit) this is not so with other security-relevant standards. Besides, numerous audits do not follow any common standard anyway. It will have its share of heavy scrutiny in the next chapter. With regard to security assessments, numerous issues the auditors might uncover are likely to require attention and intervention of the top management. Such matters are usually strategic, operational or human, but might be centred on technology if large operational changes, costs or high risks are involved. At the end of the day, the key decisions concerning security audits and their outcome would be either taken, or at least vetted at the entity's top. *'Experience in general also teaches us that notwithstanding the multifarious branches and scientific character of military art in the present day, still the leading outlines of a war are always determined by the cabinet, that is, if we would use technical language, by a political not a military functionary'* (Clausewitz).

12. *'Information security assessment should be understood and appreciated at the bottom'.*

It should not be viewed as an unpleasant distraction negatively interfering with the auditee personnel's duties. In particular, the audit must not create the impression of being an oppressive instrument of the evil managing apparatus. Life is harsh, and at times uncovered offenders are fired or otherwise disciplined because of the assessment's findings. In our practice, there were cases in which what started as a casual internal IT security audit ended up with computer forensics and legal repercussions. Firing, reprimanding and otherwise scourging employees is not some specific goal of information security assessments, however, and is a relatively rare audit outcome. The auditors should endeavour to win sympathies and gain assistance of the auditee staff by presenting themselves as friendly advisers and (where permitted by the nature and conditions of the audit – for instance ISO27001 auditors are only allowed to point at the relevant sections of the ISO27002 guideline) handy troubleshooters. They must never be smug or boss around. Active obstruction and resistance of the auditee personnel at whatever level can easily ruin any security assessment and result in a certification failure. It has to be carefully avoided from both the auditor and the auditee sides.

13. *'Information security assessment must produce transferable, communicable results'.*

Where necessary, the auditors *as a team* should be able to speak the language of operations, asset and risk management, technology, human resources, compliance and even finance. Possible implications of the assessment results for all these areas should be reviewed and appropriately presented. They should be understood top, bottom, left and right, so that the corrective actions that require collaboration are not stalled. If the assessment is technical, writing a brief, clear management summary is a must.

14. *'Information security assessment must decrease the friction of the auditee'.*

Friction is a term we have borrowed from military science. Generally, the 'friction of war' refers to the effects of uncertainty, looseness, suspense and chance. The MCDP 1 *Warfighting* has a great description of what one can rightfully call internal friction: *'Friction may be self-induced, caused by such factors as lack of a clearly defined goal, lack of coordination, unclear or complicated plans, complex task organizations or command relationships, or complicated technologies. While we should attempt to minimize self-induced friction, the greater requirement is to fight effectively despite the existence of friction.'* All we need is to apply this description to corporate or organisational information security is to replace "to fight" with "to operate". *Figure 1* depicts factors that typically contribute to internal friction within a company.

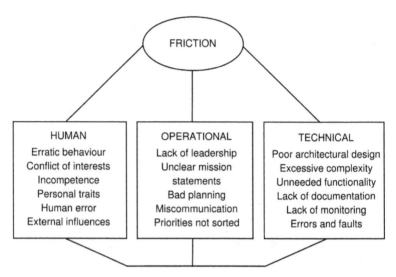

Figure 1: Typical elements of internal friction

Note that these factors are interconnected and, in combination, might give rise to a general detrimental result. By finding and eliminating various flaws and gaps, a thorough information security assessment and its follow-up can reduce internal friction and diminish FUD, at least within its sphere of immediate application. It is a way of monitoring, which implies it being a way of observing and viewing, including of the implementation effectiveness of controls.

15. *'Information security assessment should promote security awareness and initiative'*.

Another useful military term closely related to friction is 'fog of war'. Fog of war refers to the unknown and concealed. It seeks to capture the uncertainty regarding your own capability, the potential adversary capability and adversary intent. From the IT security viewpoint, the

Internet – or any other untrusted public network – is covered with a thick fog of war, condensing into both public and not-so-public clouds. There is a certain amount of this fog clouding your systems and networks, your ISMS, your employees. When information and systems are outside your perimeters – as in the case of work from home and business travel – the volume of this fog grows in geometrical proportions. By dispelling it and increasing security awareness, information security audits curtail friction and FUD. Clarity, knowing more, and understanding what to do stimulates initiative. In contrast, not knowing is often synonymous with not acting.

16. *'Information security assessment always operates with probabilities'.*

Information security audits are a highly practical and effective way of evaluating security risks. Everything else is either a guesswork, or (if based upon incident statistics) reactive. Even when the vulnerability or gap is clearly defined, the risk it presents would always be 'fuzzy'. To measure this risk in a specific real life situation, the auditors will need to weight and gauge numerous variables, some of which are ambiguous, outside the audit scope, or not fully known. Due to the inevitable effects of friction, it is typically senseless to express risks in some absolute 'all-or-nothing' values. Besides, it is not possible to predict the adversary acts with absolute certainty. Thus, any analysis of the estimated attack scenarios can only state which scenarios are more likely to occur, and why.

17. *'Information security assessment is mainly a proactive countermeasure'.*

Sometimes, security incidents trigger information security assessments, which provide a level of support to forensic investigations. Once we performed a penetration test that uncovered the vulnerability through which the attackers got in and which could not be discovered by the usual forensic methods alone. Nevertheless, security audits are casually done to prevent incidents, or soften their impact, and not to react to them. As such, they deprive potential attackers of opportunities and initiative. *'If you can always remember danger when you are secure and remember chaos in times of order, watch out for danger and chaos while they are still formless and prevent them before they happen, this is the best of all.'* (Ho Yanxi)

18. *'Information security assessment must be impartial'.*

This is one of the major reasons why the majority of information security audits are outsourced to third parties. It is more difficult to ensure neutrality of the internal auditor team. In the case of the majority of SMEs, having fully neutral internal auditors is simply unaffordable, and separation of duties is generally a problem. However, the auditee should also watch out for any suspicious involvement of the third-party consultants with their personnel and, especially, competitors. It also pays to have vendor-independent security auditors that would not aggressively push through any specific services or products of other companies for a commission. Of course, this depends on the audit type and is, for example, far more likely to occur with PCI DSS than SSAE16 or ISO27001. In such a case, the auditors would be tempted to twist the assessment conclusions and recommendations to present the solution they promote in a favourable light. You hire the auditors to assess and analyse, not to advertise and sell!

19. *'Information security assessment must be dissociated from the checked system(s)'.*

By 'impartiality' we mean not taking any parts. By 'dissociation' we mean *not being a part oneself*. This is often an issue with the in-house auditor team. Outside the scope of its immediate tasks, it should be kept as isolated from its customary targets as possible. One of the evident reasons why it ought to be so is to avoid the development of any interfering mutual relations between the auditors and the audited. But there is more to it than meets the eye and is an issue of *dissociation, not impartiality*.

The infamous Gödel's second incompleteness theorem can be stated as follows: *'For any formal effectively generated theory* T *including basic arithmetical truths and also certain truths about formal provability,* T *includes a statement of its own consistency if and only if* T *is inconsistent.'* Gödel has proved that the internal consistency of a system can never be proven except by employing reasoning which is not expressible within the system itself. Thus, you cannot determine the consistency (or inconsistency) of a system from within and have to be free of its constrains. If possible, *the in-house auditors should think and operate as if they were an independent third party*. But there is an even broader application of this reasoning. The best way to disassociate oneself from the auditee mindset and acquire clear external range of vision and perspective is to wholly, unreservedly think like the adversaries: *'We should try to "get inside" the enemy's thought processes and see the enemy as he sees himself so that we can set him up for defeat. It is essential that we understand the enemy on his own terms. We should not assume that every enemy thinks as we do, fights as we do, or has the same values or objectives'.* (MCDP 1 *Warfighting*)

20. *'Information security assessment results must be strictly confidential'.*

What could be a better gift to a foe than a document describing in detail which security gaps your company or organisation has and how to exploit them? That adversary can be internal. Life goes on. Love can turn to hate, happiness to dissatisfaction. A member of staff who is trustworthy today can become totally disgruntled tomorrow, or lose their job. The fewer people have access to any information that demonstrates your potential weaknesses, the better. Also, be careful with properly sanitising any reports you have to provide to outside parties – such as customers – under NDA when this is unavoidable due to contractual obligations. Even the metadata in such a report may have to be checked not to divulge unnecessary information. As Bruce Schneier emphatically pointed out, "probably the safest thing you can do with the (security audit) report, after you read it, is shred it".

On aggressive defence

> *'Because we typically think of the defence as waiting for the enemy to strike, we often associate the defence with response rather than initiative. This is not necessarily true. We do not necessarily assume the defensive only out of weakness.'* – MCDP 1 *Warfighting*

Countering active security incidents is the most interesting part of it all. After all, it involves the clash of wills. Add skills, knowledge and understanding to the concoction, and you will get the whole picture. If one is able to fend off determined, deliberate, planned attacks – in particular the so-called APT (advanced persistent threat(s) – reducing the number of passive security incidents and diminishing their impact should be a cakewalk. Or so the theory goes.

Great military minds have pondered the subject of offence versus defence for millennia. It appears that eventually they worked out an admissible and respectable theoretical framework that addresses the issue in a variety of situations. In the field of information security, we see nothing of the kind. At best, there are disparate glimpses of what can be the fabric of such an endeavour. For example, security specialists often hum "the best defence is offence" mantra. Fine. But what exactly does it imply in practice? Are we supposed to hack the hackers? Or publish private gossips about nosey, disaffected employees on Facebook before they do the same to you or your enterprise? This doesn't make much sense.

An information security professional is engaged in a form of continuous warfare which is defensive by its very nature. The aim of this 'combat' is not to give an inch of the protected 'territory' (data, systems, services, applications, other assets) to the adversaries. The latter come of all breeds and can be positioned both outside (the 'invaders') or inside (the 'infiltrators' or 'insurgents'). Information security audits are an important way of shaping this engagement. They should not be under- or overestimated.

Based on what we could learn from military masterminds, there are three *interrelated* key strategies of successful defence:

- *'Build up strong, multilayered resistance without overstretching or overspending'.*
- *'Readily adapt to the opponents and environmental change'.*
- *'Compel the enemy to follow your rules of the game'.*

The optimal defensive strategy adapted to a given situation should effectively combine the elements of all three.

Defence-in-depth

The first strategy seems to be very straightforward. Beef up your defences on many existing levels while involving policy, process, operational, human, legal and technical elements. Such levels will have their sub-levels nested within. Try out a simple exercise: count in your mind the points required for a proper echeloned defence of a large network. We estimate that at least the following are absolutely necessary:

1. Redundant load-balanced connections to multiple ISPs (to counter both denial-of-service and technical failures; mind that at least a tier 3 ISP can in itself fall prey to a massive DDoS).

2. Fortified network perimeter (nowadays, that includes at least gateway IPS and may be WAF – the bulk of modern firewalls support at least IPS functionality).

3. Secure separation of internal networks (do remember that VLANs are network management and not a security solution: 'VLAN-hopping' attacks are well-known and should be guarded against where such risks are significant).

4. Protection of traffic streams and infrastructure protocols, including wireless traffic and protocols.

5. Protection of all separate systems, including servers, workstations, mobile computers and various network appliances. Mind the BYOD!

6. Secure, redundant 24/7 monitoring and logging applied to everything listed above.

7. Trained technical personnel who are up to task and end-user security awareness training.

8. Capable security management.

9. Appropriate vendor support contracts, SLAs/MSAs and NDAs. Verification of supplier security is desirable – the relevant sections of ISO27002 could be consulted on this topic.

10. Security policies, procedures, guidelines, instructions, inventories, network diagrams and technical manuals covering all aspects of the above (including change control, incident response, vulnerability management, etc.).

How many points did you come up with? What was missing? Are these security elements also missed within a real network infrastructure of your company or organisation?

Not understanding and servicing such hierarchical structures in a befitting way usually leads to a major strategic fault we call a 'Maginot line mentality'. As Clausewitz pointed out a century before the actual Maginot line was built, '*if you entrench yourself behind strong fortifications, you compel the enemy to seek a solution elsewhere.*' The unblessed fortification line had "On ne passe pas" ("they shall not pass") engraved on it. And they did not: Erich von Manstein outflanked the line through the Ardennes.

Despite Cloud networking, remote employees, BYOD and BYOA (bring your own application), and various forms of wireless connectivity, some information security specialists still view what they protect as some kind of a medieval fortress with walls, ditches, watchtowers and sentinels at the gates. This is evidently a manifestation of the Maginot line mentality. For a long time, the real borders of the 'fortress' are blurred, nebulous, fluid and continuously fluctuate. We would rather call it an 'information security zone':

- *'An information security zone is everywhere your sensitive data, systems and other valuable assets are. This is the territory you need to defend. It continuously expands and contracts'.*

You have telecommuters – it expands to their homes and means of travel. You have employees with company mobile computers and smartphones on business trips – it expands anywhere they go, including planes, hotels, taxies, cafés or all other places you can (or cannot) imagine. The mobile computers and smartphones can be attacked at any time via (wired or wireless) hacking and plain old theft. The employees themselves can be attacked via social engineering, blackmail, bribery and so on. The growing popularity of Cloud computing and software-as-a-service (SaaS) makes further enormous contributions towards reshaping information security zones for subscribers to these services, their partners and customers. They might increase *friction* by orders of magnitude. The Cloud and fog of war go hand–in–hand.

In the introductory part we noted that the experienced security auditor should be able to recognise and condemn the prevalent 'cataclysmic approach' of the auditee. The Maginot line mentality is another strategic blunder of a similar scale the auditors should be looking for. It is vital to understand that an information security Maginot line can be created nearly anywhere. On a technical side, the most common occasion is still the network perimeter. Sometimes it is end-host security. Some may put all of their eggs into the basket of applied cryptography. Have you ever heard something along the lines of "we don't care whether our data are lost, they won't be able to decrypt it anyway"? Keystroke loggers and social engineering are just two of the many approaches the assailants can adopt to outflank encryption and avoid frontal, brute-force cracking attacks. There could be security policy, process, operational or human resources Maginot lines. A trusted third-party hosting, Cloud, SaaS or security services providers (ironically, including suppliers of information security audits!) can become one. Be vigilant and watch for its obvious signs of 'bare flanks' and highly uneven security control distribution. Knowing the background of the manager ultimately responsible for the organisation's information security helps. Something truly remote from this background is likely to have insufficient attention paid to it.

Adapting to adversaries

The two remaining 'dynamic' or 'adaptational' strategies of defence are similar in their dependence on:

- *knowing the enemy.*
- *maintaining the tempo.*
- *initiative.*

For them, timely information security audits and well-prioritised corrective actions play a truly pivotal role. We shall briefly examine this role here.

The 'adapt to the adversary' approach is by no means new. Nearly two-and-a-half thousand years ago, Sun Tzu exalted it saying that *'the ability to gain victory by changing and adapting according to the opponent is called genius'*. He has also underlined that such adaptation must be creative and continuous: *'Therefore victory in war is not repetitious, but adapts its form endlessly'*. In the introduction, we stated that:

- *'To assess the probability and impact of active security incidents, a more aggressive and all-encompassing path must be taken'.*

Such a path signifies that a robust security assessment should simultaneously analyse the auditee's defences and potential assailants' capabilities. From the defender's viewpoint it can be worded as *'assess yourself and your opponents'* (Ho Yanxi). Other relevant discourses from the Chinese strategy sages sometimes quoted by information security experts are:

- *'So it is said that if you know others and know yourself, you will not be imperilled in a hundred battles; if you do not know others but know yourself, you will win one and lose one; if you do not know others and do not know yourself, you will be imperilled in every single battle'* (Sun Tzu)
- *'When you know yourself, this means guarding your energy and waiting. This is why knowing defence but not offence means half victory and half defeat'* (Zhang Yu)

"Half victory and half defeat" is not what we aspire to. Recall that the fog of war reflects *'the uncertainty regarding your own capability, the potential adversary capability and adversary intent'*. Thus, it has to be removed not only from your own, but also from the opponent's capabilities and designs. To do so, the auditors must thoroughly research the means different attacker species have using all sources of information available at their disposal, as well as their own experience and imagination. Then the established offensive means should be applied to test the auditee's information security at different levels and points, and without causing unacceptable disruption or damage.

Technical penetration testing or social engineering specialists will now predictably say that this is exactly what they do. But the scope of applying this logic can be broader. Just as we split all security incidents into active and passive, we can describe all information security assessments in exactly the same way:

- *'A passive information security assessment is based upon verification against prefabricated checklists'.*

- *'An active information security assessment is based upon vigorously searching for vulnerabilities and gaps employing all relevant knowledge, experience, creativity and insight'.*

One can be highly imaginative, dynamic and resourceful when analysing security policies, procedures or any other pertinent documentation. On the other hand, a penetration test or a social engineering check can be reduced to an application of a limited set of 'canned' cookbook gimmickry. This is saving time (and most likely, but not always, the budget) at the expense of depth. It has its place under the sun.

It should be emphasised that both passive and active assessment classes are effective, proactive ways to discover and analyse risks. It is only the scope and type of risks that differs. So, you should not disdain the passive approach. While it certainly does not look artistic, it is much easier to calibrate and standardise (did it occur to you that there is no formal, universally accepted standard on penetration testing and social engineering?). It is very useful at establishing information security baselines (in military terms, 'lines of retreat'). It can extend the breadth of an audit by checking more targets in a given period of time. To stress it again, the passive approach can also reduce that period, and getting ahead of the opponents is vital. What it won't do is help to prevent sophisticated and determined attacks centred around the element of surprise. Thus, you have to gauge the probability of such a threat prior to selecting the passive or active option. Do not forget that any sane attacker will go for the low-hanging fruit first, and the chain breaks at its weakest link.

Compelling adversaries to adapt

The third strategy of aggressive defence – forcing the opposition to adapt, or accept your rules of the game – certainly requires application of the active approach. Historically, this is also the latest strategy. At the time of Sun Tzu, skilful adaptation to your foe was sufficient to be a strategy genius, although he did state that '*those skilled in war bring the enemy to the field of battle and are not brought there by him*'. Nevertheless, even Clausewitz wrote that '*while on the defensive, our forces cannot at the same time be directed on other objects; they can only be employed to defeat the intentions of the enemy.*' Nothing is said about shaping these intentions in a needed direction. This is not so nowadays.

Revisit the introductory thought that information security practices have plentiful logical and strategic similarities to counter-intelligence and counter-insurgency efforts. USAF Colonel John Boyd (1927-1997), whose observations and thoughts we have already employed on multiple occasions, starting from the epigraph to the whole book, is considered by some to be a modern-day Sun Tzu. Being a jet fighter pilot, he was deeply exposed to the high-tech, high speed manoeuvrable combat action of his times. Besides, John Boyd took an active part in developing F-16 and F/A-18 Hornet fighter planes. His ideas heavily influenced MCDP 1 *Warfighting* – another frequently quoted source of inspiration for this work. Colonel John Boyd vigorously contemplated on modern counter-blitz and counter-guerrilla action. We find his conclusions to be highly applicable to today's information security 'combat'. Below, some of them shall be meditated upon.

- *'Blitz and guerrillas, by operating in a directed, yet more indistinct, more irregular, and quicker manner, operate inside their adversaries' observation-orientation-decision-action loops or get inside their mind-time-space as basis to penetrate the moral-mental-physical being of their adversaries in order to pull them apart, and bring about their collapse. Such amorphous, lethal, and unpredictable activity by blitz and guerrillas make them appear awesome and unstoppable which altogether produce uncertainty, doubt, mistrust, confusion, disorder, fear, panic.'*

Replace "blitz and guerrillas" with "malicious hackers, insiders and cyber criminals" and you will see the main reasons for their apparent success (and for the accompanying media hype). Also, remember the FUD game. This is how they win it. Of course, the offenders rarely want your entire collapse, although this is possible in the cases of revenge, direct competition or politically motivated attacks. Most likely they are after more specific aims, financial or not. The observation-orientation-decision-action (OODA) loops (*Figure 2*) introduced by

Colonel Boyd reflect the following stages of any complete interaction process that involves decision-making:

1. *Reconnaissance and data gathering (observation)*
2. *Analysis and synthesis of gathered data (orientation)*
3. *Determining the course of action (decision)*
4. *Physical, technical, process, organisational and other forms of implementing the decision in practice (action)*

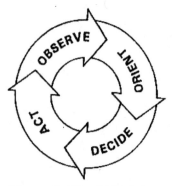

Figure 2: The OODA loop

We will make extensive use of the OODA loop concept in the upcoming chapters of this book.

So, which suggestions did John Boyd provide to counter the foregoing threats?

- *'In dealing with uncertainty, adaptability seems to be the right counterweight. The counterweight to "uncertainty" cannot be "certainty."'*

The applications of this principle to information security auditing were already discussed in the Fundamentals section when we elaborated on the inherent incompleteness of security audits, and so on. It will resurface elsewhere. Remove just enough fog of war to enable sufficiently effective observation. Throw just enough fog of war at the adversaries to make them confused and blur their vision.

- *'To shape and adapt to change one cannot be passive; instead one must take the initiative.'*

Active information security assessments require higher initiative. So does preparation for them and reaction to their outcome on the auditee's side. Aggressive defence is proactive, instead of a 'cataclysmic doctrine' that waits for a security accident to happen so that something can be done about it afterwards, as if we can't learn until it occurs. Building rigid 'fortification lines' is not aggressive defence.

- *'Idea of fast transients suggests that, in order to win, we should operate at a faster tempo or rhythm than our adversaries – or, better yet, get inside adversary's observation-orientation-decision-action time cycle or loop.'*

If information security auditors are more resolute, vigorous and knowledgeable than the attackers, and the assessment follow-up corrective actions do not lag, this is certainly possible. Attackers have their limitations in time, resources and skill, especially when countered by full-time, well-organised and motivated specialist teams.

- *'The ability to operate at a faster tempo or rhythm than an adversary enables one to fold adversary back inside himself so that he can neither appreciate nor keep-up with what's going on. He will become disoriented or confused.'*

This amounts to winning the FUD game and completely thwarting the attack. Disoriented offenders also turn into soft targets for punishment via disciplinary actions and law enforcement acts.

- *'spontaneous, synthetic/creative, and flowing action/counteraction operation, rather than a step-by-step, analytical/logical, and discrete move/counter-move game.'*

Plain and simple, this is the pattern an organisation's information security must follow. This is what the well thought-out ISMS should promote. This is how an effective information security assessment must be executed and reacted to.

There could be multiple specific applications of these principles in various spheres of practical information security. On a technical side, by uncovering vulnerabilities and designing whole new methods of attack before the adversaries do, security researchers frequently overrun the opposition effectively by getting inside their OODA loops. Needless to say, many novel methods of attack were discovered in the process of performing security audits. Numerous new forms of defence were also devised while reacting to security assessment outcomes, often because a compensating control had to be quickly designed and deployed. Rapid inclusion of new heuristics (not simply signatures!) into intrusion prevention and anti-malware products might also allow us to get ahead of numerous attackers. When organisational and technical measures converge to create an effective monitoring and logging system, punitive action against in-house offenders can be taken before they do any actual harm. They can now be caught red-handed with ease. This means the attackers will be forced to react instead of the company or organisation reacting to them. Social engineering can be met with counter-social engineering against its perpetrators, and the possibilities for sting operations are endless. We used social engineering against assailants in the past to find out their future plans and targets, and to determine their present capabilities and skills. In one such case, we could not technically discover a backdoor installed by a hacker team while performing computer forensics until the required information was obtained . . . from the team itself via social engineering directed at one of its members.

To summarise, blitz can be successfully met with counter-blitz, guerrilla-like tactics can decimate guerrillas. These are the key lessons from Colonel Boyd's strategic research. Contemplate it with utmost thoughtfulness, and you will find how it might apply to your particular situation and assigned information security tasks.

On counteroffensive

'We conclude that there exists no clear division between the offence and defence. Our theory of war should not attempt to impose one artificially. The offence and defence exist simultaneously as necessary components of each other, and the transition from one to the other is fluid and continuous.' – MCDP 1 *Warfighting*

The discourse of the previous section automatically brings the question of whether it is possible to counterattack. This topic was speculated about by many information security professionals, again without producing any definite results. Nothing has changed since. Military strategy actively contemplates and uses counter attacking even in the most bluntly defensive standoffs:

- *'The ultimate aim of defensive war can never be an absolute negation, as we have before observed. Even for the weakest there must be some point in which the enemy may be made to feel, and which may be threatened'* (Clausewitz)

- *'A rapid, powerful transition to the attack – the glinting sword of vengeance – is the most brilliant moment of the defence. Anyone who does not think of it from the very beginning, or rather, anyone who does not include it within the concept of defence, will never understand the superiority of defence' (Clausewitz)*

Note the key point in the second excerpt: *the capability of counterattack must be included within the system of defence for it to be truly superior.*

The main ways of bludgeoning in-house attackers are disciplinary and, sometimes, legal. Recall that at least two-thirds of serious information security incidents are internal, caused by disgruntled employees and clashes of corporate or organisational politics. The main way to sledgehammer external offenders is via law enforcement agencies, although you can sue the offenders or smear them by an effective media and word-of-mouth campaign in social networks, and so on. All these situational possibilities are fully, entirely dependent on your present information security defences. Which, by way of reminder, are policy, operational, technical and human, and should be regularly verified and continuously improved employing appropriate security audits.

Let us review the classic example of a specific common 'technical' countermeasure – the logs. To be taken seriously by law enforcement agencies' representatives or accepted as secondary or hearsay evidence in the court of law, a set of defined conditions must be met:

1. There must be appropriate security policies covering audit trails in the company or organisation.
2. There must be a suitably qualified person responsible for maintaining and reviewing the logs.

3. Logs must be reviewed regularly.
4. The integrity of logs must be well-protected.
5. Logs must be correctly timestamped.

To meet these objectives effectively, logging should be centralised. Having redundant centralised log servers helps. Having reliable and secure backup of logs helps a lot. When an internal information security audit is performed, all these elements should be thoroughly verified via sampling. When technical security testing is done, it should be used as the opportunity to check how running vulnerability scanning or other attack tools is reflected in the logs. The absence of or a flaw in any of the objectives listed above can easily make logging a useless, time- and resource-consuming exercise, especially from a legal viewpoint.

This 'technicality' brings us to some important general conclusions:

- *'Information security assessments must verify the auditee's incident prevention and response capabilities and procedures'.*

In more specific terms:

- *'Information security assessments should identify loopholes that can allow offenders to erase their tracks and get away'.*

As you can see from the example above, such loopholes can be (surprise!) policy, technical, procedural and human. If you try to present as valid evidence any audit trails that are not a part of a continuous and documented process, but were specifically collected to react to a single security incident, the court won't take them.

1: Information Security Auditing and Strategy

The offenders do have strategic gaps that can be and are successfully exploited. At the moment of writing the first edition of this book, the TJX case (which had then led to the amendment of PCI DSS standard) was still making big waves in the news. TJX hackers managed to get in – a battle won. Then they managed to retrieve the money – a decisive battle won. A great deal of cyber criminals fall exactly at this stage (for instance, the infamous attempt to retrieve money from Sumitomo bank in London after the successful keylogger attack assisted by a corrupt security guard). That is, if they are not a part of a well-developed international crime organisation with established channels of money laundering- – and these are many. But at the end 'Maksik', 'Segvec' and at least some of their accomplices got caught. A decisive battle lost, and for these TJX hackers it nullifies the results of all battles previously won. Even if they did manage to stash some of the stolen cash somewhere, they are not likely to enjoy it. Not for a few decades, anyway.

One of Sun Tzu's basic teachings is that you have to hit the adversaries where they do not defend. Thus, legal, enforcement and disciplinary means are very efficient against the majority of offenders who are strongly technically inclined. They seldom understand and pay attention to procedures, company policies and regulations, laws, financial elements and instruments, the ways that law enforcement agencies operate. By concentrating on technology only, one also becomes highly vulnerable to social engineering. On the other hand, for a great deal of internal wrong-doers technology is the Achilles' heel. They think that no one is watching. They think that if they have copied confidential data no one would spot it or prove it. They still think that if they have deleted a file, or even formatted the whole hard

62

drive, it cannot be restored. And so on. We have helped to bust such offenders many times. While you may think that this discussion has deviated from this book's theme into the realm of computer forensics, consider the following statement:

- *'Information security assessments should be able to identify suspicious behaviour and signs of malevolent acts.'*

This is similar to financial audits uncovering fraud such as salami slicing. Information security assessments can and sometimes will trigger forensics. While the statement above appears to be mainly applicable to the internal audits, experience shows that it's not always so.

The above discussion is centred on legal, enforcement and disciplinary paths of counteroffence. But can you counterattack technically? There is (or at least there was) a curious appliance or two that were advertised as 'active defence' safeguards. That is, they launched denial-of-service (DoS) attacks against assailants. This is a very bad idea. The obvious problem is that hackers can easily fake someone else's address to force such an appliance to attack it. Envision a situation in which two such devices belonging to different entities are tricked into playing a 'DoS ping-pong' one against the other. Besides, from the auditor's point, how does one run a security scan of a network border device that tries to knock you offline? Turning off the device for the time of scanning doesn't sound great if we are talking about frequent automated scans. Thus, if anyone offers you such an idea of active defence in any form or shape, stay away. The fog of war that clouds the Internet makes it entirely unfeasible. Even automatic shunning of offending network addresses is generally a bad idea. No one can stop attackers from abusing it by faking source addresses and forcing the shunning gateway to block access to resources critical for your business or network connectivity.

On the other hand, in applied wireless security the coverage zone of your network is somewhat limited and, at least, can be reasonably monitored. If its security system is properly configured, all legitimate users must be authenticated. Thus, knocking off unauthorised users and misconfigured devices makes certain sense and can be applied. Nevertheless, when performing wireless security audits, on several occasions we have effectively tricked such systems into smiting rightful devices and users. What could be the lesson?

- *'Information security assessments should verify that countermeasures are not excessive and cannot become the source of problems themselves.'*

Recall the eternal 'difficult password problem'. If the passwords are too long, too complex, or are changed too often, users forget them or write them down.

On the conditions of success

'. . . on the defensive, there is no great gain to be won except by a great stake' – Carl von Clausewitz

To conclude this chapter, we would like to say a few words on what should be considered a successful defence. The end results of auspicious information security actions are:

1. *Preventing passive security incidents.*
2. *Preventing and repelling attacks.*
3. *Humiliating and apprehending offenders.*
4. *Successfully passing all the required security audits.*

Point one is about attention, awareness and appropriate controls. The two following points are a resolution of the 'clash of wills', while the fourth point acts as a check against the three prior points. As Clausewitz has specified, *'mere endurance would not be fighting: and the defensive is an activity by which so much of the enemy's power must be destroyed, that he must give up his object.'* In information security, we are not fighting some brutal war of attrition. The "enemy's power" that "must be destroyed" is, above all, the power of their will, their desire to launch or resolve to carry on with the attack, or perform any other malicious acts.

One of the major compliments a technical attacker can deliver is "this network (or system, or application) is boring". Boredom is the sister of unwillingness. Note the 'will' in the latter word. Unwillingness signifies unpreparedness, thus telling that you have prepared better than the opponents. From their point of view, a 'boring' system or network is the one that does not have easily discoverable and exploitable gaps. This is only possible if a prior audit has identified all such gaps and the follow-up reaction has led to their complete elimination. Security by default is a sales myth. Insecurity by default is far closer to reality.

Sun Tzu stated that *'in the case of those who are skilled in attack, their opponents do not know where to defend. In the case of those skilled in defence, their opponents do not know where to attack'.* Thus, the conditions of victory in terms of attack and defence are that:

- *you know where (and how) to defend.*
- *the adversary does not even know where (and how) to begin.*

In relation to information security auditing, it signifies that the previous audits have properly identified and verified all these 'wheres' and 'hows', and the latest monitoring audit was, well, unbelievingly boring. This, of course, applies to all major areas of our *information security zone*: policy, operational, technical and human. The auditee has reached the state in which, in the words of Sun Tzu, '*even if the opponents are numerous, they can be made not to fight*'. Now they have to maintain this state, '*be orderly within, and watch for gaps and slack*'. (Mei Yaochen)

CHAPTER 2: SECURITY AUDITING, GOVERNANCE, POLICIES AND COMPLIANCE

'. . . in strategy everything is very simple, but not on that account very easy.' – Carl von Clausewitz

In the previous chapter we emphasised that the most dangerous flaws are the flaws of security strategy. We have also discussed a few examples of such flaws. Strategic failures generate chain reactions of secondary and collateral shortcomings, many of which eventually become exploitable vulnerabilities – technical, process and human. This is common sense that applies to numerous fields of expertise:

- *'When your strategy is deep and far reaching, then what you gain by your calculations is much, so you can win before you even fight. When your strategic thinking is shallow and near-sighted, then what you gain by your calculations is little, so you lose before you do battle. Much strategy prevails over little strategy, so those with no strategy cannot but be defeated'* (Zhang Yu)

We have also underlined that quality information security assessments should aspire to identify these strategic flaws by cutting through the dusky thicket of details and assembling the whole picture of the auditee's security state as much as possible. Thus, the progress of hands-on audits is usually moving in the 'bottom-to-top' direction from software applications, systems, networks, people, processes and documents to the governance of the whole information security structure. The organisation and maintenance of this structure, as any CISSP exam prep guide will stress, must flow in the opposite direction. After all, *'the one who*

*figures on victory at headquarters before even doing the
battle is the one who has the most strategic factors on his
side'* (Sun Tzu). But is everything as straightforward as
both textbooks and sages of the past tell?

On evaluating the top-down approach

'*The subordination of the political point of view to the
military would be contrary to common sense, for
policy has declared the war; it is the intelligent faculty,
war only the instrument, and not the reverse. The
subordination of the military point of view to the
political is, therefore, the only thing which is possible.*'
– Carl von Clausewitz

A thorough information security assessment should seek to
verify that:

- the top management of the auditee cares about the
  organisation's information security, rather than adopting
  a laissez-faire attitude.

- it is reasonably aware of the *major overall* security
  issues and risks the company or organisation is facing.

- there is a good level of bi-directional communication
  and mutual understanding between the board and the
  manager responsible for corporate or organisational
  information security (usually the CISO).

- general information security strategies and programs do
  exist, are documented and *followed through*.

ISO27001:2013 heavily asserts the above points in the new
section 5 on leadership added to the body of the Standard.
One of the most obvious things to check first is whether the
information security policies include appropriate clauses on

senior management support and are endorsed and signed by a representative of the board or, at least, a C-level exec. This was the main topical requirement of ISO27001:2005, but it is no longer sufficient in order to conform to this Standard. When writing security policies for our clients, we casually align them with the ISO27001. The same applies to our domestic set of policies. ISO27001 templates suggest that the opening chapter of any compliant security policy should be dedicated to information security organisation and include a section on senior management support. This is what this section may typically look like:

- <section number> **Senior Management Support** *<insert company name>'s Information Security Policy is fully endorsed and supported by the company's Board of Directors.*

- *This Information Security Policy becomes effective immediately after it has been approved and signed by <insert Senior Management representative position>.*

- *The <Senior Manager> has direct responsibility for maintaining the Information Security Policy and providing advice and guidance on its implementation.*

- *<Insert the representative position, usually the CISO> shall be the principal Senior Management contact and representative overlooking corporate Information Security Policy matters.*

- *All <insert company name>'s Managers are directly responsible for implementing this Information Security Policy within their business areas, departments and teams, and for the policy's adherence by their staff.*

- *The Information Security Policy review procedure shall be endorsed and supported by <insert company name>'s <Senior Management positions>, and signed-*

*off by the company <insert senior manager position>
prior to initiation.*

- *<insert company name>'s Senior Management shall
ensure a proper level of inter-departmental collaboration
in relation to the Information Security Policy compliance
and support throughout the company.*

So, always check that the auditee's security policy contains
similar opening statements (easy!) and they are adhered to in
practice (difficult, although the introduction of a compulsory
management review of ISMS in SO27001:2013 helps).

A mistake that is sometimes made is picking on the auditee's
management regarding various operational, process,
technical, physical and human resources information security
details. The auditors might do it out of arrogance to
demonstrate their prowess in a beloved specific field of
knowledge. This is not the senior or even specialised
manager's job, however, and not knowing about many of
these things is not their fault. The CIO, or even the CTO, can
be highly regarded in the company. They can be on the board
of directors, as commonly happens with high-tech IT-centred
enterprises. They could also be information security gurus,
but obviously don't have to. The CISOs are often expected to
possess specific in-depth knowledge of different security
methods, technologies and tools. For these important security
professionals, however, it is far from being an absolute
requirement despite the common perception of it being so.

We could not resist the temptation to cite quite a lengthy
excerpt from Clausewitz's *On War* discussing the qualities
top military commander should wield:

*'The Commander of an army neither requires to be a
learned explorer of history nor a publicist, but he*

*must be well versed in the higher affairs of State; he
must know and be able to judge correctly of
traditional tendencies, interests at stake, the
immediate questions at issue, and the characters of
leading persons; he need not be a close observer of
men, a sharp dissector of human character, but he
must know the character, the feelings, the habits, the
peculiar faults and inclinations of those whom he is to
command. He need not understand anything about the
make of a carriage, or the harness of a Battery horse,
but he must know how to calculate exactly the march
of a column, under different circumstances, according
to the time it requires. These are things the knowledge
of which cannot be forced out by an apparatus of
scientific formula and machinery: they are only to be
gained by the exercise of an accurate judgement in
the observation of things and of men, aided by a
special talent for the apprehension of both.'*

This, in our humble opinion, is a very precise description,
which is easily transferable into the language of modern
technology. The CISO should be able to identify five AES
(Advanced Encryption Standard) selection finalist ciphers,
but does not need to know how many rounds of iteration or
S-boxes these ciphers have. They should know the
difference between WPA (Wireless Protected Access)
versions one and two, and the distinctions between their
SOHO and Enterprise implementations. Detailed knowledge
of the RADIUS (Remote Authentication Dial In User
Service) protocol used by WPA Enterprise, however, is not
needed. They should understand the principles behind buffer
overflow, SQL injection, cross-site scripting and other
common software-centric attack methods. Nevertheless, a
CISO does not have to read, write, patch or even execute

code. Where in-house software development is done, a CISO is expected to be versed in SDLC security and common development methodologies such as Agile, but they are neither a security programmer nor a security beta tester. Of course, baseline knowledge and understanding of Cloud security issues (Cloud Security Alliance documentation helps a lot) is expected when such technologies are employed, but a CISO is also not a Cloud security expert. Rather, a good CISO should be able to select security solutions, methods and approaches that fit with Cloud/SaaS use by the particular company. Speaking of the 'management part' of the aforesaid excerpt from *On War*, you only need to replace the "State" with "company" or "organisation" to apply its intended meaning to our situation. The parts dealing with the human issues can be safely left intact.

The real role of the CISO is the one of a bridge or, to be more technically meticulous, a *router* that supports multiple communication protocols. The CISO 'routes' information between those who operate on a large scale and know *what* to protect in general terms and *why* (the top management), and those who function within more limited scopes and know the details of *where* and *how* to safeguard it in practice. The CISO must be able to capture senior management's directions and intent, and translate them into clear and precise language of security policies, standards and guidelines. Then they have to work on implementing, enforcing, maintaining and improving these policies and their operational applications with more junior security specialists and professionals from other departments. These departments typically include, but are not limited to, human resources, IT, risk management, legal and compliance. *Figure 3* shows the classical top-down flow of information security guidance and intent in a large entity, the CISO being its 'core router'.

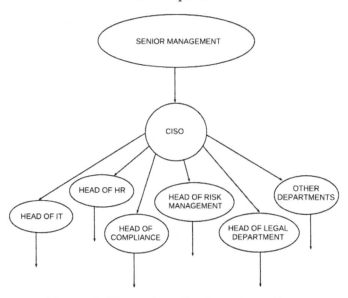

Figure 3: The personalised top-down flow

To summarise, the role and expected skill set of the CISO must be clearly understood by information security auditors of all specialisations and backgrounds. The same applies to the organisation's senior and departmental management. This is absolutely crucial for the success of the assessment and its follow-up corrective actions, since the auditors will closely work with the auditee CISO from the very beginning to the very end, and probably afterwards.

As for the company directors and other top managers, they should have some understanding of general information security principles and issues. For example, as primary data owners they should be well familiar with how the company information is classified to assign and alter appropriate classification levels themselves or authorise others to do so. Overall, this is similar to what Clausewitz said about the Cabinet members of a state: '*a certain knowledge of the nature of war is essential to the management of political commerce'.*

By the way, did it cross your mind that since "any action is reciprocal and triggers reaction", the scheme in *Figure 3* is fundamentally flawed?

When things go bottom-up

> *'The occurrences of war will not unfold like clockwork. We cannot hope to impose precise, positive control over events. The best we can hope for is to impose a general framework of order on the disorder, to influence the general flow of action rather than to try to control each event. If we are to win, we must be able to operate in a disorderly environment.'* – MCDP 1 *Warfighting*

Information security management, unfortunately, tends to lean to one of two extremes. One is to be too lax. Another is to be too severe. 'Taking information security seriously' is usually associated with the latter – the stricter, the better. If you ask many security specialists what is most vital in their field, you will no doubt receive plentiful answers like 'control', 'discipline', 'enforcing the policies' and 'that the rules are followed'. Some may recall the infamous 'deny all' principle. Building and maintaining a viable ISMS, however, is not configuring a firewall.

Surely, unrestricted top-down flow of intent and control is highly important. As Sun Tzu pointed out, *'maintain discipline and adapt to the enemy in order to determine the outcome of the war'*. The aforementioned "flow of intent and control" and following the established rules maintains that discipline. But what about adapting to the enemy?

2: Security Auditing, Governance, Policies and Compliance

In his *Patterns of Conflict*, Col. John Boyd stated: *'Napoleon, Clausewitz, and Jomini viewed the conduct of war and related operations in essentially one direction – from the top down – emphasizing adaptability at the top and regularity at the bottom'*. This is the essence of the 'top-down' principle. The 'top' adopts, writes and edits policies and standards. The 'bottom' must follow them with the utmost precision. If this is how you think the effective ISMS should work, than you are in company with Napoleon, Clausewitz and Jomini (a famous 19th century French strategist). But don't be so proud. Recall that we have previously compared active adversaries to guerrillas or insurgents. Marching in perfectly organised columns against mobile guerrilla groups is utterly useless. They will dissipate and wait for an appropriate moment to strike. The moment will come. This effective approach decimated Napoleon's armies in Spain, Russia and Austria. He did not know how to address the problem and likened the guerrilla warfare that the Grand Armee faced to an ulcer.

This, and not the lack of specific technical skills, is often the reason why malicious hackers and cyber criminals sometimes mock security systems and infrastructures they face, as well as professionals who oversee them. Attackers view these systems as bulky, inflexible and slow to react, with the costs of implemented safeguards not justifying their practical worth. The only real danger modern-day guerrillas face when encountering a Napoleonic-era column charging towards them is to die from laughter. Yet this is, metaphorically speaking, what numerous information security specialists and whole organisations are still doing. This is what it looks like from the outside attacker's perspective. When discussing absolute command and control (many CISO's sacred dream!), Col. John Boyd astutely pointed out that the traditional '*C&C* (Command and Control) *represents a top-down mentality applied in a rigid or mechanical way that ignores as well as stifles the implicit nature of human beings to deal with uncertainty, change, and stress*'.

These factors of "uncertainty, change, and stress" bring to attention the issue of friction. As we have previously discussed, friction is something we should strive to diminish. *Figure 4* demonstrates that it could be completely the opposite if one adopts the 'control freak' or, to put it more politely, the 'rigid C&C' paradigm.

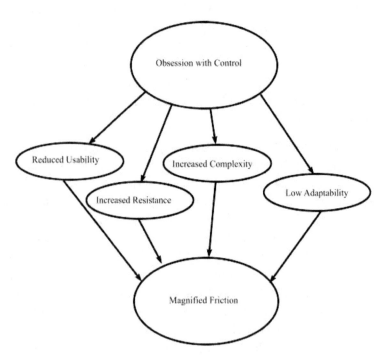

Figure 4: Friction and excessive control

The most commonly addressed technological manifestation of this issue is 'security versus usability'. Recall the 'difficult password problem'. The majority of security professionals will suggest using two-factor authentication to resolve it. This suggestion is generally correct – but we have seen people literally wearing necklaces of authentication tokens like stereotypical tribal chiefs wear shark teeth. The accursed complexity has returned, albeit on a different level.

Using soft tokens and a mobile phone as the authentication device, a practice that became very common since the last edition of this book, mitigates this problem but introduces an additional weak link in the chain: the phone itself. This technology allows us to receive authentication PINs via SMS, or to generate them with an authenticator app. Thus, all PINs should be received or generated by a single device. In practice, using the phone to authenticate to numerous accounts may be a technical problem, especially when these accounts are for the same service or application. Besides, to simplify matters, phone-based two-factor authentication systems often allow the user to reuse the PIN. That is, the same PIN can be utilised several times, or multiple times for a pre-defined duration. No doubt, many companies and organisations are opting for it. However, such implementation is less secure than the more traditional hardware authentication tokens.

A mobile phone is not a little specialised dongle without network connectivity. Expensive smartphones are lucrative targets for thieves. They can also be hacked into via their Internet connection, local connectivity using WiFi or Bluetooth, and/or get infected by malware. The latter becomes exceedingly widespread as smartphones are now used for banking operations including contactless payments and bank transfers. If the PIN is reusable and did not expire, an adversary who has (or has got into) the phone can abuse it. An authenticator app can also be hijacked or replaced by malware. A keystroke logger can be installed. Turning phones into portable computers, even running exactly the same operating system a typical laptop does, exposes them to exactly the same security risks any networked, wireless-enabled system is facing. The same tools and approaches used by cyber criminals to obtain authentication credentials to online banking from the phone can be used to obtain your valuable corporate resources. Thus, a very thorough analysis of benefits and risks must be performed prior to deciding which authentication system is optimal for every specific case. More modern does not always mean more secure.

This was a purely technical example. At times, technology can resolve such issues by applying unorthodox (at their introduction age) means. Before the event of asymmetric encryption, a common way to protect the shared keys was by using a KEK (key encryption key). But then, logically, the problem of enciphering the KEK with some KEKEK would arise, and then the KEKEKEK and so forth towards the infinity. The introduction of Diffie-Hellman and similar secure mutual authentication algorithms has successfully solved this issue. However, there is no magical silver bullet for eliminating its human counterparts.

When employees are exposed to harsh and obstructive regulations and controls, the following can, and will happen:

- They passively resist (ignore) the controls.
- They actively resist (circumvent) the controls.
- They obey them to the letter, which usually comes down to endless execution of mindless drills that may lower productivity and will be eventually opposed by the management for doing so.

At the end of the day, they will completely lose any initiative to use the control and become dissatisfied, if not disgruntled.

Contemplating flexible command and control

MCDP 1 *Warfighting* asserts that *'we must not try to maintain excessive control over subordinates since this will necessarily slow our tempo and inhibit initiative'*. It also reinforces this thought with the following statement: *'The senior intervenes in a subordinate's execution only by exception. It is this freedom for initiative that permits the high tempo of operations that we desire. Uninhibited by excessive restrictions from above, subordinates can adapt their actions to the changing situation'*. Surely, what is acceptable and recommended for the Marines should satisfy even the most authoritarian CISO!

Figure 5 shows the 'Boydian' reciprocal approach to information security management as we see it.

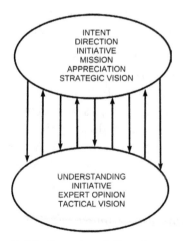

Figure 5: Bi-directional flow in a nutshell

The 'top' should generate intent, provide direction and formulate overall missions to accomplish. It must see the entity's information security as a whole and from the business perspective. The 'bottom' should clearly understand these intent, direction and mission assignments flowing from the top. But it should not be silent. It has the expertise that the top lacks. It can determine and execute specific tasks that the top is not even aware of, and may never be. Thus, it should provide an upward flow of such expertise, and the management should actively appreciate and encourage it, rather than ignore as some sort of background noise that accompanies execution of business processes. Technical, human resources and other specialists know the details that senior management is naturally unable to see. And, as the folk wisdom goes, the devil is in the details. The bottom is obliged to listen by the rules that the top sets. The sensible 'top' is obliged to listen by reason and circumstances. An auditor can be such circumstance that makes the bottom heard via the assessment report and its recommendations. *Lack of effective communication in any direction is a serious security gap.* Finally, but most importantly, both the bottom and the top must exhibit appropriate initiative.

When outlining a possible solution for the 'top-down-top' question, Col. John Boyd has proposed that the inflexible top-down command and control should be substituted with a swiftly adaptable 'leadership-monitoring-appreciation-error correction' circular flow. This is a highly sensible approach, which is fully applicable to modern information security management. As MCDP 1 *Warfighting* precisely formulates, '*we seek unity not principally through imposed control, but through harmonious initiative and lateral coordination within the context provided by guidance from above*'.

To conclude, what is casually viewed as the most stringent and hard-boiled 'thou shalt not' structure of enforcement and control should be, to the contrary, one of the most flexible corporate or organisational management systems. In its rapid adaptability to changing environment it can, perhaps, be compared to stock market trading. Thus, the auditors must verify that the ISMS and the way it is run maintains the necessary degree of initiative, flexibility, fluidity, adaptability, harmony and pace to be truly proficient. This could easily be the main strategic goal of any ISMS assessment. Meanwhile, *'the autocratic control and drill-machine approach'* has just joined the club of glaring strategic faults to look for during information security audits. This could be compared to a well-known anti-pattern jokingly called 'management by perkele' a Finnish swear word shouted at soldiers by their commanders in the days of old when soldiers disobeyed orders. Another relevant organisational anti-pattern is 'mushroom management' referring to the management keeping their staff in the dark by making decisions without consulting the employees affected, and possibly not even informing them until well after such decisions are made. Finally, there is an anti-pattern called 'stovepipe organisation' which mainly refers to restriction of horizontal (such as in inter-departmental collaboration), rather than vertical communication flows. The name of this anti-pattern originates from every home (department, group, team, service line) having its own 'stovepipe' (line of control). Note that, in relation to information security, the role of CISO as a 'router' previously outlined in this chapter and depicted in *Figure 3* must prevent this anti-pattern from occurring. Also note that the strategic flaws we flag out in this book could be rightfully designated 'information security anti-patterns' by analogy to their managerial and engineering counterparts.

On analysing ISMS strategies and flows

> *'It may sound strange, but for all who know war in this respect it is a fact beyond doubt, that much more strength of will is required to make an important decision in strategy than in tactics.'* – Carl von Clausewitz

If we know what to assess and how it should function to be effective, the audit is seemingly not a difficult task. Assuming that the auditors are familiar with how a robust ISMS is constructed and should operate, the major obstacle to auditing information security strategies is the situational orientation and taking into account all relevant environment variables. The latter must be the hardest part of all, taking into account the limited time the auditors have and the complexity of modern organisational structures, even in modestly-sized companies. Ideally, all of an organisation's security programs and strategies should be in perfect resonance with its business model, modes of operation and aims. Prior to performing the assessment of actual security processes and controls, the auditors should learn as much as possible about these decisive factors. They should get a good grasp of corporate politics and study the 'terrain', as *the first step of any ISMS audit shall always be analysing and verifying the aforesaid resonance.* Something that truly helps the auditor and the auditee alike is when the auditee has clearly identified and documented any external requirements that drive its security programs. If it is legislation and compliance, a list of appropriate laws and compliance demands matching them with the necessary security elements shall be made. If it is contractual requirements of the auditee's customers, then a similar list of customers and their security needs listed in the signed contracts, any relevant addenda, and may be even expressed in less formal communications, will be very helpful. If information security strategies and programs do not properly correspond to such requirements, the overall business model and planned developments of a company, they are non-viable and there is no point in studying them any further. The same applies to their accord with operational models and strategic aims of any non-commercial organisations from charities to government agencies.

What about real-life examples of such situations? We can recall a corporation that has built its ISMS and security infrastructure in accordance with the textbook rules. It did not truly take into account the fact that about 70% of its staff were temporary contractors who, on average, didn't stay employed for more than a year. This was overlooked on all levels from security policies to access lists, authentication methods, personnel monitoring and physical controls. As a result, they had at least a few cases of major confidential data leaks, as well as rampaging plain old theft of IT equipment, stationery and other goods. Another instance that can be rather illustrative is a company that was undergoing a major merger, which was not sufficiently addressed in its information security programmes and plans until it actually happened. Then the management of the new entity had to restructure the ISMS *reactively* and in haste. As you might expect, this created multiple security shortcomings, few of which – including physical access control issues, which allowed intruders to get through by claiming to be employees of the other half of the merged entity –remained unresolved a year after the merger took place.

To outline *the next strategy assessment step*, we would have to return to the previous section's discussion topic, namely the 'leadership-monitoring-appreciation-error correction' flow. The first question is whether it exists at all. If it appears so, check its functionality and sufficiency, starting from the leadership part.

There are plentiful modern definitions and theories of leadership that are useful to know, but are clearly outside this work's scope. One such definition, coming from Warren Bennis and Dan Goldsmith's book *Learning to Lead*, is that '*a good manager does things right. A leader does the right things*'. It underlines initiative and active decision-making instead of following the prescribed word. Sun Tzu provided probably the most ancient definition of 'leadership': '*The Way means inducing the people to have the same aim as the leaders*'. His follower Cao Cao later commented: '*This means guiding them by instruction and direction*'. All this requires having a strategic goal or goals that can serve as rallying point(s) of effective strategic information security programmes. As John Boyd pointed out, '*for success over the long haul and under the most difficult conditions, one needs some unifying vision that can be used to attract the uncommitted as well as pump-up friendly resolve and drive and drain-away or subvert adversary resolve and drive.*'

Such rallying points must be clearly defined, explained and communicated. Compliance can help, especially if it is strongly ISMS-related. In fact, ISO27001:2013 requires clear and measurable security objectives to be defined in the security policy chapter or section on information security management and organisation. Becoming ISO 27001-compliant within a year in itself is a perfect rally point. Making all employees security aware and able to spot and duly report all suspicious activities is a good rally point, providing it can be effectively measured. To do so, simply providing awareness training and ensuring that 100% of all staff did participate while all newcomers receive such training within a month may not be sufficient. A good measurement criteria may require introduction of post-training security awareness tests (such as via online multiple-choice questions) to be based upon their pass/fail rates. These tests can be generic (based on a ready third-party solution), bespoke (based on the company security policies and requirements) or both.

Recalling the aforementioned negative example, in case of a merger or acquisition creating an effective ISMS for the new-born corporate entity by absorbing the best from the amalgamating companies is an excellent rally point, providing there is a measurable security baseline to be achieved. Reducing the number of information security incidents below a certain level can be a good rally point, if one is able to define this level with clarity and sound reasoning. Our division of security incidents into passive and active may help. The management could first address the reduction and mitigation of the former, and then deal with the latter. A common approach is to aim at reduction of incidents according to their severity classification. For instance, a company may aspire to have no more than 1% of severe- and 19% of medium-impact incidents as gauged against the overall incident number within a defined period of time. Another possible approach can be based on classifying incidents by type. For instance, all security incidents can be categorised into those occurring due to neglect and those occurring due to other reasons (such as technical faults or zero-day vulnerabilities). Then the objective can be reducing the percentage of the former below the defined level. Talking about vulnerabilities and their remediation, fixing X% of

2: Security Auditing, Governance, Policies
and Compliance

vulnerabilities within a given time (for example, a week) can be a good specific technical security objective (and, generally speaking, the same can apply to resolution of any information security tickets in the company). In contrast, reducing the number of vulnerabilities, or the number of specific vulnerabilities (such as severe-impact ones) below some defined level is not as good security objective as it might first appear. The growing number of vulnerabilities may simply reflect better detection capabilities and, thus, could be a sign of an improved security system rather than its deterioration. To underline, without quality security metrics at hand, setting workable, achievable security objectives is next to impossible. Hence, when performing the assessment, auditors should carefully match the defined objectives with the corresponding metrics and vice versa. Lack of such correspondence is a non-conformance.

The following excerpt from MCDP 1 *Warfighting* provides a good summary for this discourse on security objectives as rallying points:

- *'top-down flow of intent provides consistency and continuity to our actions and establishes the context that is essential for the proper bottom-up exercise of initiative. A subordinate should be ever conscious of a senior's intent so that it guides every decision. An intent that is involved or complicated will fail to accomplish this purpose.'*

Providing that such a flow of direction and intent exists, the strategic goals and plans are reasonable, the objectives are clearly defined, and are thoroughly synchronised with their governing 'political' counterparts, what remains to *assess* is *whether it all actually works as intended*. This relates to the 'monitoring-appreciation-error correction' part of our flexible security management chain. Its analysis amounts to reviewing information security processes and their end results. In this chapter we shall concentrate on the former, leaving the latter for more technical discussions to follow.

High level dissection of security processes

The peculiarities of separate specific processes – for example the processes of secure software development, incident response, personnel termination or change control – belong to the realm of tactics. This section is dedicated to the strategic dimension, which covers the ISMS as a whole. ISO27001:2005 explicitly stated that ISMS processes must follow the classical Deming, or PCDA (Plan-Check-Do-Act), cycle. This is not so with ISO27001:2013, which gives you the flexibility to adapt any other relevant process framework, such as COBIT, instead. Of course, you can still stick to the tested and proven Deming. Alternatively, it can be modified, expanded and adjusted to better suit the information security field. This is exactly what we did below; effectively merging the Deming with Colonel Boyd's OODA loops. To refresh your memory, the Deming cycle is shown on the *Figure 6*.

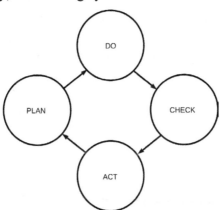

Figure 6: The all-familiar PCDA

In practical terms, a typical Deming cycle of the ISMS process is characterised by a combination of relatively large amplitude and slow pace. In particular, thorough planning and in-depth checking must absorb and analyse large number of variables, which inevitably consumes plenty of time. An information security audit can fit the Deming cycle well when looked at from the auditee's perspective. This is, as we noted in the beginning of the first chapter, *more strategic in nature*. The assessment is first planned, then executed, then its outcome is studied, and finally appropriate follow-up corrective actions are performed. From the auditor's viewpoint, however, the OODA loop appears to be more suitable to describe and structure the process of assessment. Also, take note that typically the attackers operate in OODA loops rather than follow the Deming. OODA loops can be slow and fast, covering vast or narrow ranges; they can be tactical or strategic. So, how do OODA loops and the Deming cycle mix together on the grand scale of things? *Figure 7* depicts our vision of this dynamic union.

While the Deming cycle is more global, there is an OODA for everything. The flexible 'command and control' in the centre of the scheme spins its own OODA loops. There are OODA loops within every single stage of the Deming cycle. There could be as many of them as necessary both in the 'C&C centre' and within the separate cycle phases. They can be nested, one within the other, like Russian dolls. A very important part of the scheme is that the central flexible C&C loops influence every Deming cycle stage and its inner OODAs. Even more, they also influence the transition between the phases, which is represented in the scheme by the diagonal arrows. By 'influence' we imply a whole plethora of possible effects: trigger, direct, control, monitor, measure, correct, appreciate, accelerate, delay, and

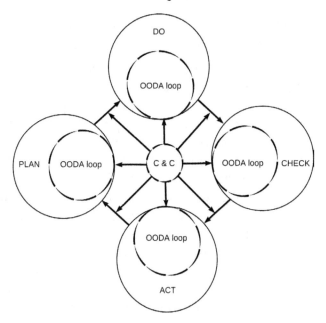

Figure 7: Unfolding of a complete strategic process

so on. This is how, in highly simplified terms, such a process would work in the ideal world:

1. The central C&C OODA loop revolves. Its Action becomes the Deming PLAN stage.

2. The PLAN OODA loop now spins. The end results of its Action (plans) are fed back to the C&C.

3. The C&C OODA loop revolves. If the plans are disapproved, we return to 2. If the plans are deemed satisfactory, its Action becomes the Deming DO stage and triggers the inner DO OODA loop.

4. Repeat this block for the whole Deming cycle until its successful completion.

But in the ideal world we won't need any information security assessments whatsoever.

In reality, the auditors must check where and how our security or security-relevant process goes wrong and suggest a suitable remedy. In severe cases, whole stages of the Deming cycle, not to mention separate OODA loops, can simply go amiss. But the issues you will most commonly encounter are the problems of synchronisation. Note that the scheme in *Figure 7* looks like a combination of clocks that converge into a single, all-permeating pattern. If some of these clocks become desynchronised the whole process may fall apart, or its efficacy can be dramatically reduced. In the words of Col. John Boyd, which have actually inspired this scheme: *'faster tempo, or rhythm, at lower levels should work within the slower rhythm but larger pattern at higher levels so that overall system does not lose its cohesion or coherency'*.

Thus, look for what is missing and what is desynchronised. Check where the C&C OODA loop didn't spin to initiate a Deming phase or supervise the transition between them (laissez-faire!). Verify that nothing has stuck 'at the stuttering sound of "OO-OO-OO" as described by Dr. Ullman in his CrossTalk Journal article[2]. Examine that one loop didn't start to spin before its logical predecessor has completed its own revolution (a typical case of de-synchronisation). And so forth.

Nevertheless, always keep in mind that we are not dealing with some infallible, rigid clockwork mechanism of medieval deists or theatrical Prussian military parades. Re-

---

[2] *https://davidullman.com/uploads/OODA_Loop_Crosstalk.pdf*

read the epigraph to the "When things go bottom-up" section of this chapter one more time. Contemplate it. Synchronisation, for instance, does not mean that all our 'clocks' are ticking with exactly the same speed, or that this tempo would *always* be slow at higher levels and rapid at their lower reflections and counterparts. Our synchronisation is a matter of functionality, operability and efficacy. It is not striving for some über-Platonic perfection that would inevitably destroy all initiative. Some deviations could, or even should, be acceptable. The auditors should always keep it in mind. After all, *'information security assessment always operates with probabilities'* and is a way of analysing and prioritising risks. Low risk issues can be tolerated and retained, as eliminating them might introduce more problems than such issues present themselves.

When gauging the balance of factors, such as the discussed above, experienced security auditors firmly enter the realm of art.

On security assessments and security policies

*'War is an instrument of policy; it must necessarily bear its character, it must measure with its scale: the conduct of war, in its great features, is therefore **policy itself, which takes up the sword in place of the pen, but does not on that account cease to think according to its own laws.'** –* Carl von Clausewitz

One of the most straightforward elements of assessing the ISMS and information security strategies in general is auditing security policies of a company or organisation. Security policies are rightfully viewed as a centre and a cornerstone of any ISMS, outlining and connecting into a whole a variety of its elements. This can be compared with the role national policies have in a conduct of a state:

- *'war is to be regarded as an organic whole, from which the single branches are not to be separated, in which therefore every individual activity flows into the whole, and also has its origin in the idea of this whole, then it becomes certain and palpable to us that the superior stand-point for the conduct of the war, from which its leading lines must proceed, can be no other than that of policy'* (Clausewitz)

If you substitute 'war' with 'information security' in this excerpt, it would outline our situation very well. Being the founding father and a vigorous proponent of the political concept of warfare, Carl von Clausewitz contemplated a great deal the role of (state) policies in 'taking up the sword in place of the pen'. That is, moving from the guidance of the policies to resolute implementation. Many of his conclusions deserve honourable place in information security management textbooks. Therefore, we have decided to dedicate some of this section's space to a brief 'Clausewitz substitution exercise'. Consider the following statements:

- *'If war belongs to policy, it will naturally take its character from thence. If policy is grand and powerful, so will also be the war, and this may be carried to the point at which war attains to its absolute form.'*

If the security policies are "grand and powerful", so will be the ISMS and the entity's information security state, which can even come close to an "absolute form". By an "absolute form", Clausewitz implied a total mobilisation of all citizens and resources of the state towards a unified military goal. In our case, participation of every employee in information security programs and enabling reasonable safeguards for all involved systems, networks, physical premises and sensitive documentation would suffice.

- *'Only through this kind of view, war recovers unity; only by it can we see all wars as things of one kind; and it is only through it that the judgement can obtain the true and perfect basis and point of view from which great plans may be traced out and determined upon. It is true the political element does not sink deep into the details of war, vedettes* (listening-posts) *are not planted, patrols do not make their rounds from political considerations, but small as is its influence in this respect, it is great in the formation of a plan for a whole war, or a campaign, and often even for a battle'.*

Only through the policy-centric approach information security of an entity becomes complete and plans for effective security programs can be laid. It also enables us to see various human, technical, process and operational actions and countermeasures as "things of one kind", guided by the same direction, intent, philosophy and logic. While it is true that information security policies do not "sink deep into the details" of personnel vetting, web applications or database input validation controls, organisation and planning of all these measures and even the separate acts are still governed by the policies.

- *'If, therefore, in drawing up a plan of a war it is not allowable to have a two-fold or three-fold point of view, from which things may be looked at, now with the eye of a soldier, then with that of an administrator, and then again with that of a politician, etc., then the next question is, whether policy is necessarily paramount, and everything else subordinate to it'.*

Security policies cannot have "a two-fold or three-fold point of view", looking at the issues they address with the eye of an IT specialist, then with that of a human resources manager, and then again with that of a CEO. They must effectively translate information security intent, direction and initiative of the entity's top management into a clearly expressed written form, understood by all to whom these policies apply.

General security policy shortcomings

Having said all of the above, we did encounter numerous sufficiently large companies that don't have any information security policies whatsoever. We have seen even more businesses that have security policies to observe formalities ("the compliance demands it!" or "the customers want us to have one") or for the sake of appearance ("look, we care about security, we have a beautifully bound 400-page policies tome!"). The policies exist but are completely ignored. They are not read, updated, followed, and, of course, not reviewed and reassessed. Many security specialists, in particular on the technical side, view the policies as a mere formality, annoying bureaucracy and even simply as a waste of time. If the situation is similar to the ones we have just outlined, these opinions of policies are entirely correct. One of the key aims of information security assessments must be to ensure that such a state of affairs is avoided or abolished.

We will review more specific details regarding hands-on security policy auditing in the upcoming chapter of this book. This chapter is dedicated to security governance – the strategic side. When performing a general assessment, the first thing the auditors should look for is whether the security policies are not generated via some clueless automated tool, or by taking a publicly available template or someone else's policy and using a find-and-replace function. If you have looked at such tools and written numerous security policies consulting various templates yourself, this should not be difficult. It should not be harder than spotting plagiarism in students' works is to an experienced lecturer.

A hallmark of following a mindless template or adapting others' policies is the presence of elements that are completely irrelevant for the company or organisation. This signifies the cardinal sin of the ISMS (if actually existent!): being out of touch with the business model, modes of operation and aims of a company. The irrelevant elements can vary. It could be assigning responsibilities to positions – or even whole departments and teams – not available within the company. It might be covering areas of business operations that are completely absent. We suggest the following general set of security policies strongly aligned with ISO27001:

- Information security organisation
- Classifying information and data
- Controlling access to information and systems
- Processing information and documents
- Purchasing and maintaining commercial software
- Securing hardware, peripherals and other equipment
- Combating malware and other cyber crime
- Controlling e-commerce information security
- Developing and maintaining in-house software
- Dealing with physical security considerations
- Addressing personnel issues related to security

- Delivering security training and staff security awareness
- Complying with legal and policy requirements
- Detecting and responding to information security incidents
- Planning for business continuity
- Acceptable use policy
- Telecommuter and remote work security policy
- Mobile & BYOD security policy
- Password policy

These policies may exist as the listed separate chapters (highly preferable, not least because some of the chapters are specialised, rather than being suitable for all staff!). They can also be arranged in chapters combining several topics at once; for example, Acceptable use + Telecommuter and remote work + Mobile and BYOD policies can be one chapter that all employees have to adhere to and sign. In the past, we have audited a company that had security policies dedicated to in-house software development (*chapter 9* of the above), and another that possessed a fully-blown e-commerce (*chapter 8*) policy set. However, the first company did not develop *or even plan to develop* any software in a foreseeable future. The second did not perform *or plan to perform* any e-commerce activities. Above, we have marked the planning intent in italics because sometimes things are done in advance in the interests of scalability. These were clearly not such cases. If the Standard recommends so, it does not mean that you have to do it even if only to become compliant. Practical demands should be addressed first and, if a severe security incident takes place, being compliant can actually make things worse from a legal viewpoint.

After the auditors have finished searching for unnecessary *and clearly obsolete* elements within the policies, they should start looking for other gaps. The most obvious gap is when a whole chapter or subject section is missing. The proposed list of topical policy chapters provides a good reference point, but is by no means complete. For example, if a company relies heavily on wireless networks in its everyday business operations, then a sound wireless security policy should be created. There can be a security policy on managing security vendor relationships and evaluating security of the supply chain (proposed in ISO27001 Annex A 15.1.1), or a policy regulating security of Cloud and SaaS resources in use, or a dedicated policy on information security risks management, or a policy on implementation of cryptographic controls. The latter is also suggested in ISO27001 Annex A 10.1.1 but we humbly think that having a good cryptography standard in the company is more important. Such policy chapters are not listed in the proposed set. Nevertheless, not having them where highly relevant for business might constitute serious gaps. This underlines the necessity of security auditors having a good knowledge of their auditee's business environment and its key dependencies.

The next overall security policy review stage will need to weight the chapters against each other. You may find out that while all relevant topics are covered, this coverage is highly uneven. Such irregularity often discloses the policy author's main background, which can be management, technical, human resources or even legal. By analysing which policy chapters are well-cultivated and to the point, and which are frankly poor and were compiled in haste or not thoroughly reviewed, this background is easy to deduce. When contemplating Clausewitz's wisdom earlier in this section, we explicitly stated that "security policies cannot have a two-fold or three-fold point of view". Being the top management's written expression of information security direction and intent, they cannot afford to have one of the lower level specialist's views as prevalent. Thus, irregular coverage of various information security topics is also a serious strategic gap, second only to not covering some of the areas at all. If this unevenness is very high, it is a clear indication that the Maginot line mentality is present. Too much effort is dedicated to a specific scope of activity and field of knowledge, at the expense of its equally important counterparts. The only justification for clearly preferring one information security area over the other can be derived from thorough analysis of the corresponding security risks. In such a case it will be documented and communicated to the auditor.

When checking the policies, pay due attention to their general style and depth. Clarity is easy to verify. For instance, *'computer and network appliance premises must be safeguarded against unlawful and unauthorized physical intrusion. All visitors to these premises must be physically supervised'* is a very clear physical access security policy statement. The evaluation of depth, however, is a delicate issue that requires experience and expertise to reach the necessary balance.

It is common knowledge that information security policy statements must be general, if not generic. The 'technicalities' should be left for the corresponding downstream guidelines, standards, manuals, and so on. It is very easy to slip from the strategic level of the policies to the tactical level of such specialist documentation. This is a typical error of security professionals, who get carried away by their special background-related knowledge when composing policy statements. It is not, however, a particularly dreadful error. It only means that, as the implementation inevitably changes, the correlating policy will have to be reviewed, rewritten and reapproved. Although, when such change is frequent the policy may simply become ignored, especially since the approval from senior management is likely to be necessary.

Statements that are too general present a much larger problem. They are also a good indication that some standard policy template was used without giving much thought to its relevance for the business. *"All sensitive data must be encrypted"* is not a security policy statement, but simply an expression of common sense. *"All backups of 'highly confidential' data must be protected with strong cryptography"* is a good policy statement providing that 'highly confidential' is a designated classification level in the implemented data classification. It shows precisely which defined data classification category ("highly confidential") is covered, and where ("all backups") it must be protected. The word "strong" also makes a huge difference, providing that a downstream standard clearly defining what is acceptable as "strong cryptography" in the company, and what isn't. For example, it might say that when it comes to symmetric block ciphers, only AES with a minimal 128-bit key size can be used. This discussion has inevitably brought us to the subject of verifying whether every security policy is properly supported with all necessary downstream documentation, as well as the corresponding processes and controls. It will be reviewed in the less 'strategic' chapters of this book.

2: Security Auditing, Governance, Policies and Compliance

Addressing security audits in policy statements

To accomplish the discourse on general assessments of information security policies, we still need to address the coverage of security assessments in the policies. In the chapter on complying with legal and policy requirements, a section on complying with security policies would appear to be the most appropriate part of the suggested streamlined information security policy to cover the subject of information security audits. Just as an example, its corresponding statements might look like:

- *'The <responsible senior manager, CISO, chief compliance officer> shall initiate semi-annual information security assessments and employ trusted third-party auditors to evaluate the degree of compliance with the current Information Security Policy'.*

- *'These information security assessments can be external, internal or otherwise specialised as determined and approved by <company name>'s security committee'.*

- *'All files and documents related to the Information Security Policy compliance and audits are considered to be "highly confidential" and must be appropriately safeguarded. A register of their location and ownership is to be created, maintained and safeguarded as "highly confidential" data'.*

- *'A reassessment of the threats and risks involved relating to <company name>'s business activities must take place periodically to ensure that the company is adequately insured at all times'.*

- *'Managers and system owners must ensure compliance with information security policies and standards through regular system security reviews, penetration tests and other relevant activities undertaken by competent testers.'*

2: Security Auditing, Governance, Policies and Compliance

- *'Information security audits should be carefully planned to minimise disruption to operational processes and systems. All affected employees or other users are to be informed of any such activities at least a week in advance.'*

Periodic or triggered assessment of security policies must be covered in the chapter on information security organisation, information security policy review or similar subsections. Its statements might be akin to:

- *'<Company name>'s Information Security Policy shall undergo a review at least annually'.*

- *'The management shall form an ad-hoc review committee to create, update, or review policies when significant changes are necessary prior to the regular (annual) review'.*

- *'The Information Security Policy review procedure is to be endorsed and supported by <company name>'s senior management, and signed-off by the <responsible senior manager position> prior to initiation'.*

- *'Trusted and competent third-party consultants can be employed to assist with the Information Security Policy review if deemed necessary by <company name>'s senior management'.*

Additional policy entries might cover who is responsible for supervising information security audits depending on their scope and specific nature. More often than not this is a direct responsibility of the company's CISO.

On security assessments and compliance

'Regulation-SOX, HIPAA, GLB, the credit-card industry's PCI, the various disclosure laws, the

2: Security Auditing, Governance, Policies and Compliance

European Data Protection Act, whatever--has been the best stick the industry has found to beat companies over the head with. And it works. Regulation forces companies to take security more seriously, and sells more products and services.' – Bruce Schneier

Regulations and standards are the top-down approach taken to the absolute. The top (from which the regulations and standards are hammered down) is literally removed from the company or organisation to the realm of a higher authority. This is somewhat similar to the role of the United Nations in the world's political affairs – take it for good or bad. But at least in the UN the representatives of different nations can vote. In contrast, any down-top flow in information security regulations and standards is extremely limited. There is usually little you can do to alter them, unless you are a part of the regulatory body yourself. Sometimes, however, there is a window to contribute when the standard is still in drafts, as it was with ISO27001:2013 for a quite protracted period of time.

Compliance to industry standards and legal regulations is, overall, a good thing. As Bruce Schneier pointed out, it forces companies and organisations to do something about information security or face various penalties without waiting for an incident to happen. It aspires to provide a defined security baseline for the whole variety of business operations. It sells products, but beware the 'shiny box with flashing lights' or its more modern application or service counterpart mindset. Being compliant while some of your rivals aren't can provide a significant competitive advantage. Sometimes, it can open whole markets. For the auditors, compliance demands are beneficial not only because they provide their bread and butter by forcing companies to subscribe for security assessments. Technically speaking, at least some standards and regulations provide highly useful reference points for assessing processes and controls while streamlining them across entire industries. Or so the theory goes.

In practice, the UN analogy seems to be a reasonable one. Sometimes the intervention of the UN stops wars and mitigates disasters. Sometimes it completely fails to do so. The predecessor of the UN was completely toothless to prevent the Second World War. There are many companies and organisations that are fully compliant to various standards, from ISO/IEC 27001 to PCI DSS, and yet had severe security breaches that made large media waves. The UK FSA Detailed IT Controls Form (Annex 1) has dozens of pages dedicated to information security requirements, including independent penetration testing. Nonetheless, we have encountered plenty of companies that were fully FSA-compliant but didn't even have a security policy. We have also dealt with a bank that had it all on paper, but has been severely penalised by the FSA for lack of IT security controls which were, indeed, abysmal. In fact, we still haven't seen any detailed statistics comparing both the number and impact of security incidents between companies compliant and non-compliant to a selected industry standard. Doing such statistical research would be a difficult task. Its results could be easily biased. Besides, for the bulk of companies, incident statistics are confidential information not to be released to the outside world; in some parts, however, public release of security incidents information is a legal requirement.

The erroneous path to compliance

In some situations, regulations and standards can become part of a problem rather than its intended solution. Just like information security in general, they are frequently treated as a necessary (enforced) evil that must be shaken off with minimal resources and time expenditure. This leads to a very formal and superficial approach. The auditees build 'Potemkin villages' or, to put it more precisely, 'Potemkin fortresses' for compliance auditors to see. Unfortunately, the latter are often perfunctory themselves. They go through a prefabricated check-list of expected results, apply it to the presented Potemkin fortress, and churn out another 'everything is OK, you are compliant' report. The behaviour of such auditees is very similar to that of the crammer students who mechanically memorise answers to the expected exam questions instead of properly studying and comprehending the examined subject. When encountering real-life issues pertinent to this subject, such graduates are commonly lost, not to mention that such knowledge is quickly forgotten once the exam is over.

When the auditees are at least honest to themselves and understand that their Potemkin fortresses do not provide any *actual* protection, the aforementioned issue is half the trouble. The real calamity unfolds when the auditees start believing their own smoke and mirrors. Then the false sense of security slips in. It is your mortal foe. The military parallel is thinking that a certain section of the front line is reasonably defended while it lays bare in front of the opponent. Never underestimate the adversaries: sooner or later they will find such gaps and ruthlessly exploit them. And if we look at passive security incidents only, the thread will tear where it is the weakest. When applied to information security auditing, the 'something is better than nothing' principle is blatantly wrong. It is wrong because it is incomplete. The complete version should be '*something is better than nothing only if it does not encourage false sense of security in any shape and form*'. Thus, even if the auditee did a very good job at satisfying all compliance demands, and the auditors truly excelled at verifying every single inch of it, do not sit back and cheer. Being fully compliant to any existing information security standard should never instil a false sense of security. It is only a step on a long way to becoming adequately secure, even if making this step requires tremendous efforts from the company management and its subordinates. These pains are largely justified, however.

Keeping in mind the problems we have just discussed, perhaps there is a need to single out the narrow, compliance-centric approach as one of the strategic anti-pattern flaws to look for during ISMS assessments. Sometimes, when a company does not have a CISO or equivalent, its information security management is handled by the compliance officer. In other cases, the compliance issues are so hard-pressing that all resources are re-oriented to resolve them and to get that 'damn cert' as soon as possible. In these situations, the general security orientation may suffer from severe confusion. However harsh and unsettling the compliance auditors might be, they are not the enemy. The main aim of any information security act and safeguard is to protect data and systems – not to get certified. Information security standards and regulations also serve the same goal: they are not a noumenalist thing-in-itself. Armies exist to fight battles rather than participate in parade displays and successfully pass inspections of the General Staff. Apart from possible disorientation, the narrow, compliance-centric approach can also promote what we have earlier called a drill-machine mentality. This is not surprising, considering that the down-top flow is restricted and the primary source of initiative lies outside the entity, being a regulatory body or a standard committee. To avoid such shortfalls, the following suggestions could be helpful:

- *'The senior management of the company or organisation must intercept the compliance initiative and become its main source'.*

- *'There must be a clear understanding that while the compliance demands shape security programs and systems, their 'command and control' are still internal and must serve the specific aims of the business first'.*

- *'An attitude of getting the most and the best out of any security compliance audits and their follow-up reactions **in terms of actual/practical information security** should be developed'.*

In our earlier metaphor of world politics, the UN undoubtedly shapes the political landscape, but does not violate the sovereignty of its member states (with a few possible *force majeure* exceptions). The states, on the other hand, are trying to get maximal benefits for themselves out of different UN initiatives.

Getting down to earth

The paradox of information security-related standards and regulations is that, while being stringent and rigorous in essence and on the paper, they can be very lax when it comes to practical implementations and their assessments. The main reason for this looseness is that they are too general and do not go deep under the bonnet from many security specialists' perspectives. On the other hand, some of the regulations address only the limited areas of information security, and don't even do so directly.

One should always keep in mind, that at the end of the day regulations like the Sarbanes-Oxley Act, Basel Accord, Solvency and GLBA are financial by their very nature. For them, information security is auxiliary. It should be reviewed, but is not likely to be the decisive factor in getting compliant. It is one thing among the great many. Sarbanes-Oxley 404 assessment approach is a very good illustration of this statement. These regulations do not explicitly enforce specific, highly relevant types of hands-on information security audits like penetration tests or social engineering checks. In our experience, sometimes auditors that verify compliance to such regulations pick on such matters, but more often they do not. In a similar manner, FSA auditors in the UK often ignore the presence or absence of specific security assessment services. Auditors from one of the Big Four once ran FSA compliance-triggered security assessment of a company we had been supplying with internal and external penetration tests for years. They were totally unaware of these tests and didn't even ask the auditee for the most recent test report. If they did, it would have saved them plenty of time. Besides, they could have synchronised with us in verifying whether various security issues we had previously discovered had been fixed prior to the next planned penetration test. The auditee company could have gained numerous benefits from such collaboration.

Now let us turn to information security-specific standards, namely ISO/IEC 27001 and PCI DSS. ISO/IEC 27001, as one would expect, is fully ISMS-centred. There is no point reiterating the whole ISO 27001 certification process in this brief section. Its descriptions are widely available in the public domain, just search for the '27001 implementers forum'. With regard to building and assessing an information security management system, ISO27001 does a pretty good job, and there don't seem to be any viable, widely recognised alternatives. What is important to understand, though, is that the ISMS is only a part of the overall information security of a company. A crucial, backbone, core, organising, structuring part, but not the entire thing. While this could sound highly obvious, at least some security professionals with mainly managerial background tend to neglect this basic truth. Returning to our warfare analogy, the ISMS can be compared to the C&C chain, and security policies to military regulations, codes of discipline and field manuals. History knows many great armies that possessed the most perfect chain of command, organisation, orderliness, the books . . . and were completely defeated at the end.

ISO27001 compliance audits traditionally concentrate on policies, other security documentation, ISMS processes and only then the controls themselves. Assessing the actual implementation of controls is frankly not their strongest trait. Nor should it be. Security policies, standards and guidelines have to prescribe more specific implementation-centric audit types. Reviews of these important documents must verify that these are prescribed correctly. Such specialised security assessments, like penetration testing and social engineering checks mentioned above, must compliment verification of ISMS. In fact, they are a down-top (implementation – process – policy) hands-on method of this verification. Only when the harmony between both top-down and down-top approaches is achieved, with the 'security audit architecture' attain its "*absolute form*".

The PCI DSS, however, is somewhat expected to get under the bonnet with a greasy toolkit. It explicitly prescribes specific technical security controls, safeguards and their regular audits. This is what the PCI DSS states regarding the latter in accordance with the defined merchant tiers:

- *'Level 1 – Any merchant processing more than 6,000,000 transactions per year, merchants identified by any card association as Level 1 or merchants that have suffered a hack or an attack that resulted in an account data compromise. Level 1 Merchants validate by undergoing an Annual On-Site Security Audit by a Qualified Security Assessor and carry out a Quarterly Network Scan utilising an Approved Scanning Vendor'*

- *'Level 2 – Any merchant processing 1 million to 6 million transactions per year. Level 3 – Any merchant processing between 20000 and 1 Million transactions per year. Merchants with Levels 2 and 3 validate PCI Compliance by completing an Annual PCI Self-Assessment Questionnaire and carry out a Quarterly Network Scan utilising an Approved Scanning Vendor'*

- *'Level 4 – Up to 20,000 transactions per year. Level 4 merchants validate PCI Compliance by completing an Annual PCI Self-Assessment Questionnaire and carry out a Quarterly Network Scan utilising an Approved Scanning Vendor'*

Sounds good – especially considering that those who have suffered from a severe 'active' security incident are automatically assigned to Level 1.

To refresh your memories, *Table 1* presents twelve requirements for PCI DSS compliance, organised into six logically related groups called "control objectives." These are also PCI DSS audit targets.

Table 1: PCI DSS requirements

Control objectives	Control objectives
Build and maintain a secure network	1: Install and maintain a firewall configuration to protect cardholder data.
	2: Do not use vendor-supplied defaults for system passwords and other security parameters.
Protect cardholder data	3: Protect stored cardholder data
	4: Encrypt transmission of cardholder data across open, public networks.
Maintain a vulnerability management programme	5: Use and regularly update anti-virus software or programmes.
	6: Develop and maintain secure systems and applications.
Implement strong access control measures	7: Restrict access to cardholder data by business need-to-know.
	8: Assign a unique ID to each person with computer access.
	9: Restrict physical access to cardholder data.
Regularly monitor and test networks	10: Track and monitor all access to network resources and cardholder data.
	11: Regularly test security systems and processes.
Maintain an information security policy	12: Maintain a policy that addresses information security for employees and contractors.

There are also six milestones for prioritising PCI DSS compliance efforts, which are shown on the *Table 2*.

Table 2: PCI DSS Prioritised Approach

Milestone	PCI DSS compliance goal
1	Remove sensitive authentication data and limit data retention.
2	Protect the perimeter, internal, and wireless networks.
3	Secure payment card applications.
4	Monitor and control access to your systems.
5	Protect stored cardholder data.
6	Finalise remaining compliance efforts, and ensure all controls are in place.

In relation to requirement 11 (regularly test security systems and processes), the Prioritised Approach sets forth the following prerequisites:

11.1 *'Test for the presence of wireless access points by using a wireless analyser at least quarterly or deploying a wireless IDS/IPS to identify all wireless devices in use'*

11.2 *'Run internal and external network vulnerability scans at least quarterly and after any significant change in the network (such as new system component installations, changes in network topology, firewall rule modifications, product upgrades)'*

11.3 *'Perform external and internal penetration testing at least once a year and after any significant infrastructure or application upgrade or modification (such as an operating system upgrade, a sub-network added to the environment, or a Web server added to the environment)'. These penetration tests must include the following:*
    11.3.1 Network-layer penetration tests
    11.3.2 Application-layer penetration tests

11.4 *'Use intrusion detection systems, and/or intrusion prevention systems to monitor all traffic in the cardholder data environment and alert personnel to suspected compromises. Keep all intrusion detection and prevention engines up to date'.*

11.5 *'Deploy file integrity monitoring software to alert personnel to unauthorized modification of critical system files, configuration files or content files; and configure the software to perform critical file comparisons at least weekly'.*

We should note that PCI DSS requirement 12 is not only about creating and maintaining appropriate information security policies. It also covers other elements of the ISMS, even though in this aspect it is not as complete as ISO/IEC 27001 and its corresponding ISO/IEC 27002 guidelines. Besides, at least some parts of the PCI DSS requirements, such as requirements 9 and 12, address issues of social engineering attacks.

Is the PCI DSS perfect? Nothing is. One can still be technically meticulous and note a few problems lurking within the Standard. Such discrepancies happen. The matters more relevant for the current discussion are that:

- *'PCI DSS standard has a limited scope. Only the companies and organisations that accept payment cards, store or transmit card or transaction data are covered'.*

Producing a PCI DSS-like compulsory standard that would affect all industries that hold sensitive (for example, personal) data would be a tremendous step forward in upholding a high level of information security and combatting cyber crime. Even better, such a standard could combine the strengths of both ISO/IEC 27001 and the PCI DSS.

- *'This limited scope is transferred downwards within a single company or organisation. Only the systems,*

*premises and communication channels that belong to the
"cardholder data environment" (CDE) need to be
compliant'.*

This opens a potential gap for lateral attacks and may lead
to development of the Maginot line mentality within the
affected entities. We will heavily review the subject of
'outflanking' attacks in the fifth chapter of this book. By
the way, note how the 'grand politics' (the business goals
and reasons behind the PCI DSS) influence the 'battlefield
technicalities' (which parts of the IT infrastructure of a
separate company are protected in accordance with the PCI
DSS, and which are not). We have to say, though, that in
the current version of the PCI DSS the definition of the
'cardholder domain' has been expanded to include all
infrastructure close to systems where card data is stored.
For instance, if a single system on the network is holding
card data, then the entire network independently of its size
becomes a part of the CDE. If a SaaS application has access
to the cardholder domain, then it shall fall under PCI
regulations, for instance 6.6 Code security review. This
partially mitigates the problem described.

- *'At the very least, PCI DSS network scans and their
reporting formats still need optimisation and streamlining',*

This statement comes from pure experience. We have seen
many scans and reports from PCI DSS Approved Scanning
Vendors (ASVs). There are, of course, PCI Security
Standards Council requirements for the ASVs. ASVs have
to be reapproved annually. Two years ago, PCI Security
Standards Council requirements became more stringent,
particularly regarding the approved scanning tools and
methodologies themselves. Becoming an officially
registered ASV started to become more difficult, and

numerous existing vendors have lost their status and were removed from the lists. But the real quality of ASV scans and their reporting is still not the same. Some ASVs seem to perform reasonably well within the limited scope of quarterly security scanning. Others still use vulnerability scanners that are known to miss whole classes of security flaws and produce numerous false positive results. Some scanning reports are sufficiently detailed. Other may simply say "these systems are secure" and supplement it with fragments of a common scanning tool output without provision of detailed technical information, which is highly useful in fixing the discovered issue, not to mention to eliminate a false positive. Remember that in information security auditing *'something is better than nothing only if it does not encourage false sense of security in any shape and form'*. Vulnerability scanning cannot be a substitute for proper penetration testing, and has very little to do with ISO27001-style overall security audits (supposed to be substituted by answers to self-assessment questions for PCI levels 2-4, where internal audits by a visiting QSA are not required). Yet it often serves as grand management excuse not to do both: after all we are PCI-compliant, so why bother while we can save? Can you sense the ghastly spectre of the false sense of security creeping in?

CHAPTER 3: SECURITY ASSESSMENTS CLASSIFICATION

'If tactical facts in one case are entirely different from those in another, then the strategic must be so also, if they are to continue consistent and reasonable.' – Carl von Clausewitz

In theory, everything must be thoroughly assessed and verified to eliminate all kinds of security vulnerabilities and gaps. In the real world, however, there are limitations imposed by both budget and time. Because of these restrictions, the most critical areas must be identified to be audited first. Or, unfortunately, to be the only areas where the state of information security is to be assessed for the foreseeable future. Making a correct, well-informed decision concerning the necessary information security audit's scope, priorities, spectrum and characteristics can be an intricate task. We shall thoroughly address it in the next chapter of this book. To be well-prepared for it, though, the auditees need to familiarise themselves with the assessments *a la carte*. The menu is quite extensive, and on numerous occasions the differences between the starter and the dessert are blurred and vague.

There is no universal panacea against information security incidents, whether passive or active. Thus, in the words of Col. John Boyd, *'it is advantageous to possess a variety of responses that can be applied rapidly to gain sustenance, avoid danger, and diminish adversary's capacity for independent action'*. The available variety of information security assessments can be broken up into separate categories in accordance with their targets, aims, methodologies and depth. If judged by applying these multiple parameters, a specific security audit can belong to several categories at once. When selecting the most appropriate information security audit type, it is advantageous to move from the more general categories towards their specialised analogues. Accordingly, we shall review the global classifications first.

On broad categories of security audits

> *'Strategy may follow a great diversity of objects, for everything which appears an advantage may be the object of a combat.'* – Carl von Clausewitz

The systematics discussed in this section are sufficiently common to apply to nearly all types of information security assessment. Previously, we divided the assessment activities into passive and active on the basis of their approach to tackling security issues. To rehearse:

- *'A passive information security assessment is based upon verification against prefabricated checklists'.*
- *'An active information security assessment is based upon vigorously searching for vulnerabilities and gaps employing all relevant knowledge, experience, creativity and insight'.*

Another approach-based division is characterising security audits as *intrusive or non-intrusive*. Intrusive assessments can, but will not necessarily heavily interfere with the audited systems or processes, and all staff involved. As such, it is generally not recommended to perform intrusive audits against live production systems or important business processes and operations. One should be also careful with performing any intrusive auditing during business-critical periods of time (such as the annual performance review, etc.). Nevertheless, since non-intrusive tests usually lack the depth of their counterparts, and testing or pilot set-ups are not always available or feasible, the above advice is frequently ignored. When the estimated impact of a threat is incomparably higher than any disruption an intrusive audit that counters this threat can bring, such passing-by is entirely justified. In any case, intrusive assessments should be more carefully planned, monitored and supervised. Commonly, but not always, the intrusive audits are by their nature active, and non-intrusive are passive. Interviewing employees, checking the physical security of premises, vigorous social engineering and penetration tests are typical examples of intrusive assessment activities. Reviewing security documentation, access lists, audit trails and systems configuration files is usually not intrusive. On many occasions, such activities can be even performed off-site.

Based on the auditors and their target's location, all information security assessments can be divided into *internal and external*. This should not be confused with the assessments being performed by in-house or third-party consultants. There is nothing unusual about external assessments run by an in-house team using rented resources and remotely hosted systems. External assessments are often active and emulate exterior attackers trying to breach perimeter defences and penetrate into the auditee's *information security zone* anywhere it extends. As such, they are penetration testing and social engineering-centred. Regular network vulnerability scans like those required to be PCI DSS compliant and provided by the ASVs is another common example of external security audits.

Internal assessments can come in all shapes and forms, targeting policy, process, operational, human and technical security issues. They are usually done on-site, but this is not entirely obvious. The auditors can review some of the assessed data in their office, if the contract and NDA conditions permit it, auditee data classification is not violated, and appropriate safeguards are in place. It is also possible to install a separate testing system or software kit on the internal auditee network and use it to run a variety of technical checks initiated and controlled remotely over a well-protected VPN link. We strongly discourage taking any highly sensitive data, including personal employee, configuration and password files, off the auditee premises. It doesn't matter how strong the auditors' defences and controls can be, all actions that could create additional security incident opportunities must be avoided. The *information security zone* should be kept as shrunk as possible. At the end of the day, who audits the auditors? Besides, being on-site ensures robust communication between all parties involved, which is crucial in any information security audit's success.

Black, grey and white box tests

According to the initial level of the auditors' access, information security assessments are divided into *black box, grey box and white box* varieties. This classification is traditionally applied to purely technical activities from which it has originated. Nevertheless, we feel it can assume a wider scope and should be viewed as general. To define:

- *'Black box assessments refer to situations where the auditors have no access rights at all and possess very limited information about the audit targets'.*

- *'When performing grey box assessments, the auditors start with having some form of limited, unprivileged access'.*

- *'White box assessments signify that full access to all analysed data, networks and systems is granted throughout the whole audit'.*

To a certain extent, this classification can be applied to non-technical activities. For example, social engineering checks can be black or grey box. If the list of preferred targets is supplied and some physical access to the auditee's premises is granted, a social engineering check no longer belong to the black box category. In theory, ISMS reviews should always fall under the white box category. Due to time and other constraints, however, in practice many of them are closer to shades of grey. This happens because more often than not for a variety of reasons the auditors are not provided with complete and unrestricted access to all relevant processes and documentation.

To summarise, black box tests are directed at assessing risks presented by typical external opponents with no insider knowledge. A great deal of vulnerability scanning, penetration testing and social engineering audit services belongs to this category. The reconnaissance phase plays the pivotal role in any black box activities: to find gaps in the *information security zone* one has to know its boundaries and terrain very well.

Grey box tests evaluate risks stemming from adversaries who are legitimately allowed at least some access rights and admittance to internal information. Such opponents can be rogue employees, as well as customers, guests, vendors, external consultants and partner companies – or, as a matter of fact, *anyone who successfully hijacks their access, whether technically, socially or physically.* When contemplating the 'insider threat', it is of utmost importance to remember that *any external attacker who has managed to get a foothold within becomes a part of this threat.* Thus, *grey box tests are invaluable in assessing defence-in-depth countermeasures and safeguards beyond the protected perimeter.* All testing activities that involve *privilege escalation* are, by definition, grey box.

Finally, white box assessments aim at achieving the highest efficacy of discovering security flaws in a given period of time. The auditors do not have to spend any time on reconnaissance and can get straight to the unabridged matter. Thus, *white box checks present a superb form of quality control, but are usually poor as a form of practical risk assessment.* The white box approach is something of a 'testing lab exercise' that lacks situational realism. Even the internal attackers that hold highly advantageous positions do not usually have full access to anything they desire. Nor do they use the majority of hands-on methodologies typical white box assessments employ. Reviewing security policies and other relevant documentation or scrutinising source code of applications and configuration files of systems are classical examples of white box tests.

Assessments specialisations and actual scopes

The most obvious general classification of information security assessments is splitting them into technical, human resources, operational and management. This division takes into account the audit targets, methods and required professional expertise. At the same time, when discussing the fundamentals we have explicitly specified that any security assessment inevitably addresses all major information security areas simultaneously. The difference seems to be through which specific realm and its applicable methodologies it is *primarily* done in practical terms. The 'chain diagrams' in *Figures 8, 9* and *10* illustrate this point of view using typical examples of what is considered to be purely technical, human or security management auditing tasks.

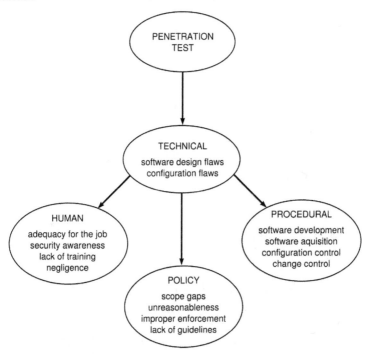

Figure 8: The 'technical' chain example

Through purely technical gaps, our penetration test evaluates other information security realms. The sources of software design or configuration flaws commonly originate from problems in these non-technical areas. For example, before the patch is released by a vulnerable software vendor, the problem is largely technical. As soon as the fix becomes widely available, the issue turns operational, as in 'not following efficient change control, or vulnerability management procedures'.

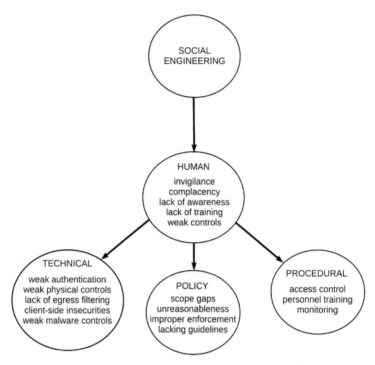

Figure 9: The 'human' chain example

Some people are naturally complacent and naive, but more often than not vulnerability to social engineering is a result of improper security awareness and related training. Also note that a variety of technical countermeasures and security procedures can be used to mitigate social engineering risks. For example, a combination of strong physical controls with strict identity verification procedures (such as those based upon biometrics) is efficient in thwarting physical intrusion attempts. Proper two-, or even three-factor authentication (what you have, what you know, and what you are) can also prevent many social engineering attacks directed at obtaining authentication credentials. End users can not fall prey to infected e-mail attachments if these are discovered and eliminated at the mail server side. Egress filtering against a list of malicious sites updated in real time can thwart many phishing attempts.

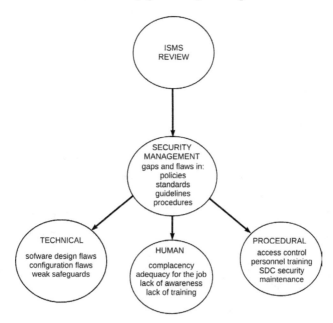

Figure 10: The 'management' chain example

The SDC on the diagram refers to the software development cycle, while the "maintenance" applies to maintaining the existing applications, systems and networks. Practically any security flaw can be (and often is) the end result of information security management gaps.

These schemes are by no means complete. You can add as many factors as you see fit. For example, far more procedures or processes can be listed in *Figure 10*. Nevertheless, the diagrams clearly demonstrate that strict separation of information security assessments into technical, human, process, policy and so on is vague from the strategic perspective. Besides, many real world security assessments can be described as semi-technical, semi-human, or semi-security management, or use a combination of these general areas approaches and methodologies. It will become more apparent in the remaining sections of this chapter.

On technical information security assessments

Different types of technical security audits are casually defined by what is assessed at the first place. The 'what' determines the 'how'. A notable exception is division between vulnerability scanning and penetration testing, which is based upon the level of assessment depth. This separation, and the definitions of vulnerability scanning and penetration testing services in general, still creates plenty of confusion for the users of these services. In his popular book *Schneier on Security*, Bruce Schneier once pointed out that *'Penetration testing is a broad term. It might mean breaking into a network to demonstrate you can. It might mean trying to break into the network to document vulnerabilities. It might involve a remote attack, physical penetration of a data center, or social engineering attacks. It might use commercial or proprietary vulnerability scanning tools, or rely on skilled white-hat hackers. It might just evaluate software version numbers and patch levels, and make inferences about vulnerabilities.'*

We believe that by introducing the overall division of information security assessments into passive and active we have successfully resolved this issue. *Vulnerability scanning is passive. Penetration testing is active.* The rest is technical detail. Thus, to *'just evaluate software version numbers and patch levels, and make inferences about vulnerabilities'* is to perform a typical non-intrusive vulnerability scan. The rest of the activities listed by the security guru are different forms of penetration testing. For the sake of clarity, we discuss social engineering and technical penetration testing as separate types of information security assessments. Thus, the latter in this book refers to the technical activities only.

Server, client and network-centric tests

By their general targets and corresponding methodologies, technical security tests can be separated into three large groups:

- Server-side tests
- Client-side tests
- Network-centric tests

In this separation we did not split application security testing into a separate category. A specific application targeted in such tests can be deployed at the server-side (Cloud servers included), client-side or both. It may implement application-specific, high-OSI layer network protocols, which can be subject to security tests. Hence, application security testing can encompass any of the listed categories, or all three at once. In *chapter 5* we will review application security testing peculiarities in more detail.

Server-side tests are the most traditional form of penetration testing and vulnerability scanning. In modern virtualised environments they can be further split into virtual server and hypervisor tests. Centralised services provided by corporate or organisational servers whenever they are hosted always presented the most lucrative trophy for any attacker. At the same time, breach of their confidentiality, integrity and availability usually has the highest negative impact for owners of these systems. A breach of a hypervisor amplifies this impact by the number of virtual servers it runs, which could well mean a thousand times. Server-side attacks (and their emulation by the auditors) traditionally involve feeding maliciously modified 'client-side' input to the targeted services. It is easier to launch typical server-side attacks since they do not require installation and configuration of any services on the assailant's systems. Such attacks are highly mature and well-researched. The countermeasures against them are also numerous and widely implemented. Due to the latter fact, in recent years the trend has shifted towards client-side (in)security.

Client-side attacks (and their emulation by the auditors) are centred on installation of rogue services that feed maliciously modified 'server-side' input to the targeted end-user applications. Web browsers are the most frequently targeted user applications of today. To execute client-side attacks with success, the assailants need to lure users of a vulnerable application to connect to their rogue servers. This is usually done via the following avenues:

1. phishing;
2. social engineering utilising e-mails, instant messengers, social networks, message boards, and so on;
3. spear-phishing (essentially, a combination of 1 and 2);
4. intercepting and redirecting network traffic so that the users end up visiting the rogue service, or receive a rogue application update.

The latter approach typically requires network traffic access, thus being applicable only when the connections are insecure (shared cable and wireless) or for internally positioned attackers. Alternatively, the assailants can try to poison DNS caches to alter the records so that the users of vulnerable DNS servers can be redirected to a malicious service. At the moment, client-side attacks that involve approaches 1 – 3 are heavily employed by cyber criminals worldwide. The last approach is mainly employed when rogue wireless access points are set to emulate public hotspots, and so on.

The network-centric tests can be subdivided into two categories: testing network appliances and checking security of communication protocols. As servers became harder to crack, the attention was diverted not only to their clients, but also to various network appliances deployed nearby. Security of network appliances is still frequently overlooked. Many system administrators treat them in accordance with the infamous 'if it works, do not break it' principle. As a result, there are still many routers, switches and more specialised appliances that run systems with known security issues. We have heavily elaborated on this problem in the earlier book, *Hacking Exposed Cisco Networks*, where we also blatantly stated that "who controls the router, controls the network". This was written ten years ago, but the problem remains at large.

As for the security of network protocols, it has entered the spotlight due to two major factors:

- Comprehending and popularising the 'insider threat'.
- The spread of wireless networks, including Bluetooth, near-field and other personal area (PAN) wireless connectivity, including for wearable gadgets, sensors and sensor networks, and so on.

While network appliances security can be assessed from anywhere providing the connectivity exists, to check for network protocols vulnerabilities the auditors must be directly plugged into the auditee's network. There are few notable exceptions to this statement, but we won't go into the technical details here. As a general rule, network protocols assessments belong to the realm of internal and wireless security audits.

IT security testing levels and target areas

There are three general levels to which a variety of IT security checks can be applied. These levels are shown in *Figure 11.*

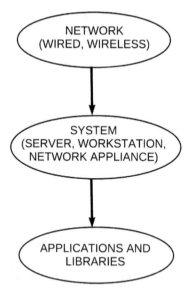

Figure 11: Three planes of technical security assessments

The highest level is the network. All access to corporate or organisational networks can be in-band or out-of-band.

In-band connections are links to the Internet and other networks casually used in everyday business practice. Out-of-band connections are auxiliary links used for specific purposes, such as troubleshooting in cases of major in-band lines failure. External wireless connectivity can be viewed as out-of-band, unless we are talking about connections to last mile wireless providers where they still exist. The most traditional out-of-band form of connectivity is dial-in via POTS (plain old telephone service). Nowadays, old slow dial-in lines for connecting remote users or, for example, payment systems are dying out, being superseded by VPNs over fast links. Nevertheless, reserve dial-in lines are still used for network appliances maintenance and some payment terminals. Thus, one of the most ancient attack types, the wardialing, should not be discarded as a source of potential risks. Where applicable, wardialing tests should be performed.

The middle level is various networked systems. This means absolutely any network-connected device, not just servers, workstations, routers and switches! To keep a wide perspective of things, these include:

- mobile hosts such as tablets and smartphones.
- networked printers and scanners, which often store scanned documents for an indefinite time.
- networked cameras, including CCTV systems.
- VOIP phones and other tele- and videoconferencing equipment.
- networked data storage and backup devices.
- networked systems of physical access control (swipe card readers, biometric systems).
- networked environment control and other sensors and automatic systems they supply data to.

- wireless access points of all kinds.
- load balancing and quality of service (QoS) appliances.
- specialised security appliances, including, but not limited to firewalls, VPN concentrators, Intrusion Prevention Systems (IPS) and their distributed sensors.
- payment terminals and other banking transaction systems.

Security gaps can lurk anywhere. If it is connected, or could be connected to any network, its security state must be verified.

Unless we look for purely configuration-centric gaps, like enabling insecure network protocols or weak authentication means, security testing of systems always ends up in searching for gaps in various software they run including libraries and other dependencies of this software. This is the lowest and the most detailed level of the three. The applications tested can be of a system (for example, device drivers), service (front-end, back-end and middleware included) or end-user types. Security of the environment in which the tested application runs must be always taken into consideration. A serious flaw in a common library used by multiple applications is major trouble in brewing.

In application security testing, the differences between black and white box approaches are probably the most pronounced. Thorough black box application security testing has to involve different fuzzing and reverse engineering methodologies, including bypassing anti-reverse engineering methods such as those based on DRM (digital rights management). We will elaborate more on fuzzing, its types and scope in the fifth Chapter of this book. White box application testing refers to its manual and automated source code reviews often outsourced to specialised vendors. Grey box application testing can apply to situations when some of its modules are open source, and some are proprietary and can't be disclosed to third parties. If the application is not open source and the auditee is not its vendor, then all application testing is legally restricted to observing how it behaves in different environments and under various types of input. Asking the auditors to perform even the most minimalistic reverse engineering of proprietary software is pushing them to break the law. This can be reported. On the other hand, if the auditors themselves offer to reverse engineer a closed source application, the situation is fishy and you should stay away from it as far as you can.

A casual overall technical information security assessment evaluates all three levels progressing in a top-down direction from scanning the network to verifying separate systems, their configuration settings and applications they run. This provides a good slice across the general technical information security state of a company or organisation, and is instrumental in realistic assessment of related risks.

In the majority of situations, however, you cannot have both the all-encompassing scope and breathtaking assessment depth. Not with the imposed limitations of budget and time, anyway. Typically, external and internal tests are treated as completely separate categories, and rightly so. Black, grey and white box audits are also performed separately, or in stages proceeding from black to white. For instance, after security scans of the internal network infrastructure (black or grey box testing), a thorough review of hand-picked appliances configuration files can be performed (white box). Nevertheless, these general classification-based split-ups can be insufficient.

So, highly specific technical security audits are sometimes called for to address what is perceived as the area of highest concern. Most commonly encountered types of such specialised assessment services are selected application or database security testing and wireless network audits.

Above, we have already reviewed application security testing in brief. When a specific application is crucial for business operations and carries significant risks if compromised, its detailed security assessments are routinely ordered. Such audits must be performed at the pre-production stage against pilot installations of the tested application. They should be repeated as a part of the change control process when significant alterations to the application's architecture and functionality are introduced. Casually, these audits are supplemented with penetration tests of the infrastructure that supports the application in the production environment. There is no point in having strong security of the application itself if the server it is hosted on or a back-end database it communicates with can be successfully breached. More often than not, the applications that are explicitly assessed are on-line shopping cards and other software used to perform financial transactions or collect customer data over public untrusted networks. Although in practice it can take all kinds. For instance, we once performed an in-depth evaluation of a novel wireless authentication software that aimed to bring the benefits of WPA Enterprise security for SOHO users.

If you subscribe for a SaaS application that is critical for business, it is vital to understand that its vendor puts it through security scrutiny outlined above. Hence, it comes down to performing appropriate supplier security verification emphasised in ISO27001:2013 A.15.2. Has it been security reviewed? By whom? At which stage? What was the scope of the review? Did it cover all infrastructure supporting the application? Which security controls are implemented to protect the application against all relevant threats? Is security addressed in the application change control? Who has access to the production systems running the application? Is any of its development outsourced to third parties? What are the agreements with such parties and do they cover security issues? Was the security level of such parties verified and how? Which resilience and redundancy measures have been built into the application and its supporting environment? Is the vendor going to report to you any security incidents affecting the application and its milieu? How quickly and in which form are they going to be reported? What are the expected incident and other issues' resolution time? These are but a few questions that must be asked to the supplier of such a service if it has any criticality for your operations and processes.

Talking about wireless security assessments, they do imply using highly specific methodologies that strongly differ from their wired counterparts. It is even difficult to say whether wireless assessments are external or internal. The auditors must be present within the coverage zone of the analysed network, which typically spreads across and beyond the auditee premises. The exception is near-field comms, including those used by physical access control systems at the entrance. Physical location is important. Wireless network defences can be analysed in a more comfortable manner while staying in the auditee offices. However, we recommend running off-premises tests using specialised equipment such as antennas and amplifiers. This allows you to discover where the fuzzy borders of the network or wireless signals from standalone client devices spread. It means knowing where the attackers can position themselves. Are such locations, such as the company's car park, within the security guards' reach or do they have outdoors CCTV coverage? Can an attacker remain there indefinitely without being challenged or even spotted?

At least some wireless security issues are physical, as in radio physics, and require a degree of knowledge in this subject. The encryption protocols employed by WPA and other approaches designed to protect wireless networks differ from their wired siblings. Most importantly, wireless security testing is typically fully black box, with the auditors not having any initial connectivity to the assessed network at all. To emphasise once more, while the majority of today's wireless tests are WiFi-centric, the issues of wireless security are not limited to WiFi. Bluetooth and WiMax, near-field comms and ZigBee also present their share of potential security risks. Below we will also mention security problems of commonly used wireless keyboards. In the future, the number and type of wireless connectivity means will only increase. The same applies to their criticality: we can already see wireless-enabled cardiostimulators (hacking into which can literally kill), wireless BCI (brain-computer interfaces) access to which can allow some rather futuristic forms of social engineering, and numerous personal health sensor wearables. The access to data produced by the latter is going to be particularly interesting for health insurance companies. Perhaps it is time for the current legal definitions of 'personal data' to be redefined.

'Idiosyncratic' technical security tests

There are whole ranges of technical information security assessments that sometimes have little or no relation to any networks and networked hosts. These assessments can include:

- technical evaluation of physical premises controls including monitoring systems such as alarms and CCTV.
- verifying security of RFIDs.
- TSCM (technical surveillance counter-measures) or, to put it simply, bug and frequency sweeping.
- various radio communications security across the entire spectrum.

A lot of corporate physical entry controls are still based on RFIDs, and only some are biometric. RFIDs, obviously, have plenty of other uses from asset tracking to mobile and transportation payments. They also have their growing share of insecurities, mainly directed towards cloning the actual RFID tag or reproducing its signal. Then, in our example, successful unauthorised entry becomes possible. Fully blown RFID exploits are reported, and the talk of RFID viruses and worms is in the air. Thus, if a company or organisation depends on the heavy use of RFIDs – for instance, use in large warehouses for asset inventories and control – and any disruption or compromise of this use may present high impact risks, auditing security of the deployed RFID solution becomes a priority. In general, RFID security is an increasingly popular and actively developing field. Pay attention to what it brings, especially if you are a professional technical security auditor or manage the auditor team. It could be that you will have to expand your arsenal of everyday tools and techniques soon.

TSCM, though, is an entirely different ball game. Electronic surveillance is usually of a great concern when industrial espionage from powerful competitors or even foreign governments is high on the list of risks. In such cases the premises must be built with blocking all compromising radio, optical and acoustic emanations in mind. All unauthorised electronic devices, such as personal phones or tablets, must be banned. Power and phone lines must have appropriate filters and/or white noise generators applied. And so on, until it becomes a fully-blown TEMPEST bunker. TCSM sweeps must be performed by highly professional teams that possess very costly equipment. In the past, the NSA stated that a qualified TSCM team must spend at least $250,000 on necessary hardware. Since then, this sum has probably gone up by quite a margin. Operating this hardware requires skills that need formal engineering training and years of experience to hone. Do not be deluded by someone who will offer you a spy shop tools-based sweep. It might only discover bugs you can buy in a local Maplin or RadioShack store.

We are not TSCM experts and do not perform professional bug sweeps. There are two relevant issues we would like to address, however. The first is that you might, after all, encounter the use of low grade, spy shop bugs within your corporation. It would be 'personal'. Driven by internal skirmishes and squabbles, employees can use them to snoop on their colleagues. Most likely you don't even need a proper TSCM sweep to discover these feeble devices. Your technical specialists would be able to do so with some exciting bed-time reading and an inexpensive wideband radio frequency scanner. Or, most likely, they would be discovered physically after the unusual leaks of information become apparent. Casually, their discovery results from purely human failures of the corporate James Bond wannabes.

The second issue is far more interesting and challenging. Ten years ago we used to amuse guests by playing music with a PC monitor and a free software tool that controls it. The signal could be picked up in a neighbouring room with a wideband scanner at about 10 MHz frequency. Wrapping the screen in a tin foil did not help. A few years later, one of the authors was informed of a software backdoor that employs a PC serial port to transmit stored keystroke data, also at about 10 MHz, by manipulating voltage at its pins. While it is likely that the receiver has to be positioned in the next room across the wall, this is still a rather unconventional mode of out-of-band information leakage. Then, this year, there were a few proof-of-concept demonstrations of out-of-band communications employing ultrasound generated by in-built laptop sound cards. Again, while the other node will have to be positioned in the same room with which the node communicates, risks presented by such unconventional backchannels cannot be discarded. A room in question can be a large conference, lecture or airport hall. The trend of 'traditional TSCM' steadily merging with 'conventional IT security' becomes progressively evident. For example, keystrokes can be relatively easily captured and decoded by:

- intercepting signals sent by wireless keyboards, mostly operating using Bluetooth.

- directing an invisible infrared laser beam at the back of a laptop, or at the table surface next to it.

- monitoring the minute voltage changes of a power line to which a computer is plugged.

Meanwhile, passwords can be captured via hacked (or provided as a gift, or 'incidentally' found 'lost') smartphones cameras, and a smartphone gyroscope has been already transformed into a microphone by Stanford security researchers who produced an app called Gyrophone to do so.

All of this could be done using cheap DIY hardware and public domain open source software tools to go with it. There is far more to it than we have touched upon. For instance, we did not outline hacking into GPS (could be critical for logistics companies) and other satellite communications (a channel frequently overlooked by corporate security teams, yet the volumes of sensitive data still carried via satlinks in plain text remains astonishing!). To conclude, methods and approaches that firmly belonged to the realm of government agents or professional corporate spies in earlier times are becoming fully accessible to Joe the hacker from a local 2600 or Defcon group. It should not be ignored. When internal and physical premises security audits are performed, the auditors should look out for all unusual activities and contraptions they might encounter. The latter are easy to discover. For now.

On non-technical information security audits

Just like their 'geekier' siblings, all non-technical information security assessments are subdivided in accordance with their primary targets. These targets inevitably determine the methodologies utilised. A non-technical security audit can concentrate on:

- premises and other physical security.
- people.
- Documentation.
- operations and procedures.

With the previous section finishing on auditing wireless security, some aspects of physical access control and

TSCM, it makes perfect sense to proceed with the premises reviews first.

Premises and physical security checks

Assessing the security of premises can be a standalone task. But most of all it is an important element of more general internal information security audits, or certification audits including ISO27001. As such, it supplements their technical, human, policy, process and operational components, and is reciprocally reinforced by them. A word of warning: physical security issues often stick out like a sore thumb. They are the easiest to discover in the limited audit time. They tend to be those making the first impression on the compliance auditor. So, do not underestimate them when it comes to formal certification or customer audits, even though in the reality they may present lower security risks than, for example, malware.

Figure 12 depicts the main areas addressed by security assessments of corporate or organisational premises.

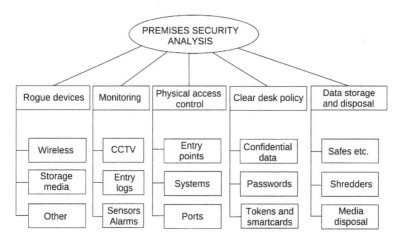

Figure 12: Five domains of premises security checks

Physical access control means having control over all forms of physical admittance to premises, printed information, systems, data storage and networks. It does not limit itself to doors, receptions, keys and swipe cards/employee badges. Of course, all traditional physical entry points must have sufficient authentication and supervision means. The strictest controls must be applied to:

- all outside entries.

- all entries to server rooms.

- all entries to other premises where confidential data and critical systems are stored.

Such entry points must be constantly monitored. The doors should withstand all unlawful entry attempts that do not involve serious welding job or dynamite. If an entry code is used it must be difficult to guess. Check how often this code is changed, who is allowed to know it and why. These 'who' and 'why' also apply to all other physical authentication means including ID and swipe cards, RFID tokens and biometrics. How are they issued and withdrawn if an employee leaves? What are the procedures for cancelling and replacing stolen or lost tokens and cards? How third-party and guest access is granted and supervised? Is there an open badge-wearing policy so that the trespassers can be easily recognised? Is it actually followed? Does the badge allow clear employee identification (name, photo ID)? What kinds of badges are there (employee, visitor, vendor, anything else)? What access level to which premises do different badge types provide? Who controls it, and how? Does it actually work as intended? Are employees taught to counter tailgating and have they learned their lessons well? As you can see, we have already crossed the border into the realm of physical access control policies, guidelines and correctness of their implementation.

Controlling physical access to systems most commonly means that:

- mobile computers and other media cannot be stolen.
- unsupervised systems are protected with a screen lock.
- bootloader and BIOS passwords are applied (optional, but rather useful control).

Using biometric (fingerprint-based) and two-factor authentication for physical computer access is gaining popularity and will hopefully join the above list soon. When verifying security of physical system access, always check that:

- the screensaver would lock the screen in ten minutes or so.
- screen lock, BIOS or bootloader passwords are strong.
- computers are configured to boot from the hard drive first.
- when dealing with multi-boot computers, boot time protection is equivalent for all operating systems installed.

Besides, if countermeasures against connecting USB and other devices are implemented, their efficacy should be verified.

Controlling physical access to ports means that unauthorised devices cannot be plugged into the network. In particular, this includes physical ports in all public access areas – lobbies, canteens, halls, corridors, meeting rooms. Ports used for VOIP phones connectivity are not exempt. As a general rule, all physical ports which are not in use must be turned off on the corresponding switches. All physical ports used to manage network appliances or for monitoring purposes (e.g. Cisco SPAN) must be adequately protected. At the least, strong passwords must be applied. When analysing physical access to systems and network ports we inevitably plunge into the realm of technical internal audits. And, of course, all of these vital countermeasures against physical intrusion must be reflected in the relevant security policies and guidelines.

Monitoring goes hand in hand with physical access control. Traditionally, physical monitoring refers to CCTV coverage of physical points of entry and all areas where confidential information and critical systems are present. When reviewing CCTV security it is important to check:

- which areas are properly covered.
- whether movement sensing and night vision functionalities are implemented.
- how secure the communications between CCTV cameras and monitoring stations are.
- who is reviewing CCTV records and how often it is done.
- who has access to the records *and systems that store them.*
- whether the records are properly timestamped.
- how the records are kept and backed up.

In a nutshell, CCTV records should be treated in a similar manner with systems logs. Unlike logs, however, video clips take plenty of space. We have seen many companies where the server storing the records ran out of space. As a result, older records were simply being overwritten by more recent ones. A correct implementation of the system must include secure regular backups of the older records, as well as *redundant servers* in case a crash happens. Another problem we have regularly encountered is access to record-storing systems being granted to anyone in the IT support team. This is not a good security practice. The records should be treated as confidential data with need-to-know, role-based access to it.

In a very similar way, all logs from physical entry control systems must be maintained, protected and preserved. Since these logs are not video or audio data, encrypting them would not present any technical inconvenience and is highly recommended. From our practice, we recall a forensic investigation in which the entry logs were decisive in determining and later prosecuting a malicious insider. He had actually managed to delete the logs, but in the process of investigation they were successfully restored.

Quite often, both monitoring and physical access control are run by the facilities management of a landlord company. Besides, nowadays it is common to outsource monitoring and even physical access control maintenance to a third party that has no relation to the facility. All of these must be scrutinised as any other third-party security vendor is. The key points to pay attention to are:

- How fast and how often such a company will provide records and logs of physical monitoring and access control, including ad-hoc requests in incident cases.
- Their quality, clarity, integrity protection and level of detail.
- How quickly amendments to physical access control are made (for example, if an employee leaves, how long will it take to cancel their physical access?).

- If physical access control is supervised by facilities management, whom else do they allow through (their personnel, cleaners, technicians, vendors, anyone else) and how such access is controlled.

How such systems behave in emergencies (for instance, if they are maintained remotely via the Internet, will they completely go down if the Internet connection is lost? What will happen in the case of power failure?). A few words should be said about verifying environment monitoring and controls. While this may not sound like a relevant security subject, don't be so sure. First of all, availability is still a part of the CIA triad. If environment support systems fail, a major collapse of servers and appliances is likely occur, resulting in severe disruption of availability, or even loss of valuable data. After all, CISSP textbooks do always include a section on fire, flood and other disaster and elements-related issues. Do you actually have a fire extinguisher not further than 30 yards away from the server room?

What makes this topic a much hotter one is that nowadays many environment monitoring and control systems operate via IP networks. As such, they present a very interesting (and often insufficiently defended) target for hacking. Evaluating this issue properly belongs to the area of internal penetration testing. When performing physical premises audit, do not limit the checks to verifying that the environmental and building control systems are operating as expected. Verify whether they are managed over a wired or wireless IP network. If such is the case, enquire how the management access to such systems is protected and who is authorised to access them.

Another important domain of physical information security audits is to assess that the clear desk policies are followed.

Unattended confidential data should not tumble about in any shape or form, on paper, written on whiteboards, or in electronic format. This applies not only to the employees' desks, but also to networked printers or scanners, often positioned in corridors accessed by unauthorised persons, where such documents are sometimes forgotten or lie for a long time before being picked up. It helps to have a separate 'confidential' printer or scanner, which is physically supervised. Alternatively, it could be protected with a PIN and supervised via CCTV. It is generally recommended that HR, finance, senior management and departments that deal with sensitive R&D information have their own printers and scanners not shared with anyone else, whether physically or over the network. Also verify whether wireless connectivity of such office appliances is either disabled or protected, strong passwords to access them over the network are set, and they do not store any confidential documentation without a clear business need.

Passwords are, of course, confidential data. Since the problem of them being written down is so excruciatingly common, in *Figure 12* we have placed passwords into a separate box. Below, authentication tokens, smart cards and, potentially, other physical authentication gimmicks are noted. Whether used for the premises entry or system and network access, they must be kept in a secure place where they cannot be stolen or lost.

Two remaining domains of physical information security checks are in a way related to clear desk policies. If confidential data is not lying around, then where is it stored? Is it properly locked? Is the location supervised? Who can access it? Are there backup copies? How these copies are secured? How all of this is inventoried? After checking for these basic facts, verify if such data is disposed in a secure manner. Technical destruction of sensitive data in electronic format can be logical or physical. Here we are interested in the latter. In a nutshell, it comes down to mechanical grinding of data carriers, like hard drives or CDs. We can recall an instance of a company that had a room literally filled to a ceiling with old hard drives awaiting physical destruction to be done by a third party. In a meanwhile, the room was not properly secured and any employee could pick up a hard drive or two.

Both paper documents and CDs, as well as unneeded or obsolete credit cards, are destroyed by shredding. It is a good practice to have separate 'confidential' shredders and bins. Having separate shredders for the departments listed during printer and scanner discussion (HR, Finance, senior management, R&D) also helps. Office shredders are not considered a good icebreaker topic at a party. It is useful to know that different types of shredders exist, however, and there are currently six security levels of their classification in accordance with the DIN 32757-1 standard:

- Level 1 = 12mm paper strips
- Level 2 = 6mm strips
- Level 3 = 2mm strips (confidential)
- Level 4 = 2 × 15mm paper particles (commercially sensitive)
- Level 5 = 0.8 × 12mm particles (top secret or classified)
- Level 6 = 0.8 × 4mm particles (top secret or classified)

So, a shredder for confidential documents should at least satisfy level 3 requirements. It must not be one of the cheap strip-cut devices which slice pages into narrow strips as long as the original sheet of paper. It should, of course, support the shredding of CDs.

Finally, the premises must be thoroughly checked for rogue devices. In general, the term 'rogue device' can apply to any unauthorised equipment that presents security risks. In the past, the accent was on rogue modems that could fall prey to wardialing. In this day and age, the term became nearly synonymous with 'wireless rogue device'. By providing unaccounted out-of-band connectivity, *both rogue wireless access points and unauthorised client devices* constitute a grave threat. The best way to discover and pinpoint them is, of course, thorough wireless security scans and/or wireless intrusion detection systems. However, to some extent physical security checks can also counter this nuisance.

One of the most blatant issues to check for when performing a physical premises audit is the presence and use of various removable storage media. Nowadays, it ranges from the ordinary USB memory sticks and external hard drives to media players, mobile phones and digital cameras. These humble rogue devices present one of the most formidable security threats of today. Via them, confidential data trickles out bypassing any egress filtering, and malware crawls in outflanking gateway antivirus controls. Prior to performing a physical assessment, the auditors should consult existing security policies to find out the auditee's position on using removable storage media on their premises. If the policies are lax, they should at least enquire whether there are any specific systems to which connecting removable media is highly undesirable, or whether a permission to use mobile media at work has to be received from line management or IT. If the policies explicitly forbid the use of removable media, then any suspicious device must be scrutinised. It does not matter if a discovered USB stick, external hard drive or *any other removable storage media* merely lies on a desk not being plugged into a nearby computer. In Anton Chekhov's words, *'one must not put a loaded rifle on the stage if no one is thinking of firing it.'* In a similar manner, do the acceptable use policies allow employees to burn CDs (which are still a source of sensitive information leaks)? If not, check for any computers that have CD burners. What about copying data to wireless-enabled mobile media – tablets and smartphones included? *Physical security assessments are immensely policy-driven.*

What are the other types of rogue devices one should look for? When discussing TSCM, we have stated that the auditors should always expect the unexpected. However, physical keystroke loggers are a danger you should always expect and check for. Usually, these minute nasty devices come in four possible varieties:

- USB-to-USB
- PS/2-to-PS/2
- USB-to-PS/2
- PS/2-to-USB

It is possible, however, to buy a whole keyboard with an in-built keystroke logger. If all keyboards in a large office are of the same make and type, but a single one sticks out like a sore thumb, we, as auditors, would start asking questions.

Similarly, if there are three laptops on the system administrator's desk it looks perfectly normal. At the same time, if three laptops lie on a desk of an accountant or sales manager, there is a good probability that at least one of the three is personal. Are employees allowed to bring in and connect their own computers? Again, enquiries will follow and the policies will be consulted on the subject of BYOD and BYOD controls. The latter will range from which

BYOD are allowed and for what, how are they scrutinised by IT prior to connecting to internal networks and storing company information, whether BYOD are inventoried, how do they fit with the company end-host security baseline, the level of access company system administrators may have to BYOD, change control and vulnerability management of such devices, how an incident involving BYOD will be investigated, and so forth. Now you can see why ISO27001:2013 explicitly mandates having a strong policy on mobile and BYOD use.

Two factors seem to be of the utmost importance when security assessments of premises are performed. The first is verifying if all necessary controls are in place and humming. The other is being able to spot things that somehow break the general pattern and are out of place. The former requires very thorough checklists, as premises assessments are usually *passive*. Hopefully, the information discussed in this section can help you to create or improve these lists. The latter challenges this view, as the sense it requires grows with experience and is on the verge of art. Besides, it is closely related to social engineering tests centred on physical access.

Social engineering tests

Information security assessments that centre exclusively on the human factor involve different forms of social engineering. Additionally, ISMS assessments commonly have a strong human component dictated by relevant policies, standards and guidelines. Recall the proposed ISO/IEC 27001-aligned security policy set. Two chapters listed (personnel security issues and security awareness training) are fully directed at the human security problems, while the rest inevitably address them to a larger or smaller extent. Likewise, assessing actual information security operations and procedures is impossible without auditing performance of all employees involved in their execution, either by observing or by interviewing them.

A considerable volume of information security publications is dedicated to discussing social engineering and emphasising that 'humans are the weakest link'. We wholeheartedly agree with this statement – for as long as it out-steps any specific boundaries and applies to the overall human folly and its role in allowing security incidents to occur. As far as social engineering is concerned, it is simply the oldest and most tested and tried method of breaching confidentiality, integrity and, at times, availability of any imaginable target. Or, to simplify and resonate with the introductory discourse, of bending and overcoming the opponents will by deceit. Practically any social engineering attack can be described with a simple scheme shown in the *Figure 13*.

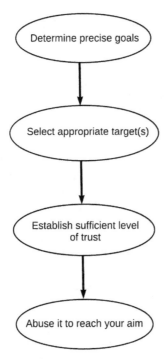

Figure 13: A general outline of social engineering attacks

That is, you decide what you want, select the most appropriate person that can lead you to it, establish the necessary level of trust, and then abuse this trust when the time is due. Unlike legitimate security assessments, real life social engineering attacks have an additional stage – getting away with what you've got. This can be more difficult if compared to purely technical security breaches. Social engineering casually involves a much higher degree of interpersonal contact and interaction, which often leaves a pronounced giveaway trace. In contrast, remote attackers that rely on technical means only are completely faceless until caught.

Practical social engineering methodologies are very strongly affected by its defined aims. Compare the following tasks a

3: Security Assessments Classification

physical access social engineering security test can be expected to complete:

1. Getting into the company premises.
2. Getting into the server rooms.
3. Getting into the server room and retrieving a configuration file (or any other data).

The first is easy to accomplish, providing that sufficient public information about the auditee's employees, suppliers, customers, and so on is available (just try LinkedIn). The second significantly raises the bar. People are not expected to hang around server rooms without a valid reason, and the attacker will have to pass for a member of the IT team or a vendor support technician. As we have already reviewed, such premises must be protected with strong physical authentication means and stay constantly monitored. The third option inevitably brings in the element of technology. Our social engineer will have to be able to bypass physical authentication of a system and copy the file. This may require some specific technical skills and appropriate console cable in the pocket. It also takes time. "Hey, you, what are you doing there?" The more specific is the aim faced by a social engineer, the harder it is to accomplish. This is precisely the opposite in many other areas of information security testing. Non-specific goals, such as gaining any foothold on the target's systems and networks, could be surprisingly easy to accomplish via social engineering means. All you may need is to find a single gullible person among thousands of employees.

Major goals of social engineering tests are summarised in *Figure 14.*

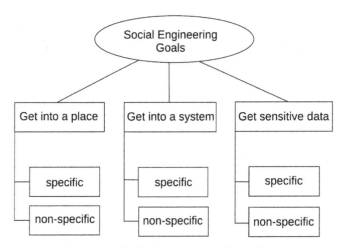

Figure 14: Social engineering aims

An attack may reach them directly or via a chain of intermediate targets. Through the social engineer's sights all people can be subdivided into three large categories:

1. Those who possess desirable data or access rights.
2. Those who are trusted by the first category.
3. Those who are highly susceptible to social engineering tricks

When a single person belongs to groups 1 and 3 at the same time, it is called luck. Or negligence on the part of those who entrusted valuable data or systems to such employees and did so without providing necessary security awareness training. As one cannot base effective attack strategies and tactics upon the assumption of favourable fortune or complacent opposition, a correct approach of getting to 1 from 3 via the 2 must be found and successfully exploited. This might require a hefty dose of elaborate planning and research.

In establishing the necessary contact with the targeted employees, contractors, vendor and customer reps and other relevant persons, all types of communication channels can be used. The more of these channels are open, the better for the attacker. This allows sufficient manoeuvring space while increasing the area of possible influence (what is commonly called the 'attack surface' in technical penetration testing). Quite often, the behaviour and perception of people strongly differ between personal, telephone and online intercourse – especially social networks. In the process of developing rapport and gaining trust, all three ways can be tried to select the most optimal one. Common sense dictates that the online – phone – personal contact sequence should be followed where possible. The earlier in this chain the breakthrough occurs, the more insecure our targets are. In practice, however, such succession may not be the best, or might not work at all. Technology also imposes its mighty amendments. Nowadays, the quality of streaming video-conferencing can be so high, that it comes close to a personal contact. Alternatively, there are numerous remote employees working from their home offices for whom personal contact with their management and other colleagues is already minimal, and may not be highly important for their duties.

Just like with 'conventional' IT security and electronic surveillance, we are observing active interpenetration between social engineering and technical attack means. In some areas this transfusion is practically complete. Above, an example where some technical skills are needed to bypass system authentication after physical access has been gained was noted. Now we would like you to consider the following looming factors:

- RFID hacking can be employed to assist in physical premises penetration.
- Rogue wireless devices of all kinds can be plugged in by physical intruders to provide out-of-band connectivity.

- Client-side attacks, spear phishing included, often rely on social engineering means. The opposite is also true.

Currently, the latter case seems to be of a particular relevance. Old good social engineering tricks using e-mails claiming to be the IT department representative asking to change passwords or click on the attached 'update' file may still work. Some people just never learn. Nevertheless, an explosion in client-side attack methods and techniques allows far more efficient ways of exploitation. A link to a phishing or browser exploits-hosting site can be carefully hidden in a long URL of a well-composed 'click-this-and-receive-a-candy' e-mail. Even better, it can be well-hidden behind the embedded image with a button to click. It can be posted to social networks, blogs or sent through instant messengers and SMS. Flaws like cross-site scripting (XSS), cross-site request forgery (CSRF) and URL splitting allow attackers to steal authentication cookies to your corporate or third-party sites as soon as such a potentially interesting link is clicked. And do not forget that nowadays trojans can be concealed in practically any file format. Would you resist if an mp3 of an as yet unreleased hit by your favourite band is sent to you by this exceptionally friendly young lady you enjoyed chatting with on Skype so much? A pity her microphone is broken. She absolutely adores the same band and this is why, obviously, you have met online. Don't you have the band listed in your profile? Would you not listen to that mp3 'she' has just sent? It is only a double-click away. Peer-to-peer networks are, of course, a divine gift for spreading malware-patched content that can also be abused by social engineers with ease. All one needs is to distribute a malicious file and send a link to its torrent to the intended target person providing there are reasons for the target to upload such file.

For example, he or she could have been asking to find it online, and a social engineer has discovered such a post.

We shall return to the subject of social engineering in the fifth chapter of this book, where some applicable terminology, strategies and tactics will be introduced.

Security documentation reviews

The final class of non-technical information security assessments that needs to be reviewed in brief is auditing ISMS of a company or organisation. It was already covered in the previous chapter on the strategic scale. Verifying the 'tactical ISMS level' means checking that all agreed strategies are effectively implemented in everyday practice. After all, *'the art of war in its highest point of view is policy, but, no doubt, a policy which fights battles, instead of writing notes'* (Clausewitz).

In terms of assessing security documentation it all comes down to verifying whether the policies are supplemented with all necessary downstream documents and these documents are feasible and correct. Besides, the auditor must check whether the data classification rules in the company are followed and all the required classification labelling is in place. Access rights to the documents, in particular stored at resources that allow public sharing (such as Google Drive), must be verified to match their classification level. Whether key security documentation is inventoried properly, approved and reviewed by appropriate persons, has designated owners, and version control is working are other key areas of document management to verify, at least when ISO27001 audits are concerned. However, this brief discourse on document control is not related to the main topic of this conversation, namely the documentation content and its correctness.

Figure 15 outlines the 'classical' security documentation chain.

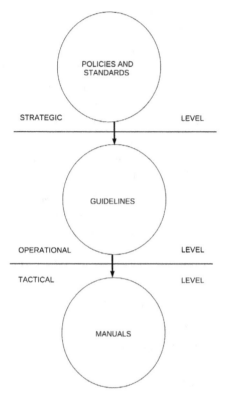

STRATEGIC ... LEVEL

OPERATIONAL ... LEVEL

TACTICAL ... LEVEL

Figure 15: Three planes of security documentation

Take note that the standards are placed at the strategic level together with security policies. While being subordinate to and driven by the policies, information security standards are casually company or organisation-wide and must affect all relevant areas of practice. For example, data classification standards apply to all data within an entity. Cryptography standards apply to all use of any ciphers for any purpose. Weak or lacking standards are just as disastrous as poor security policies can be.

Analysing the standards requires specialised expertise. When checking the cryptography standards mentioned above, the auditors must know which encryption algorithms *and their applicable modes of operation* are considered to be strong and weak in today's industry and government sectors. Even more, it is highly advantageous to be able to forecast which ciphers are unlikely to be broken in the near future. Such ciphers are expected to have *high security margin*, implement *whitening* and *avalanche effects*, allow for *large key sizes* and have tested and tried structural elements. Apart from defining what is strong cryptography and cryptography implementation for the entity, and what is not, a good cryptography standard (or a policy, if one wants to follow ISO27001 Annex A to a letter) must also cover various key management issues, including:

- how the keys and certificates are distributed, stored, and revoked.
- key recovery and escrow keys (if present).
- good key management practices (such as mutual authentication in key exchange, strong Diffie-Hellman types, not storing the key at the same place with the material encrypted with it, etc.).
- if any software developed in-house implements cryptography, good implementation practices for developers.
- relevant roles and responsibilities.

Figure 15 positions guidelines at the intermediate *operational* plane. In military terms, the operational level lies between strategy and tactics and deals with campaigns, rather than the whole conflict or its separate battles. Guidelines apply to specific information security areas, for example, an employee vetting guideline, a secure password guideline or an incident response guideline. They define and shape separate processes and operations that can consist of multiple individual elements. Thus, the guidelines are clearly not strategic in nature, but nor are they tactical – the manuals are.

For instance, a firewall configuration guideline should state which particular networks, systems and services are allowed to be accessed, and from where such access is permitted. It can go into great technical detail outlining which types of network traffic are considered to be malicious and must be blocked under any circumstances, or how complex protocols are to be handled. For modern firewalls, extensive coverage on additional supported functionalities (application filtering, egress content filtering, intrusion prevention, antimalware gateway functions) may be required. The guideline ought to cover how all access to the firewall itself must be protected, its configuration management run, and how various event logs generated by the firewall should be handled. However, such guidelines must be applicable to all major firewall types of any make, whether Cisco ASA, CheckPoint, Microsoft ISA, Juniper, Linux Netfilter or anything else. So it should not contain commands, screenshots or chunks of configuration files. This would turn it into a manual.

- *'The auditors should always point out if a guideline is too generic, like a policy, or, in contrast, is too manual-like. In other words, it should not slip up or down, into the strategic or tactical planes'.*

In the first case it will completely fail to fulfil its purpose. In the second case it can become obsolete and incorrect if the specific means it addresses change. Just like the

3: Security Assessments Classification

policies, you don't want to rewrite security guidelines with every upgrade. And, just like the policies, sufficient attention should be paid to their clarity. When looking through the guidelines always think whether a newcomer employee with relevant background will understand them without additional instructions and explanations.

Auditing security guidelines is 'semi-technical' in the sense that it demands necessary specialist knowledge in the applicable area. It is not necessarily *passive*. Having detailed checklists may not cover all aspects of a proper guideline assessment. When analysing security guidelines, sometimes you have to think out of the box. Consider the following typical password guideline excerpt:

- The password must not be in any dictionary.
- The password must be at least eight characters in length.
- The password must contain both lower case and capital letters.
- The password must contain numbers.
- It must strongly differ from the previous password.
- It can not contain the words like 'password' or 'qwerty'.

Is it reasonably complete? Is it secure? If you think so, have a look at these ways of generating passwords:

- CompanyName01(2,3,4,5 . . .)

Providing that the name of the company is dissimilar to a previous password, is not in a dictionary, contains at least eight characters and is written using caps, this password fully satisfies the above criteria.

- SystemDomainName01(2,3,4,5 . . .)

This would also fulfil them.

- DeviceVendor01(2,3,4,5 . . .)

Is the vendor name not in the dictionaries? Is it longer than eight characters and has caps? Fine.

We can also recall many passwords that contain, for example, fragments of employees' names or the system's IP addresses. All of them are unsafe. Current password list generating tools are very powerful and can easily make extensive dictionary files filled with such passwords in minutes, if not seconds. When performing various internal and external security audits, we have successfully cracked thousands of such passwords without spending much effort. What is the actual source of this security issue? Incomplete, poor password guidelines. In your spare time, think what this guideline must contain to avoid these and similar problems. How it should be worded? How else could seemingly complex, yet profoundly insecure passwords come into existence?

Manuals usually come from vendors and are straightforward. Unless there are clear indications that a source of insecurity can be a manual error, they are rarely checked. The real tactical level verification of the ISMS and its documentation cascade is assessing all nuts-and-bolts implementations and processes. "By ye fruits shall you know them". In practice, it comes down to security scanning, penetration testing, social engineering, physical security checks and other hands-on activities we have already discussed. However, separate detailed audits of information security processes can be also performed. In a nutshell, they aim at detailed verification of how the unfolding of a strategic process (*Figure 7*) is reflected on all interrelated planes. In an ISO27001 audit this is typically done by interviewing the responsible employees and records sampling.

Assessing security processes

Unlike security documentation, we cannot really divide security processes into strategic, operational or tactical. Rather, a separate process would permeate all three levels having strategic, operational and tactical parts (*Figure 16*).

Note that the flow on the scheme is bidirectional. This reflects the previous chapter's discussion of the top-bottom relationships and resonates with *Figure 5*. It would have been tempting to speculate that specific positions of responsibility can correspond to our process levels. It is even more enticing to superimpose it onto the *Figure 7* scheme and state that the central C&C OODA loop is 'strategic', the Deming cycle is more 'operational', and its separate stages loops are 'tactical'. That would be an oversimplification, however, and a fatal one indeed. There are information security processes of different scale, involvement, depth and scope. Applied information security itself is a process. Information security auditing is its subprocess. There is a great deal of specific processes that must be assessed security-wise, such as access control and identity management, change control, configuration and

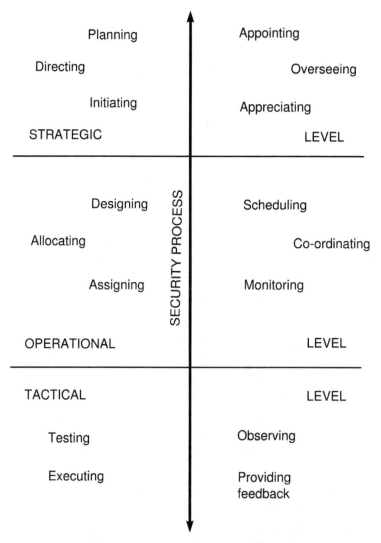

Figure 16: A typical process flow

patch management, vulnerability management, software development and acquisition, classifying information and data, incident response, security awareness and training, personnel screening and vetting, supplier security evaluation, business continuity and disaster recovery, and so on. An individual approach to every process is required. Overall, a process assessment is threefold, as *Figure 17* shows.

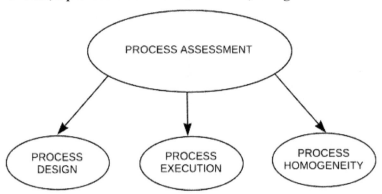

Figure 17: Three components of a process assessment

Auditing the process design concentrates on verifying its completeness, correctness and feasibility. Does it have all the components needed to be workable and effective? Are these elements efficiently interlinked? Do they correspond well to the environment in which the process operates? Are roles and responsibilities for executing different stages of the process correctly assigned? Is it all properly documented? The full *Figure 7* strategic cycle is most evident, manifested and should be verified when you analyse the process design from the very conception to the minuscule technicalities and latest improvements. Designing a fully-fledged process inevitably requires going through the Deming cycle or equivalent. In contrast, when auditing processes execution and processes homogeneity, you are more likely to encounter a collection of OODA loops.

A process execution review aims at checking whether different stages of a selected process are performed in practice without unacceptable shortfalls. In a more active form, it also means verifying if these stages can be successfully circumvented or abused by attackers of all kind. We will use the access management process as an example.

The ITILv3 "Service Operation", paragraph 4.5.1, states that *'Access Management provides the right for users to be able to use a service or group of services. It is therefore the execution of policies and actions defined in Security and Availability Management'.* Further it continues that *'Access Management does not decide who has access to which IT services. Rather, Access Management executes the policies and regulations defined during Service Strategy and Service Design. Access Management enforces decisions to restrict or provide access, rather than making the decision'* (paragraph 4.5.5.3). Thus, when elaborating on Access Management ITIL deals only with the *operational* and *tactical* stages of a much larger *information security process* of access control. If we were to review the process design, we would have to assess the whole access control without such limitations, review the relevant policies and regulations, analyse decision making, and walk through all the Deming stages. However, assessing the access management process execution can be limited to the ITIL-defined scope. It includes the following parts:

1. Requesting access.

Verify how access request generation mechanisms work. Take into account not only the requests to obtain access, but also requests to restrict it, or to change (especially, elevate) access privileges. Can anyone fake access requests? How?

2. Request verification.

How does it work? Can it be tricked and deceived by any technical or non-technical means?

3. Providing rights.

How does it operate? Which roles and groups exist? Can extra rights be easily granted to someone by mistake? Can deliberate attempts to get extra rights succeed?

4. Monitoring identity status.

How is it performed? How often access rights reviews are done? Is it equally applicable to all user types and groups? Can any changes of status be missed? Can employees do something to conceal such changes, especially if they are related to demotion, disciplinary action and dismissal?

5. Logging and tracking access.

How does it work? Can these activities and mechanisms be circumvented? How the exceptions and alarms are handled?

6. Removing or restricting rights.

How is it done? Is it easy to remove or not to remove someone's rights by error? Are the restrictions as tight as they should be? Is it possible to avoid or reverse removal or restriction of rights?

A *passive* approach to auditing such a process would be to go through a specific and extensive list of 'must dos' and 'must nots'. An *active* approach is separating OODA loops for each process part (if you look at these stages carefully, you would clearly see these loops) and analysing them applying a variety of 'what ifs'. Is observation done properly? Is orientation complete? Is the decision right? Was the action seamlessly performed? What if we submit a fake request? What if we alter a legitimate request to get into a user group we are not authorised to be in? What if we try to copy another user's data without authorisation? Would this attempt trigger an alarm? What if . . .

If a process appears to work fine, it does not mean it will do so the next time. Or with someone else. Or anywhere else. Verifying such things is what we refer to as assessing process homogeneity. A process must be reproducible. It must work in a virtually identical way when applied to different departments, company branches, other employee roles and teams, contractors and authorised guests. As pointed out by Chinese strategist Du Mu, *'when it comes to establishing rules and regulations, everyone, high and low, should be treated alike'*. The same applies to processes that put these rules and regulations to practice. Exceptions do happen, but must apply to equally exceptional circumstances, be strongly justified, documented and endorsed at the very top.

Assessing and judging process homogeneity can be tricky. Heraclitus observed that we can never step into the same river twice. Nor would it be the same up- or downstream. Demanding that a process must be reproduced every time and in every department in exactly the same manner down to every microscopic detail is unrealistic. Even more, it would be promoting that very 'autocratic control and drill-machine approach' we have actively criticised in the second chapter. Friction exists. *Processes should operate effectively and smoothly while being affected by friction.* In fact, they should have a needed degree of friction resilience and redundancy built-in. The auditors must sound the alarm only when the homogeneity deviations threaten to impede the process or clearly increase the risk of a security incident.

We must note, that concentration on and understanding of the processes involved give additional impetus and direction to other information security assessment types. When you audit any security elements, you always assess a part of some staged process, and usually more than a single process at once. You also assess the interaction between different processes and all friction born from it. This would be taken into account when we will discuss the nature of different vulnerabilities and evaluating risks they present.

The final ISMS-related subject that needs be addressed here is the matter of secrecy. No aspects of your ISMS including security policies, standards, guidelines, procedures, descriptions of processes and so on must be disclosed to any outsiders, or unauthorised persons, unless required by law. Sometimes, security policies are disclosed to partners or customers, the disclosure being subject to a specific contract condition. In such case the receiving party is authorised, and an appropriate NDA must be signed prior to granting the authorisation. All of this is, generally, common sense known from the ancient times:

- *'Matters are dealt with strictly at headquarters'* (Sun Tzu)
- *'Strictness at headquarters in the planning stage refers to secrecy'* (Mei Yaochen)

Nevertheless, we often find various companies' and organisations' security documentation being published online. Some of these policies, guidelines, schemes, and so on sometimes contain definite security gaps. We can see these gaps. So can the potential attackers. Besides, you have spent effort, time and money developing these documents, as well as the ideas, plans and processes they describe. Now your competitors, who probably operate in a similar manner, can copy and adopt them for free. When any ISMS assessment is performed, the auditors must verify that such information is appropriately classified and is not unnecessarily exposed.

CHAPTER 4: ADVANCED PRE-ASSESSMENT PLANNING

'It is best to thwart people by intelligent planning'.
– Wang Xi

Planning is vital. Planning is vision, direction and structure incarnate. In the rapidly changing sphere of information security, however, it has to be done with utmost care. Plans must always make allowance for the turn of the tide and our inevitable companion the friction. If they fail so, plans will become rigid. From a strategic advantage they will turn into an obstacle of equally grand proportions. There are situations in which having inadequate plans is worse than having no plans at all. At least, in the latter case there are still some possibilities of swift adaptation. Enforcement of stagnant plans will kill any useful initiative at spot.

Different versions of the *"no plan survives contact with the enemy"* statement are ascribed to a disciple of von Clausewitz, Prussian Generalfeldmarschall Helmuth von Moltke the Elder. This is what this renowned strategist actually wrote on the subject:

- *'No plan of operations extends with certainty beyond the first encounter with the enemy's main strength. Only the layman sees in the course of a campaign a consistent execution of a preconceived and highly detailed original concept pursued consistently to the end. Certainly the commander in chief will keep his great objective continuously in mind, undisturbed by the vicissitudes of events. But the path on which he hopes to reach it can never be firmly established in advance. Throughout the campaign he must make a series of decisions on the basis of situations that cannot be foreseen. The successive acts of war are thus not premeditated designs, but on the contrary are spontaneous acts guided by military measures. Everything depends on penetrating the uncertainty of veiled situations to evaluate the facts, to clarify the unknown, to make decisions rapidly, and then to carry them out with strength and constancy'.*

Helmuth von Moltke was obviously inspired by the following thoughts of his fellow countryman and strategy guru:

- *'War is the province of chance. In no sphere of human activity is such a margin to be left for this intruder, because none is so much in constant contact with him on all sides. He increases the uncertainty of every circumstance, and deranges the course of events. From this uncertainty of all intelligence and suppositions, this continual interposition of chance, the actor in war constantly finds things different to his expectations; and this cannot fail to have an influence on his plans, or at least on the presumptions connected with these plans'.*

- *'. . . in the course of action circumstances press for immediate decision, and allow no time to look about for fresh data, often not enough for mature consideration. But it much more often happens that the correction of one premise, and the knowledge of chance events which have arisen, are not quite sufficient to overthrow our plans completely, but only suffice to produce hesitation'.*

The modern take on this formidable issue is perfectly summarised in MCDP 1 *Warfighting*:

- *'Because we can never eliminate uncertainty, we must learn to fight effectively despite it. We can do this by developing simple, flexible plans; planning for likely contingencies; developing standing operating procedures; and fostering initiative among subordinates'.*

Perform the 'substitution exercise' against the aforesaid meditations. Its results shall be the philosophic backbone of our discussion of information security assessments planning and preparations in this Chapter.

On pre-audit gap analysis

'Every war should be viewed above all things according to the probability of its character, and its leading features as they are to be deduced from the political forces and proportions'. – Carl von Clausewitz

The first thing to do prior to any information security assessment is to determine its scope, objectives and targets. The scope is characterised by both width and depth of the audit. If we talk about formal certification, such as PCI DSS, it is mainly the width. If it is about technical vulnerability assessments depth is critical. The objectives could range from meeting specific compliance or customer demands to assessing risks presented by deploying a novel process or technology. The targets can be anything that presents information security risks, from systems to people and organisation of processes. As heavily emphasised in the previous chapters, with a proper auditing approach more targets, than defined by a narrow initial scope, would be verified and, ultimately, different aspects of the ISMS will be assessed.

The scope of an audit is heavily shaped by its budget, time frame and objectives. If the objectives are to generate an overall security baseline of systems and networks, a sweeping vulnerability scan will suffice. In a same manner, a mass-mailing social engineering test can be applied to all employees to see how many of them would open an attachment or click on a supplied malicious link. Then the results of such test can be used to verify efficiency of the existing security awareness program and pinpoint at staff in need of additional awareness training. On the other hand, if the objective is to test a crucial system, application or process, the assessment must concentrate on this element going into maximum depth and possibly including white box testing.

The four-stage framework

Ideally, you would want to go as wide and as deep as you can. In practice, some form of a gap analysis is required to define the assessment priorities, and thus – its type, scope and targets. The audit itself is, of course, the pinnacle of analysing information security gaps. Prior to its solicitation, however, the auditee team has to do some important homework. This is similar to a common academic opinion that a good student comes to a lecture or seminar already knowing at least some of its material and with a few topical questions prepared. A proposed pre-audit gap analysis four stage general framework is shown on the *Figure 18*.

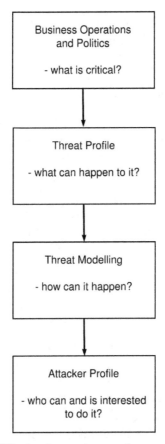

**Figure 18: The basic anatomy of a pre-assessment
gap analysis**

The first step is to find what is most vital for the company
or organisation. Is it a certain trade secret? Is it the
customer database? Could it be the company's public image
and customer trust? Or, perhaps, being compliant with
specific standards and regulations? What about personal
records covered by the Data Protection Act in the UK or its
equivalents abroad? Such critical elements can be both
tangible and intangible. They may, or may not be related to

any estimated monetary values. The key is the seriousness of damage that can be done if they are affected by a security incident of any kind, whether passive or active. Try to compile a priority list going from the most to the least critical factors and components.

The next step is to estimate and prioritise the threats. A threat is an action that leads to a security incident. You should not confuse threats with their sources (attackers, accidents), which is a common error, or their permitting factors (vulnerabilities and gaps). A threat in information security terms is similar to 'infection' in medicine, which is nether the germ nor the lack of immunity, but "the growth of a parasitic organism within the body" (Webster's Medical Dictionary). In relation to active security incidents, a threat is what the assailants want. This could be selling confidential data to competitors, fraudulent transaction, ruining the company image, blocking access to online resources, and so forth. Reviewing the entity's information security history could be a good starting point in estimating threats. Which incidents did happen in the past? What was affected? Are such issues still challenging? Assign the appropriate threats to the priority list of critical factors compiled during the previous step. It is also advisable to prioritise the threats assigned to every single critical factor on the list.

Once you have reviewed and prioritised a variety of threats, think of how your information security nightmares can become reality. We are not talking about any actual vulnerabilities and the ways to abuse them. Finding and assessing them is the auditor's task. When discussing social engineering in the previous chapter, we noted that often to get what the social engineers want they have to exploit a chain of opportunities moving from who is vulnerable to who has the desired trophy. If you substitute 'who' for 'what', this approach is fully applicable to any technically-centred attack. Thus, review (and if you don't have them – create and review) data flow, process, network and other applicable diagrams and schemes. You can construct a personnel communication diagram to understand how confidential data flows between people and how the employees are interconnected in overall terms. This can be called a human data flow scheme. Think what is exposed, where it is exposed, how and to whom. Relate it to the critical elements and threats evaluated during the two previous gap analysis steps. Then attempt to build the attack trees. Think through which specific points and in which particular sequence either external or internal adversaries can get what they want. Draw these points and connect them. Remember, that both the points and links in between can be technical, operational, human, or combined.

Finally, it is time to make some educated guesses about the nature of conceivable adversaries. The following main characteristics must be taken into account:

• *The starting position*

Are the most likely attackers external, internal, or both? How much can they know about their presumable targets? What level of access do they have? Can they open guest or customer accounts? Are outsiders casually permitted to enter your company or organisation premises?

• *The motivation*

Remember, it's all about the clash of wills. If the motivation is low, a general technical or social engineering sweep and its follow-up actions should be sufficient to prevent most attacks from such people or malware they use.

If the motivation is high, only active in-depth security testing designed to match the APT (advanced persistent threat) will suffice. Motivation, based on personal or political hatred directed against the company, organisation, or its selected employees is usually strong. If you are a lucrative target or a chief competitor, greed can also be the source of a powerful motivation. Impersonal motivations, like trying to steal what is easy to get one's hands on, are weak.

- *The inclinations*

Are the presumed assailants technically inclined? Or are they more likely to exploit the human factor? What about physical premises intrusion? Can they combine these approaches? While this may be hard to forecast for the external adversaries, as the fog of war is dense out there, this is not so with various types of internal malcontents.

- *The means*

Try to guess what the likely opponents may have at their disposal. Are they resourceful? Are they technically savvy? Are they experienced? Can they work as a team? Can they have or gain internal allies within your company or organisation? Would they be willing and able to pay highly skilled professionals in networks, systems and applications hacking, electronic surveillance or social engineering to do the job?

Different types of adversaries can be distinguished by a combination of these important characteristics. Their conjunction is situational, however, even within a separate attacker group and may always change. For example, typical cyber criminals are usually external, technically inclined and sufficiently technically savvy, but have weak motivation hunting for a low hanging fruit, although some could specialise in social engineering instead of the technical attack methodologies. Should any of them realise that your company is a very fruitful, profitable target, however, their motivation can sky-rocket. The felons will try everything to become intrinsic, which may even include attempts to get employed to gain internal access, or at least try to become authorised visitors. Besides, if the motivation is high, but the actual skills are insufficient, the opponents will thrive to learn, or enlist someone with the required skill to assist. So, do not let estimated low skills of the potential attackers put you off-guard.

Selecting the targets of assessment

If you have vigorously followed these four steps of the pre-assessment gap analysis, you should have at least approximate answers to the four main questions they pose. Then you can draw the plans outlining what should be audited, how (in general terms) it should be audited, and in which depth. When it comes to the actual selection of specific security assessment targets, the following approaches are casually applied:

1. Audit what is valuable.
2. Test what is perceived as potentially vulnerable.
3. Check what is exposed.
4. Assess what is unknown.

The first approach is most commonly recommended in all relevant information security publications. It is highly sensible, being directly related to the step one of the pre-assessment gap analysis. Alas, it is not infallible. The issue, which has already received extensive coverage elsewhere, is estimating the value of data or systems that hold it. Sometimes, it is easy to do (e.g. trade secrets, or downtime of the e-commerce service of an online shop). However, there are multiple cases of intangibles that are hard to measure in monetary terms, for example, those related to company image or customers trust. There are also situations, in which data classification policies and standards are either incomplete or not properly enforced. This leads to confidential data not being labelled as such, which means it will be treated with laxity.

Using the example of a trade secret, there can be bits and pieces of information which do not constitute it directly, but can provide competitors with a hint to what the secret can be. Are they labelled as highly confidential or, at least, confidential data? Are systems that store them and channels that transmit them sufficiently secure? Are people who know them reliable and security aware? And how do you value such fragments of data monetarily? They may supply outsiders with important clues that will allow them to reconstruct your most guarded treasure. Then again, they may not.

This brings the discussion to the matters of friction and its close associate, the fog of war. Are you sure that the systems which store valuable data are the only systems to hold it? Are you completely confident, that it was not disseminated to any other systems including public storage services such as Dropbox or Google Drive? How about paper documents, removable media and people? Did you ever perform a thorough data discovery exercise? Data tends to spread across the *information security zone*. It shrinks and expands with it. It propagates along the interlinked chains of computer and human hosts. It's fuzzy. It's chaotic. It's often cloudy. Confidential data, unfortunately, is not exempt from this observation. At times, it can be found in places you would never expect it to be. This must be taken into account when you zero on the security assessment targets on the basis of their value and criticality.

Also, what about neighbouring systems or people? All right, they may not hold highly sensitive data. For now. But can it leak to them? Besides, they can make perfect proxies for attacks against their secret-holding counterparts, bringing the assailants much closer to their aim and dramatically increasing their chances of success. Check your attack trees. How spacious the *secure buffer* around the most critical points should be? Does it have to cover only the most valuable and crucial elements? Do you really need to expand it further? How far? Can you afford such an expansion and thus, the corresponding scope of any security assessment-to-be? *Figure 19* is there to provide some food for thoughts, with few of the possible secure buffer borders drawn in dashes and labelled with question marks.

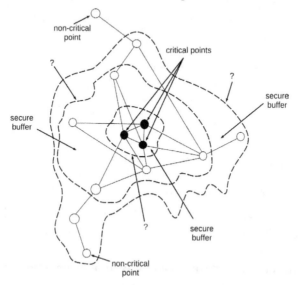

Figure 19: Where does your secure buffer spread?

The second approach is based upon either the expert advice of internal specialists, the history of security incidents, or both. It does not appear as sensible as its predecessor on the target selection list. However, it may well be justified. If the problem was not completely resolved, it is likely to repeat again. Besides, technical, human resources, or other professionals of the auditee can be completely right. But since they don't view themselves as security experts, they would like to see an independent verification of their worries. Perhaps, as a manager *you should listen and appreciate such top-bottom initiative.* In addition, there are information security zone elements which are commonly and rightfully perceived as potentially unsafe. On the human level, this applies to contractors and temporary workers. On the technical level – to complex web applications, wireless networks, BYOD, and various forms of telecommuter and other remote employee access. It makes perfect sense to include such shaky borders of the information security zone within the scope of a security audit.

The third approach is highly common and is one of the major justifications for subscribing to external security audits of all kinds. Testing the defences that the attackers will encounter first is perfectly reasonable. Provided that the opponents are outside, of course. Check the security of all entry points, be that physical doors, employee vetting, remote connections, or application front-ends, but do not fall for the Maginot line mentality. Always keep the defence-in-depth doctrine in perspective. What if the pre-assessment gap analysis indicates that an internal incident is more imminent and certain? What if the externally exposed systems are not highly valuable and critical, and do not communicate with any important internal networks and hosts? This scenario is perfectly possible if a company web site is very simple and hosted by a third party. At the same time, there are no public services open on the internal company network. What about the ever-present fog of war? Are you sure, that you are fully aware of all externally accessible services and points of entry? What about possible out-of-band channels? Should you impose any scope limitations on external security scans? Or, in contrast, give the auditors complete freedom of trying to get in anywhere by any possible means, social engineering included? These issues must be seriously weighted prior to making your final decision on the assessment scope and type.

Finally, you can opt to target what is the least certain and understood. This usually means the areas and segments where the internal expertise and corresponding controls are lacking. As compared to the three previous target selection points, this one might appear to be rather strange. Yet, when we recall our military strategy implications, it is perfectly logical. If security assessments reduce friction, and this is what we want, targeting the spots where the friction is at maximum and fog of war is immense is wise. Recall our example of IT security director who ordered a wide scope internal security assessment to get a good grasp of what is going on on the network from an independent source. This was a good decision that helped him resolve multiple issues, some of which were not directly related to security. Reconnaissance is a vital part of any information security audit. It must be put to an effective use anywhere the intelligence data is lacking and unexpected can lurk.

The four target selection approaches we have listed work in perfect concert. They can be employed to create a simple point-based system. Make a list of potential security audit targets. Place the criticality/value, perceived vulnerability, exposure and uncertainty against them as table rows. Give one to each of the criteria if you think the target is critical, potentially vulnerable, exposed to attacks, and you are not really sure about security risks it may present. This basic exercise is represented in *Table 3*.

Table 3: A possible way of selecting feasible audit targets

Criteria	Target 1	Target 2	Target 3	Target 4
Criticality or value	0	1	0	0
Perceived vulnerability	1	0	0	1
Exposure	1	0	1	0
Uncertainty	1	1	0	0
Total	3	2	1	1

The more points a potential target scores, the higher should its assessment priority be. In the illustration of *Table 3*, targets 1 and 2 should be security verified. Targets 3 and 4 can probably wait. You can always devise a more complex target selection grading that will use, for example, marks from one to ten if you see it as more fitting.

On auditing the auditors

– *'Maestro, what is more essential in art: "how?" or "what"?'*
– *'The most essential is "who".'*

Pierre-Auguste Renoir to one of his disciples

Once you have decided on the scope, objectives, targets and other desired characteristics of a security assessment, it is time to pick the most appropriate auditors. This task can be far more complex than you might think. It is critical not only for the planned assessment and it's follow up, but for the future information security projects and plans of the entire company or organisation. Thus, it must not be taken lightly.

If the audit team is internal, then all you must do is to assign its members to the tasks in accordance with their specialisations and abilities. A most suitable selection of the team personnel should have been done beforehand. Nevertheless, if the scope and character of the planned assessment is dramatically different from what the internal team usually does, hiring new professionals or, at least, providing additional training must be considered. This is not so with the more common third party security audits. You cannot rely on advertisements that companies proudly parade. Naturally, everyone would claim they are the best. Of course, sales people do not lie, they just exaggerate a bit. And often, they don't have exact technical or operational understanding of the specialised services they advertise. How can we approach this problem?

First of all, having a long-term overall information security program that covers the assessments as its important part is the key to many gates. Today, you may need one type of an audit. Tomorrow, it could be completely different. Unless absolutely necessary, or you can afford the luxury of one auditor company verifying the results of another, you would want to work with a security company that can provide for all your assessment needs. Having multiple suppliers for different types of assessment increases costs and bureaucracy, while diminishing the possibility to standardise the audit results. In one word, it's an overhead. Unless you need top-notch specialists for a highly peculiar task, it is best to avoid it.

Evaluating what is on offer

In the previous chapter we thoroughly discussed various security assessment classes and types. In fact, information security assessments are like . . . pizza. In a good pizzeria you would be offered a set menu of options, as well as the wide selection of separate pizza toppings to make your own for a fastidious taste. Of course, you also need a delicious crunchy pizza base for all of these. The fundamentals we have discussed in the first chapter form this base. They must go with any choice you make. The classes and types outlined in the second chapter allow an educated selection of the 'toppings'. However, we did not discuss the 'set menu'. Here are the standard audit types you can find in information security companies adverts:

- ISMS audits
  - documentation reviews
  - process reviews
  - overall security management reviews
- Human-related audits
  - social engineering
  - relevant process reviews
- Premises and physical checks
  - overall premises security audit
  - physical systems security audit
  - social engineering
- Technical security audits
  - external penetration testing
  - external vulnerability scanning
  - internal penetration testing
  - internal vulnerability scanning
  - application security testing

- database security testing
- configuration and standard build review
- source code security review
- wireless security testing
- other specialised technical tests

These are the most common pre-set combinations of our 'toppings'. If you are not a security auditor, practice going through this list analysing which typical assessment types can be black, grey or white box. Guess which are likely to be passive or active, intrusive or non-intrusive. But the specific point to make here is: *the selection offered by a security company you consider must contain all audit types that are, or can be demanded by your long-term information security program.* The more extensive the spectrum of specific audits offered by a company, the better. Things change, and you cannot be sure what exactly would you need in a longer run. Alas, we do acknowledge that even a specialised security company cannot cover everything and may itself resort to outsourcing. And, in some cases, narrow scope, highly specific security assessment services offered can bring great advantage. For example, there are security companies that are based around a team of highly skilled programmers which specialise on source code reviews for software vendors.

The second point is: *a security company must offer both the 'set' and the 'custom' menus.* If all they have available is the set, then it is a good indication that all testing is done in a mechanical way. In other words, it can only be *passive.* This is not a good sign. Because we operate in a fluid, rapidly changing, highly variable environment, security testing procedures often need to be modified in accordance with the auditee's peculiarities and unfolding circumstances.

Sometimes, they may need to be adjusted on the fly. A rigid selection of predefined services will not meet such purpose. There must be a possibility of mix-and-match, of a transition in the flow. A typical technical example of such situation would be if potentially insecure wireless connectivity is detected during an internal penetration test. Then the test will have to involve at least partial wireless security assessment and a brief security policy review. Finally, if the testing has specific implications for compliance, they must be addressed. For instance, PCI DSS security scanning must be done by the registered ASVs, and it is only among them that you can make your choice. Then you could check whether they offer an original scanning methodology or are simply a reseller of others' services getting a margin from it. You probably don't want to pay that margin. This concludes the part of the discussion dedicated to the offered security assessments scopes and types.

Judging the assessors suitability

The next issue is rather tricky. Somehow, you need to estimate the potential security auditor's skills. Note, that this is pertinent for both the auditee and the auditor (when hiring the personnel). We will briefly review it as such. But before delving into the skill sets of people and teams, remember to do at least some background checks to avoid unpleasant surprises. Background checks can vary from applying to specialised companies like Kroll and PeopleCheck to googling and using more attuned online people and companies search sites. Note that in some countries, such as Russia and other CIS states, background checks are legally curtailed. At the very least, sweep for common public knowledge regarding companies and people whom you are reviewing as potential security auditors. The auditors will inevitably access and handle sensitive data. The assessment report itself is highly confidential. You can't risk it. So, check if the companies and people you are reviewing were involved in any scandals, machinations, major security incidents and so on. Are there any publicised customer complaints? If you know the names of the auditor candidates, verify whether their reputation does not include any malicious hacking, cybercrime or other fraudulent activities. You might be astonished. We knew and reported entire companies operated by scammers and looking legitimate at the first sight. Alas, they weren't information security specialists.

Probably the most reliable way of determining the auditor's knowledge and skills is to have appropriate and trusted professionals from your company or organisation to check them. This means bypassing the auditor marketing team and arranging a direct meeting between the specialists from both parties. Typically, it should not present a problem. If it does, then, perhaps, the auditor company is doubtful about their experts' proficiency, and has instructed the sales reps to hold the ground, which is also not a good sign. Note, that apart from fitting the profile of the audit (e.g. network engineers if it is network security-centred), the internal professionals selected to communicate with the potential auditors must be trusted. In the context of this discussion it refers to their genuine interest in getting the best assessment results. A situation in which the company specialists may try to favour weak auditors out of fear that the assessment can uncover their faults is entirely possible. It must be taken into an account when you pick personnel for this specific task and debrief them afterwards.

Professional certifications and education

Next you need to look at different credentials and other achievements the auditors possess. These may include:

Certifications

- Education
- Publications
- Tools and exploits

The relevant certifications provided by the industry, standard bodies, and so on can be divided into three major categories:

1. General information security certifications.
2. Specific information security certifications.
3. Specific security-centred technical certifications.
4. Other professional certifications.

Currently, there are far too many applicable certifications to be reviewed in this book. We suggest studying the appropriate certification authority sources to gain necessary knowledge about each particular instance. However, some pertinent common examples need to be addressed.

CISSP and its concentrations is a good example of the category one. The concentrations make it more area-directed, but only in rather general terms. SANS GIAC is closer to the category two with its separate specialisations in security administration, security management, software security and security auditing, with further subdivisions within these spheres of knowledge. Another example of a certification par excellence directed at technical security auditing is Certified Ethical Hacker (CEH) from the EC-Council. ISECOM (Institute for Security and Open

Methodologies), most known for providing and maintaining OSSTMM (Open Source Security Testing Methodology Manual), also certifies security assessors in accordance with the OSSTMM practices. The cert is OPST (OSSTMM Professional Security Tester); other ISECOM certifications are Security Analyst, Security Expert and Wireless Security Expert. Other valuable certifications which specifically pertain to penetration testing and include hands-on practical tests apart from theory questions in their examinations are Tiger and CREST. Note that there are two types of CREST: network security-centric and application security-centric, with the corresponding two types of exams. GLAS-certified experts in the UK must have either Tiger or CREST accreditation.

Security+ is an example of an entry-level certification covering various technical aspects of information security. More specific security-centred technical certifications can concentrate on separate technology or vendors. CWSP (Certified Wireless Security Professional) is an instance of the former, CCIE (Cisco Certified Internetwork Expert) Security of the latter. Nowadays, practically all major security equipment and software manufacturers offer certifications pertaining to their blockbuster products. Also, vendor certifications not centred on information security still include significant parts on it that pertain to the specific technologies and products the cert addresses. There are security sections within MCSE, CCNP, RHCE (Red Hat Certified Engineer) and so on. Such certs form the fourth category listed above.

Apart from a huge variety of professional certifications, there is higher education in information security or relevant specific areas ranging from human resources management to software engineering. MSc programs in information security became highly popular, with more and more universities around the world following the trend. The 'academic' areas in which these programs are typically strong are information security organisation, management and principles, relevant theories, cryptography in both theory and practice. Sometimes, university programs do concentrate on specific technologies subject to lecturers' expertise, available sponsorships and grants. But in general, we tend to view current information security MSc degrees as 'CISSP on steroids'. In fact, many such programs automatically enlist their students as CISSP associates.

When assessing security auditors' credentials like certifications and degrees, whether for signing a service (the auditee) or an employment (the auditor) contract, one has to take into account a variety of factors. Some of these factors, more pertinent to the auditor party, will be reviewed in more detail in the last chapter of this book. For the purpose of the current one the following matters are essential.

- *'It is better to have certifications and degrees than not. At least, they provide reasonable proof that a certain proficiency baseline exists. In this case, something is clearly better than nothing'.*

- *'More often than not, certifications and degrees relate to knowledge, rather than skills'.*

Very specific accreditations that require passing practical, hands-on exam tests are the possible exceptions.

- *'Despite what many technical specialists think about their usefulness, having general information security certifications and degrees is advantageous for the auditors'.*

Finding vulnerabilities is one thing. Establishing their true sources and evaluating risks is another. The former firmly belongs to the realm of tactics. The latter crosses into the strategic domain. Both must be present, operating in concert. Nevertheless:

- *'for executing specific audit types highly pertinent qualifications and respective accreditations are vital, even if they are not security-centred'.*

For a source code security review, a good degree in software engineering is likely to be far more important than any information security-centred education or cert.

- *'Having too many certifications and (more rarely) degrees is suspicious, especially if the declared work experience period is rather limited'.*

Is this person really walking the talk? Is it not the case of cramming-for-the-exam we have used as an allegory when discussing compliance issues in the second chapter? How much is too many? We have seen people boasting to have more than a dozen of certs in totally unrelated areas. But cramming in a bootcamp does not make one an expert, only extensive experience in the area does. On the other hand, if a professional is known to work with specific vendor solutions for a decade and has plentiful certifications from this vendor, it makes perfect sense. Study it because you like it and need it in everyday work, not for the fancy letters on a business card.

- *'Some of the best hackers known or unknown to the world have no relevant certifications and degrees. The same can apply to prominent security researchers and developers'.*
- *'Finally, there is no specialist cert in social engineering'.*

Publications and tools

Apart from certifications and university diplomas, the auditors can also demonstrate a variety of publications, software or hardware tools, and exploit code. In our opinion, these are highly important since they clearly point at ongoing hands-on work. Publications are casually divided into:

- journal articles and books.
- security advisories.
- posts on professional forums and groups.

Articles demonstrate knowledge (or, at times, lack of thereof) in a specific area they cover. If they are written in a HOWTO style being essentially printed manuals, they indicate practical skills as well. Alternatively, a security team can release a specific tool and supplement it with detailed manuals. Check what the tool does. Think whether it, or any similar applications, can be used to assess your systems and networks addressing the likely problems they might face.

Of course, *the ultimate publication you should ask for is a sample of the relevant assessment report.* A security company must be able to provide it ASAP and for every specific audit type they advertise. It should not be obsolete, reflecting methods and vulnerabilities of a lustrous past. It must not contain any sensitive *or potentially sensitive* data related to current or previous customers. Such information can often include network addresses and diagrams, or employees' positions. If it contains theirs, then where is the guarantee that someday it would not embody yours? While it sounds all too obvious, we did encounter such cases in the past. Analyse the assessment report together with the respective specialists. Is it what you expect to receive from the planned audit? Does it correspond well to the descriptions and requirements we outline in chapter seven, entirely dedicated to reporting security assessments outcome?

Books are similar to articles, but have much wider scope and often go into more depth. They casually hint at long-standing experience or original research, since respected publishers would not accept a proposition from just anyone. Quite often, practical books are supplemented with a few tools, or whole toolkits. Speaking of which, you may encounter an information security company centred around producing and maintaining a powerful and complex tool. Again, verify what such tool does and which specific or unique abilities that you need it offers. Authoring a mighty security tool clearly shows profound knowledge and skill in the area to which these abilities pertain. On the other hand, it may also turn the company into, essentially, the tool vendor. This will undoubtedly limit its assessment's scope, strongly relating it to the tool capabilities.

Security advisories indicate *active* hands-on investigations and are, in this sense, similar to the exploit code. In fact, they are regularly supplemented with the exploit code. Check which specific issues are reported in the advisories and are targeted by the exploits. Is it somehow relevant to your networks, systems and critical applications? Also, check the element of open disclosure ethics. A standard procedure is to report a new vulnerability to the affected software vendor, communicate with its specialists, wait until the patch or fixed version is released, and only then publicly disclose the information, not to mention the exploit code. Disclosing vulnerability information before the fix is out for the sake of personal fame indicates serious ego problems. Stay away from such people, since they can put your systems at risk by making their flaws public before they are eliminated. To do this, they don't have to publish a full advisory to open disclosure mail lists or groups. Bragging to friends about "how masterly did we get in" is more than enough. There are exceptions to everything, however. If the vendor did not release the fix in a year or so, deciding to publish information about the flaw is entirely justified. Vendors should be reprimanded for their negligence. If it was a serious bug of utility or function, the customers would have already switched to a different supplier or even sued. Why should security, an essential part of warranty according to the ITIL, be any different?

In the recent past we would have said: if the auditor company has continuously published new security advisories, exploit code, and tools, go for it if technical assessments are all you need. Nowadays, things are not so simple. First of all, numerous companies and organisations that buy exploit code and information about novel vulnerabilities came to life. Once it is bought, it becomes a property of such a company and will remain confidential for a long time. Perhaps forever. So, many security researchers of today quietly sell their 'sploits and vulns' instead of publishing them to public disclosure lists like Open Disclosure and Bugtraq, or at their companies' sites. Then, more and more client companies enforce very strict NDAs that prohibit such publications. For instance, we could not disclose a few critical holes in a certain network security appliance because of such an NDA, even though the appliance was retired about three years ago and is no longer maintained. Also, do not be astonished by the sheer amount of security advisories published by some researchers and teams. Have your specialists examine them.

Currently, many security holes in web applications can be discovered by powerful scanning tools without much effort on the auditor's side. These flaws are underlined by common algorithms and are sufficiently basic to be uncovered by automated scans. Publishing them en masse demonstrates that the auditing team has a decent web application scanner, but does not necessarily indicate high level of proficiency and skill. So, '*it is always a good sign if a security company publishes some security advisories, tools and exploits. However, it does not have to spit out tons of them all the time*'.

The bottom line of this discussion is: '*if a company has released security advisories, exploits and tools, it means that its team is capable of performing meaningful and efficient **active** technical security assessments*'. Which is something you shall probably need now or in the not-so-distant future. On the other hand, it does not say a lot about its capabilities in non-technical security auditing. You should also question whether they are proficient in analysing risks and establishing the actual sources of the uncovered flaws. As we have stated above, discovering the vulnerabilities is surely crucial, but at the end of the day it is only a half of the whole job. If the matters are not put into the strategic perspective, important factors can go amiss. You can get trapped in the endless scan-report-patch-scan-report-patch-scan-. . . loop while it is entirely possible to break this nagging pattern by finding and eliminating the problem's true root cause.

The auditor company history and size

What about the security firm itself, not just its auditing team's expertise? The first thing you should look at after verifying the company's and its specialists' reputation is for how long the company has been operational. Common sense tells us: the longer, the better. If it did not go out of business, despite the credit crunch, then its services are either unique and have captured their niche, or are of a high quality, or both. There are exceptions that thrive entirely on highly aggressive marketing or strong personal connections of their directors, but these are few. If the company did operate for ages, it must have developed an internal 'school of thought and skill', as well as extensive knowledge base. This ensures that newcomers to such a company would be properly trained by joining the continuity, and the contractors to whom the company may outsource some work (a common practice those days!) will be more thoroughly scrutinised. In spite of the rapidly evolving nature of the information security science and art, having a strong 'internal tradition' is worthwhile. If possible, find out about the rotation of personnel in the reviewed security company. Public searches for current and former employees are the easiest way of doing it. A high level of retention of experienced professionals within the company indicates that such tradition is present and very well alive.

Over the time of its operation the company should have amassed various references and accumulated a sizeable client base. Always ask for the references and review the client base profile. Many companies and organisations are unwilling to provide their name as a customer for privacy reasons and supply written reference letters. Information security is a sensitive area. Nevertheless, some customers may well do, or even advertise it on their web sites. You have probably seen many of these stating "this site was security checked by <company name>". Besides, references do not have to be formal. What amounts to a reliable reference can be passed by word of mouth in a private conversation or via e-mail. Apart from proving (or disproving) the quality of the performed work, the rumour mill can also provide invaluable information regarding the ethical aspects. We live in a small world. The professional information security world is even more like a village. If someone has being involved in dubious activities like leaking confidential data or charging for undelivered services, it will be known and spread from lip to lip. The more contacts you have with the scrutinised security company acquaintances, the better. Especially if they were (or are) its customers. As for the advertised base of the existing and former clients, it should at least state to which industry or government sectors they belong. Is there a certain pattern of preference? How does your company or organisation fit into this pattern?

The final question to be addressed is how large the auditor team is. The judgement by size is not straightforward. A lot depends on what kind of security assessments do you really need and what their perceived and planned scope is. The reality is that the number of highly skilled auditors in any company or organisation is going to be limited. Admittedly, there are not a lot of them on the whole and they are thinly spread around the world. Their services are usually expensive. Besides, such professionals are typically driven by passion and would strive to do what interests them the most. Thus, if some security company claims to have dozens of top-end security specialists in a team, we would naturally have strong doubts. They aren't the NSA, after all.

Most likely, there is a small dedicated yolk surrounded by a mass of the less knowledgeable and skilled colleagues, who in the best case can be the disciples of the core 'maestros'. No one has ever managed to assemble an entire army of 'ninjas'. Nor is it likely to happen in a foreseen future. So, providing that the presence of necessary expertise is evident, the actual choice is between the 'naked' core and the core enveloped by numerous acolytes. If you opt for the latter, you will have more people to do a massive scope job. If you chose the former, you can be more confident that you are getting the service from the wizards and not the apprentices. It is reasonable to assume that *active* testing is going to (and should) be performed by the first, and *passive* – by the second. So, if you need wide range passive checks, especially if they demand physical presence of the auditors at your premises, a large team is a definite advantage. If limited scale but great depth active testing is required, however, a small highly professional team could be a better option. Remember, that many wide scope technical or semi-technical passive tests can be successfully performed by a smaller team employing effective automation (scripting). Nevertheless, as the classic Chinese strategist Wu Qi pointed out millennia ago, *"when employing a few, concentrate upon narrows"*.

On arranging the audit process

> *'First establish your plans, then prepare your equipment'.* – Li Quan

Once the assessment characteristics are decided upon and the appropriate auditors are selected, it is time to pull up the sleeves to plan and arrange the assessment process. On the auditor side it is straightforward:

1. Review the customer requirements and all information (schedules, deadlines, target lists, etc.) provided.

2. Make sure everything is understood, agreed and no arrangements are unrealistic.
3. Select specialists and assign their roles for the upcoming assessment.
4. Select who is going to communicate with the auditee during the whole process.
5. Select appropriate methodologies and techniques.
6. Now select the tools, if the assessment is technical.
7. Make sure that all chosen tools are fully operational, stable and are updated and upgraded to the latest versions. You don't want to tweak, update and reinstall during the tests. Time is precious.
8. Wait for the green light and go.

Verify that you clearly comprehend all the objectives and aims of the audit. Check that the timetable for it is reasonable and won't force you to rush with either the assessment itself or with producing the audit report. Ensure that all necessary instruments are humming smoothly. Finally, check several times when exactly you can kick off. We have seen far too much confusion when the audit began earlier than the auditee personnel was prepared for. Of course, by preparedness we do not mean any frantic attempts to 'clean up' and conceal possible issues just before the testing or other auditing starts. Such behaviour must be strongly discouraged, not the least because it is actually more likely to introduce more errors and gaps than existed before. What we imply is simply being ready to react to the assessment process and its immediate discoveries. The key words are 'effective communication'.

Final auditee preparations and planning

The auditee arrangements and planning tasks carry a higher responsibility and involve greater decision-making. First of all, is the assessment done against live or testing environment? This applies to technical audits only. If the assessment targets the testing environment, its milieu must be created beforehand allowing sufficient time for the construction and review. Then it must be thoroughly verified to emulate the real thing to the maximum possible extent. If the assessment targets live environment, always prepare for the unexpected. What if the tested systems collapse? What if a social engineer is caught red-handed and reported to the police (give the 'get out of jail' waiver to the auditor beforehand)? What if the internal audit turns out to be too disruptive for business? What if key participants of the audit fail to turn up on both sides? What if the assessment uncovers illicit behaviour or outright criminal offence? What if . . . The friction is higher at the auditee side. Always prepare for a sudden change of plans. Have spare plans. Plan for contingency.

The next thing is to decide who will communicate with the auditors and how it should be done. Common sense tells us that it should be the CISO or equivalent. It also suggests that relevant technical or non-technical specialists must be involved. Thus, define who will be in touch with the auditors. It could be more than one person, but you should avoid large communication teams susceptible to miscommunication and confusion. Three is a sensible number that ensures that someone will always stay in touch. For example, the involved trinity can be the CISO, head of the department which is most affected (e.g. IT, human resources, compliance/risk), and a selected relevant specialist, or the departmental administrator/secretary. In any case, they must be able to respond quickly to any auditor requests or status updates. Keep more than one channel of communication constantly open – phone, e-mail, instant messengers, if necessary – personal contact. Verify its efficiency. Send the auditors a few mails, or give a few phone calls asking for news and updates. See how quickly they would respond. Immediate response is highly desirable. If it lags for more than a day, it is a bad sign. Log a complaint.

Talk to the auditors and agree on the assessment phases, schedules, timetables, deadlines, debriefs and emergency breakpoint events. A protracted security audit can consist of a few phases. The separation into such stages can be done in accordance to numerous criteria and would be addressed in more detail in the next chapter. A recent audit we performed for one of our clients was split into the following steps:

- Assess a critical application.
- Debrief, wait for the follow-up reaction.
- Assess the systems that host the application.
- Debrief, wait for the follow-up reaction.
- Assess the network on which these systems are deployed.
- Debrief, wait for the follow-up reaction.
- Arrange the next round of testing to verify any corrective actions' success.

It is important to define the stages in a logical sequence and provide sufficient and meaningful intervals between them. When planning the audit schedules, think at which milestones status updates are necessary. For example, update after the reconnaissance is done, then after the vulnerability scanning is done, then after the risk analysis is performed, and finally when the report is submitted. With every status update received, ask the auditors about the estimated time of the next assessment stage. Are they ahead or behind the schedule? This brings us to the topic of security assessment timetables and deadlines.

You might have a variety of urgent pressures. For instance, a compliance check can be looming. Besides, time is invaluable anyway, and the quicker a security problem is discovered and dealt with, the lower are the associated risks. At the end of the day, it is up to the auditee to decide on both the time-frame and the deadline of the assessment process. Nonetheless, don't be mean and demand the impossible. Keep your required deadlines in sight, but also negotiate with the auditors. Find out how much time they *think* they need to do a proper job. Consult your professionals and relevant third-party information sources regarding it. There would be plenty of useful publications that describe similar testing and its peculiarities. Form your own opinion. You do not want to be overcharged or have a delayed assessment report. On the other hand, haste can be detrimental to the audit quality. *Bargain for time as you would for cash.* Decide on the absolute deadline when everything must be accomplished in full. Then consider a *realistic slack.* Shift the deadline back and present it to the auditors. Listen to their reasoning. Adjust the slack, trying to keep it sufficient. Then, as suggested above, keep your finger on the pulse checking the assessment progress with every single status update. If you see that the *very final and absolute deadline* is unlikely to be met for *objective reasons*, reconsider your plans. Perhaps, some things are not that critical and can be assessed the next time. Possibly, it is you that have overestimated the audit scope. If there are no apparent reasons for the severe delay, however, consider using a different audit supplier the next time.

Dealing with common assessment emergencies

The last topic that needs to be discussed is what we call the emergency breakpoints. *An emergency breakpoint event is the event that leads to the halt of the audit process and sudden change of plans.* Review the following possibilities, some of which we have already noted in this section:

- A severe, high risk vulnerability has been discovered.
- A critical live system has crashed.
- A clear-cut security incident has been detected.

All three issues provide strong reasons for stopping the assessment and redirecting attention and resources to their immediate resolution. They must be promptly reported by either party that discovers the problem (usually the auditors). In such a case, waiting until the planned audit process is over and the full report is submitted can do more harm than good. It risks becoming a textbook example of damage done by following rigid, inflexible plans. After the issue is successfully solved, a continuation of the audit can be arranged.

The simplest case is a critical system crash. Usually, the tests performed against such systems are non-intrusive. Nevertheless, there is always a chance of such an unfortunate event taking place. If strong redundancy and fault tolerance is built in (as it should be), and the fall-back system is not subject to similar tests, the assessment can continue. It will have to, of course, concentrate on establishing the cause of the crash and evaluate whether only availability is affected by this security problem. In other words, the auditors will have to investigate what caused an effective denial–of-service (DoS) attack and whether the issue is exploitable any further so that unauthorised access can be gained. In our practice, there have been occasions on which important systems collapsed during the security assessment. The real causes of the crashes, however, turned out to be completely unrelated to the tests. Always keep this possibility in mind: coincidence does not always mean a definite link and can be a mere manifestation of friction.

If, however, the availability is severely disrupted, the assessment will have to stop. The operation of the affected system will have to be restored ASAP. The next steps should include:

- trying to establish what caused the crash at the first place using all information at hand.

- writing a report based on the incomplete assessment results and outlining in detail what has happened.

- arranging a continuation of the checks against a standalone testing system that will completely mirror the affected one.

All of this must be done as quickly as you can. Meanwhile, the assessment report might have to point out the lack of proper redundancy and failover as a serious security gap putting data and services availability in jeopardy.

The next common type of an emergency breakpoint event is discovering a highly critical, exploitable vulnerability. Prior to the audit start, a preliminary arrangement covering this important issue should be reached. The typical action plan dealing with it is:

1. The auditors must immediately report such vulnerability to the auditee contact.
2. They must clearly outline its severity, associated impact and estimated risks.
3. The assessment must be stopped.
4. The vulnerability must be fixed.
5. The assessment can now continue, starting from verification that the breakpoint that caused vulnerability is now fully eliminated.
6. Rapid status update must inform the auditee contact that the issue is now resolved.
7. The assessment report must still outline this vulnerability and address the actions performed to remove it.

Back in university, one of the author's friends installed a new Solaris system on a network-connected server. He left it at the default configuration and went for coffee, planning to configure the box properly right after that. When he has returned, the system had port 666 open and a root shell bound to it. It took the time of drinking a single coffee mug to get hacked. If such a possibility is very likely, do not wait for the rest of the tests to complete. Inform and correct. Remember the OODA loop and getting ahead of the adversaries. If you don't, there is a fair chance that the audit will have to be followed by an entirely different service of a forensic investigation.

This is what actually happens in the third aforementioned emergency breakpoint case. Alas, the assessment is not followed by the forensic service. Rather, it flows straight into it. Imagine, that the auditors find out that one of the systems checked is already hacked and backdoored. Or highly confidential documents have disappeared without a trace. Or the auditee's employees are doing something in a clear violation of the acceptable use policy. For example, they can abuse network resources to run their own unrelated business. Or store pirated content, run peer-to-peer file exchange servers, keep child pornography or other illegal activities. The assessment will have to be stopped. The uncovered security incident must be discussed with the highest auditee contact, usually the CISO, *in strict confidence.* All evidence of the incident found by the auditors must be documented and provided to this contact in full. The rest would depend on the incident response and investigation policies and procedures of the auditee. If the auditors possess appropriate qualifications and the auditee deems it necessary, they can be employed as third party consultants to assist with incident response.

These are probably the most common examples of the security assessment emergency breakpoints we can recall. No doubt, other disruptive possibilities that can reshuffle even the most delicate arrangements and plans do exist. Nevertheless, it is entirely possible to anticipate and adapt to the inevitable interference of friction. In the words of Carl von Clausewitz, *'if we go further in the demands which war makes on its votaries, then we find the powers of the understanding predominating. War is the province of uncertainty: three-fourths of those things upon which action in war must be calculated, are hidden more or less in the clouds of great uncertainty'.* **Here, then, above all a fine and penetrating mind is called for, to grope out the truth by the tact of its judgement.**

CHAPTER 5: SECURITY AUDIT STRATEGIES AND TACTICS

'In military operations, what is valued is foiling the opponent's strategy, not pitched battle'. – Wang Xi.

The previous chapters put heavy emphasis on governance, management and policy issues in relation to assessing information security. They are also heavily centred on the issues of strategic significance. It is time to pull up your sleeves and dive into the realm of tactics. Inevitably, this means that the upcoming discourse will have to be more technically inclined. As stated in this book's preface, however, providing detailed checklists or hands-on testing manuals is not the intended goal. We are not competing with, for example, OSSTMM (Open Source Security Testing Methodology Manual), not to mention more specific in-depth guides like OWASP (The Open Web Application Security Project). Rather, we create a layer of applicable logic above and *through* such guides, by explaining how the fundamentals and strategies previously discussed can be implemented in practice.

When discussing the differences between strategic and tactical approach, Carl von Clausewitz wrote the following:

- *'combat consists of a greater or lesser number of individual acts, each complete in itself, which we call engagements, which constitute new things. This gives rise to an entirely different activity, namely, individually planning and conducting these engagements and joining them together to achieve the objective of the war. The first is called tactics, the second, strategy'.*

This provides a defined separation line between 'strategic' and 'tactical' when applied to information security assessments. A separate test, or a testing phase, amounts to an engagement in the above quote. Every engagement is an entity *"complete in itself"*, meaning it has its own OODA loop. This loop should revolve seamlessly to ensure the engagement's efficacy. *"Joining them together to achieve the objective"* of the assessment is the audit's strategy. A large part of it amounts to pulling all assessment findings together and performing an all-encompassing *synthetic* risk analysis, which is the subject of the next Chapter.

Another take on what is strategic is presented in MCDP 1 *Warfighting*, which states that *'strategy involves establishing goals, assigning forces, providing assets, and imposing conditions on the use of force in theaters of war'*. This relates to defining the objectives and planning we have already addressed in detail. Note that from the auditee's viewpoint, hopefully based upon running large scale long-term information security programs, a stand-alone audit appears to be a tactical assignment. Nevertheless, security assessments have their own, if somewhat restricted, language and logic of strategy. The aforementioned audit planning and synthesis of its approaches, methods and results to generate the whole picture are its vital parts. The same applies to all general methodologies and frameworks that can be applicable to security assessments of different nature. For instance, the basic audit sequence outlined at the very beginning of *chapter 1* is suitable for technical, process and social engineering tests. It is clearly strategic, just as all the fundamental principles discussed in that chapter are. Keep them in mind when planning and performing any information security audits, and you will find them all-permeating. No matter what you do, if you are doing it right, *'strategy can therefore never take its hand from the work for a moment'* (Clausewitz).

On critical points

'There's only one principle of war and that's this. Hit the other fellow, as quick as you can, and as hard as you can, where it hurts him most, when he ain't lookin'!' – Sir William Slim

The immediate practical aim of any information security audit is to discover as many vulnerabilities, weaknesses and gaps as possible within the defined assessment limits. In the case of an active assessment approach, simple discovery of flaws is usually insufficient. The vulnerabilities must be exploited. To do so in an effective way, it is important to pinpoint the weakest links in a chain and direct maximum effort at breaching them with further expansion of success. *'[T]here is no more imperative and simpler law for strategy than to keep the forces concentrated'* (Clausewitz) against the opponent's critical points. But how do we define them? Is it something (or someone), which is the most vulnerable? Or, perhaps, the most valuable? Or does it have a specific position in a general scheme of things? Could it possess a peculiar combination of these and, perhaps, some other important characteristics?

Centres of gravity and their types

In the previous chapter we elaborated on a possible way of allocating priority targets for an upcoming security assessment. The problem is: the perspective of the auditors on both criticality and prioritisation of specific items can be significantly different from that of the auditee. This is expected – the mindset and vision of both sides are typically highly dissimilar. Thus, there is a need to discuss the subject of critical points in more detail, this time primarily from the auditor's side. To do it in a logical and organised way without slipping into technical specificity, we shall borrow a few more important terms from military science. These terms are *'centre of gravity'*, *'schwerpunkt'/'nebenpunkte'* and *'systempunkt'*. Just as *'friction'* and *'fog of war'* are highly applicable for describing the effects of uncertainty, the unknown, chaos and chance, these terms are honed to perfection to address vital, deciding points *from the attacker's perspective*.

The modern definition of the *centre of gravity* is provided in MCDP 1 *Warfighting* (just replace "the enemy" with "the auditee", "eliminated" with "breached", and "our will" with "attackers' will"):

- *'We ask ourselves: Which factors are critical to the enemy? Which can the enemy not do without? Which, if eliminated, will bend him most quickly to our will? These are centers of gravity'.*

Thoroughly review all the information the auditee contacts have supplied. Then perform the reconnaissance testing phase, and answer these questions for yourself on the basis of its results. When doing so, dissociate yourself from the initial information provided by the auditee. You may already find that some of your answers do not match the auditee opinions. Continue with the vulnerability discovery and exploitation. During the risk analysis stage that follows, perform another round of 'centre of gravity questions'. Do their final answers correspond to the auditee estimations? What about your own post-reconnaissance assertions? How many centres of gravity were confirmed, determined or dismissed by the tests? Can you prioritise them?

Centre of gravity is a two hundred year old concept introduced by Carl von Clausewitz. He acknowledged that there could be more than a single centre and recommended to direct maximum effort at what seems to be the most vital one:

- *'Therefore, the first consideration in drafting a plan of war is to recognize the centres of gravity of the enemy power, and to reduce them to one, if possible.'*

Nevertheless, the grand strategist did realise that sometimes concentrating all effort on what is perceived as the main centre of gravity is not practically feasible:

- *'There is only one exception to the principle of directing all one's forces against the centre of gravity of the enemy force, and that is if secondary operations promise extraordinary benefits.'*

The idea of prioritising centres of gravity to determine those likely to *cause a total collapse of the opponent's defences* was further developed by blitzkrieg strategists. Blitz, as we know from history, is a highly effective offensive approach, recapitulated in Heinz Guderian's famous phrase, *"Nicht kleckern, klotzen!"* (Don't fiddle, smash!). Blitzkrieg generals used the germane terms *schwerpunkt* and *nebenpunkte* to harmonise their operations.

- *'Schwerpunkt is the centre of gravity towards which the main effort of the attack is focused so that the desirable objectives are met.'*
- *'Nebenpunkte designates secondary activities supporting the primary effort'*. These activities often involve distracting the opponents or 'softening' their defences.

In a penetration or social engineering test, *a schwerpunkt is the primary point that allows effective breach of data and systems confidentiality, integrity and/or availability.* It could be a system, application, network protocol, authentication mechanism or even someone's personal trait. The key is: *it must be more mission critical and sufficiently exploitable as compared to other identified centres of gravity.* Only that warrants the time, attention and measure of concentration it demands. Thus, like in a real war, establishing a security assessment's schwerpunkt requires decent reconnaissance and good judgement. Note that, since the concept of schwerpunkt provides a crystallisation point for mission, direction and intent, it can be highly applicable for organising any information security programs, not just running the audits. Also note the dependence of selecting the schwerpunkt on the objectives, which can differ.

In a sophisticated hacking attack, the assailants can flood intrusion detection and monitoring systems with junk traffic or fake attack signatures to render them useless. They can even try to exploit and subvert them. At the same time, the true targets of the attack are clearly not the IDS/IPS sensors or syslog servers. This constitutes a technical instance of the nebenpunkte. Emulating such subterfuge as a part of a penetration test can be highly effective in assessing the deployed safeguards. In the first chapter we noted an example of a wireless penetration test in which the IPS was tricked to attack legitimate hosts, effectively becoming a problem itself. In a real hacking attack that could have forced network administrators to turn off the 'misbehaving' IPS, thus softening the defences.

Social engineering can supply us with plentiful illustrations of using the nebenpunkte to alleviate tension, distract attention and reduce suspicion. If an astute social engineer expects that the very contact with the 'schwerpunkt person' will raise some eyebrows, she can simultaneously connect with a bunch of other people. No matter if they are totally unrelated to the engagement's aims or the person our social engineer is after. In fact, it could only create advantage by diverting attention and presenting the contact as natural and unsuspicious. All communication with the 'mission-critical person(s)' will inevitably involve lavish nebenpunkte. Further still, it might consist of 'pure nebenpunkte' without any specific attempts to get to the point, until the needed sensitive data is 'incidentally' revealed. Sometimes, the absence of any direct head-on approach to the target is the best approach of all.

The latter case is Guderian reversed: *'Fiddle until it smashes'*. One of the nebenpunkte suddenly becomes the schwerpunkt, which falls prey to an attack: bingo! It also bears associations with the fuzzing method discussed later in this chapter when addressing application vulnerability discovery. But above all, it brings into the spotlight the most modern of all the discussed terms – the *systempunkt*. It is derived from the combination of German 'schwerpunkt' and English 'system' (in general and not the IT-specific sense). A characteristic systempunkt exhibits the following traits:

- *'It is critical because of its interactions with other points in the system, rather than any specific inherent properties.'*

- *'Thus, its penetration or collapse has severe repercussions for the system as a total, often due to the avalanche or domino effect.'*

- *'An attack on it is likely to be far more damaging to the whole system than to the systempunkt itself.'*

- *'Because of that, the real value of a "standalone" systempunkt can only be measured by the total effects of its failure or breach.'*
- *'It is not necessarily the most obvious or the weakest link.'*
- *'It is usually highly reactive to many small interactions and interventions, especially if they are aptly combined.'*

In terms of chaos theory, systempunkts are vulnerabilities of complex emergent systems, appearing as side effects of the emergence. Common application libraries, code repositories, centralised version control and patch management systems, SaaS applications, routers, switches and infrastructure protocols can make perfect technical systempunkts. If information is automatically 'smeared' around the Cloud without proper security checks, any point of unauthorised entry into it could become a deadly systempunkt in waiting. Humans are inherently complex systems with plentiful weaknesses of a kind. As a little useful exercise, think who might make the best bipedal systempunkts in your company or organisation from the social engineering perspective.

Identifying critical points

Figure 20 is a slight modification of the scheme on the previous Figure we have employed when discussing targets selection from the auditee perspective.

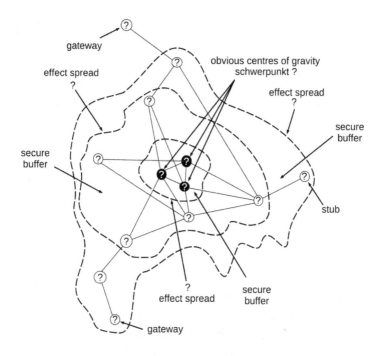

Figure 20: Where are the critical points?

For the example's sake, this time envision this illustration as a simple computer network diagram. It has two external gateways, three nodes known to hold highly confidential data, and a single stub node. The three 'confidential' nodes are the obvious centres of gravity. No third-party security assessments are required to recognise this basic fact. However, which one can be the schwerpunkt? This would depend on many factors, including:

- *The objectives of the attack.* If all the adversaries want is disruption of the external network connectivity, then both gateways *and their uplinks* are the schwerpunkt. If the attackers are after some specific employees, then these employees' workstations and communication channels are the most likely schwerpunkt. Nevertheless, the three central nodes might be also targeted if they store employee data the attacker is after. Sly internal assailants might even attack them while spoofing their victim's network address or account to frame a colleague.

- *The amount of tangible and intangible damage that can be caused by the breach.* Given the chance to protect only one of your systems storing sensitive data, which one would you go for taking into account all known and anticipated factors? Rephrasing George Orwell, all confidential data are sensitive, but some are more sensitive than the other.

- *The attacker's means.* Naturally, if the assailant is an experienced database hacker the critical node that hosts the corporate database will become the schwerpunkt. Since the ever-present fog of war prevents us from knowing what attackers can or cannot do, it is essential that the auditors possess the needed variety of skills. Otherwise, their and the assailant's perceptions of schwerpunkt may not match, leading to a predictable outcome when the attack takes place.

To summarise, while one of the three central nodes, or both gateways, or insufficiently protected communication channels to and from them are more likely to become the schwerpunkt, this is not always the case. Look around. Perhaps, you can discover a network management station (or, in case of an internal audit, sniff a management protocol) that holds the keys to all critical hosts. Yet, it might be totally missed by the auditee when doing the pre-assessment gap analysis. Can such de facto network management station be one of the system administrator's laptops?

What about any possible systempunkts on the scheme? Common sense tells that the nodes which are more interconnected should be more suitable for this role. But can the lonely stub node of *Figure 20* be the systempunkt? Envision the following scenarios:

1. The stub node is a remote workstation that has privileged access to the three central nodes or both gateways over VPN tunnels. Although, this is more of a hidden, non-obvious schwerpunkt case. It would be closer to a systempunkt, though, if we look at it as a vector of malware proliferation.

2. The stub node is the only network switch to which the attackers can gain administrative access. Then they can manipulate the STP (Spanning Tree Protocol) to redirect traffic through this switch or cause a propagating network-wide denial of service with ease.

3. The nodes on the scheme are not separate hosts, but entire BGP (Border Gateway Protocol) autonomous systems (AS). Hackers who took over the stub AS can use wily attack methods such as *prefix hijacking* or *prefix deaggregation* to wreak large scale, rapidly proliferating havoc. They can also try to suck in and intercept additional traffic by subverting the BGP path information parameter.

Scenarios 2 and 3 demonstrate the awesome, gobsmacking power of exploiting a systempunkt. All three scenarios show that systempunkt, depending on the logic of the entire system's architecture and operations, could be literally anywhere. Hence, all nodes of *Figure 20* are labelled with question marks. In fact, a systempunkt may not be the actual physical node, but a link between them or, more likely, an infrastructure protocol running through these links. Besides, by plugging in a laptop and spoofing switching, routing, redundancy, address resolution (DNS) and assignment (DHCP), or other relevant protocols, an internal attacker actually *adds or creates a systempunkt*! He or she does it by joining the attacked network and effectively emulating unauthorised access to a key switch, router or server.

Can we prioritise systempunkts and define the main one? The dash lines on *Figure 20* represent how far the repercussions of hitting a systempunkt can spread. Usually, the systempunkt with the largest dissemination of effects is the most critical. In the example scheme, that would be the point that affects all the depicted nodes, generating the outermost dash line. In other cases, look at both the reach of the aftermath and its actual impact for every confirmed systempunkt. *How many centres of gravity does it engulf, or even create?* Do the existing security buffers and zones restrict the pervasion of systempunkt effects? How? Can these restrictions be bypassed? How could the defenders reinforce them?

When criticising the classical view of centres of gravity, Colonel Boyd wrote the following:

- *Clausewitz incorrectly stated: 'A center of gravity is always found where the mass is concentrated most densely' – then argued that 'this is the place where the blows must be aimed and where the decision should be reached. He failed to develop idea of generating many non-cooperative centers of gravity by striking at those vulnerable, yet critical, tendons, connections, and activities that permit a larger system to exist'.*

Without explicitly naming it, John Boyd has essentially described utilising the systempunkt concept. In our context, "the mass" in his quote can refer to the system or data monetary or prestige value. Alternatively, it may point at the "concentrated mass" of vulnerabilities. *Neither would make a certain systempunkt on its own.* Subject to specific conditions and security assessment objectives, they may not even create a fully-blown schwerpunkt! The textbook view of prioritising targets by their value as assets can be entirely correct. But taking into account all the discussed factors, it overtly looks a bit 19th century. The vulnerability-centric view typical for many auditors might also be misleading. When exploited, a system or application with the concentrated mass of vulnerabilities makes a great beachhead for further attacks. This fully qualifies it as a nebenpunkte, the supporting effort. To become a schwerpunkt, however, it still needs to cause the exposure of sensitive data and/or collapse of the assessed defences. As far as the systempunkt goes, by definition "it is not necessarily the most obvious or the weakest link".

Another important part of the systempunkt definition is *"it is usually highly reactive to many small interactions and interventions, especially if they are aptly combined"*. In practical terms, this means that low impact vulnerabilities or feeble security weaknesses can create a gaping hole when exploited in concert. If you do not think of them in such a way, they can be easily ignored or dismissed as totally unimportant. This is the frequently overlooked and difficult subject of evaluating compound risks we will cover more thoroughly in the upcoming risk analysis chapter. Since we have already used a few network-centric scenarios to illustrate the systempunkt, here comes yet another one in a raw:

1. There is a flaw in the network segmentation mechanism, which allows unidirectional sending of traffic to a

presumably secure VLAN (virtual local area network). This is a minor vulnerability.

2. The gateway of that VLAN does not implement any egress filtering. This is not a vulnerability. Subject to the situation, it can only be viewed as a potential weakness of controls.

3. Thus, it is possible to initiate communication with external hosts on the Internet from the VLAN, but not vice versa. The VLAN address range is private and strong ingress filtering is in place. This is a feature.

4. There is a server on this VLAN which is accessed by few highly trusted and vetted employees only. Let's say, the whole VLAN is exclusively designated for the top management use. The server has guessable login credentials which the senior managers are comfortable with (and try to convince them otherwise!). This is a potential vulnerability, but the outsiders can never reach it, right?

For a non-technical reader, this is what the attackers can do:

- They will use 1 to send the requests with a fake source address into the "secure" VLAN.

- They will employ 3 to receive the replies at the external computer somewhere on the Internet.

- Thus, a bidirectional communication is effectively established, permitted by the 2.

- Now the assailants can scan the 'secure' VLAN and discover 4.

- Once it is discovered, the login credentials can fall to a dictionary attack.

The end result: employing a combination of a minor vulnerability, a commonly ignored security weakness, a feature and a potential major vulnerability even a junior employee or contractor with some networking knowledge can hack into the big boss's accounts. We will revisit various applications of the systempunkt and provide additional non-network centric examples when discussing synthetic risk analysis in the sixth Chapter. For now, it is important to state that *'low impact vulnerabilities and weaknesses that could create a critical breach when fiddled with in combination can belong to different applications, systems, protocols, or even remote networks. In fact, they can have a totally different nature, some being technical, some human, and some operations, process and policy-related.'*

The strategic exploitation cycle

Armed with the knowledge of centres of gravity definitions, types and use, take another glance at both *Figures 19* and *20*. How do they compare now? How profoundly different could the perspectives and approaches of the auditee and the auditors (or the attacker and defender) really be? Have you already encountered such discrepancies in everyday information security matters? Do you understand them better after the above discourse? Do you already find the notions it has introduced valid, helpful and applicable in security auditing practice?

To summarise the possible sequential use of the strategic critical points in performing active information security assessments of all kinds, we created the diagram depicted in *Figure 21*. We call it the Strategic Exploitation Cycle.

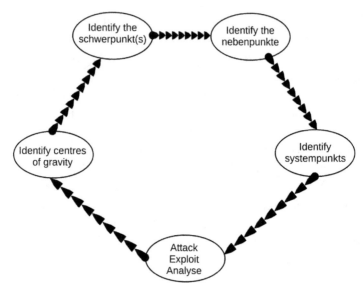

Figure 21: The strategic exploitation cycle

Later in the chapter, it will be supported by a tactical counterpart. The cycle builds its momentum towards increasing priority, reach, complexity and non-linearity of the assessment approaches and methodologies. It is live and fluid – fiddle with it! It is entirely possible to superimpose the central OODA loop together with the loops for every strategic exploitation cycle stage, like we did with the Deming cycle scheme in *Figure 7*. You can add prioritisation to or even amid the separate phases. It could be feasible to insert additional attack, exploit and analyse modules anywhere between the cycle stages. Or add new recon modules amongst them, although the operation of the whole cycle assumes continuous reconnaissance. What if you cannot pierce the fog of war and uncover the lurking systempunkts before you begin the actual exploitation? Which is, apropos, a form of aggressive recce. *What if the attack itself creates systempunkts or other centres of gravity?* This is a possibility to be reckoned with. The cycle in *Figure 21* can be utilised at any stage of active information security assessments – from planning the tests to analysing risks and even compiling the audit report. It will see heavy use throughout the rest of this book.

On reconnaissance

'If you can find out the real conditions, then you will know who will prevail.' – Mei Yaochen

Reconnaissance means finding as much information about any subjects of the assessment, from any possible sources. Apart from being an essential foundation for a successful security audit, reconnaissance on its own brings great benefits to the auditee. It reduces friction and removes fog of war by discovering functionalities, whole systems, applications, services, connections, accounts, users, information leaks and personnel deeds one could've hardly expected. By doing so, the recon provides a great contribution to reducing the element of (unpleasant) surprise. It is not uncommon to find a few security weaknesses, flaws and gaps during the assessment recon phase. For instance, quite often we used to find sensitive information lying unprotected on shared resources where it clearly shouldn't be, or even published to the Web, during early recon stage. From the reviewed critical points classification perspective it corresponds to discovering not just the centres of gravity, but obvious nebenpunkte, if not the schwerpunkt, and even the elusive systempunkts. Review *Figure 21* – everything prior to the attack and exploitation stage perfectly fits a thorough, elaborate recon phase. Besides, technical reconnaissance tests frequently uncover misconfigurations that are not directly security-related but can negatively affect system and network operations and their quality of service. By reporting and suggesting how to rectify such problems, the auditors can assist with the overall troubleshooting and contribute to networks, systems and services stability and performance.

In the terminology we use, reconnaissance is mapping the *information security zone*. Any part of it can become a 'battlefield' if attacked. In the words of the Chinese strategist Jia Lin, '*the ground means the location, the place of pitched battle – gain the advantage and you live, lose the advantage and you die*'. Knowing about the information security zone more than the assailants do is a clear advantage that allows getting inside their OODA loop with ease. They still have to do their Observations, but yours are already done. Your Orientation is based on better intelligence data. Thus, both Decision and Act will be superior.

Different assessment types demand a variety of recon approaches, and tactics shape its scope and depth. Black box audits are the most reconnaissance-dependent. In our experience, the recon phase of a purely black box penetration test can easily take half of the time of the whole assignment, if not more. In wireless security testing the recon can be even more time and effort-consuming as sufficient volumes of traffic may need to be collected. Typical white box assessments require relatively little intelligence gathering, but it is still clearly needed. For example, if you are analysing application source code it is useful to know as much as possible about its SDLC (software development life cycle) peculiarities and development procedures. Was it already security tested during the development? How? What do the secure software development guidelines of the company say? Are they somehow enforced? If configuration files of servers and network appliances are reviewed, find out about the people who configured them. It could turn out that some of them are internal, some are third party consultants, some are skilled, and some are evidently not. Also investigate configuration management procedures and techniques. Don't forget to consult all relevant security policies, standards and guidelines of the auditee, as they will inevitably affect configuration management and control peculiarities. All of these can explain and even predict many configuration discrepancies, weaknesses and flaws you might see.

External technical assessment recon

In an external black box assessment, all you can probe are the fuzzy borders of the information security zone. Any further investigations become possible only if successful penetration is achieved. If the external assessment is grey box, the auditors are provided an indentation in these borders to begin with. This amounts to a nebenpunkte, and only the following hands-on tests will tell whether it is a more critical centre of gravity that presents significant risks. When the assessment is internal, the borders of the information security zone still need to be investigated. But this time, from within. For instance, the auditors can analyse egress filtering rules and gateway redundancy protocols security. If an insider can claim the role of the corporate network gateway, that's some bad news. The information security zone itself is rarely homogeneous. It will inevitably contain different security level areas within. During the recon phase of the internal assessment the auditors must determine the borders and other important characteristics of such areas prior to commencing separate systems scans.

A typical sequence of an external black box penetration test recon is shown in *Figure 22.*

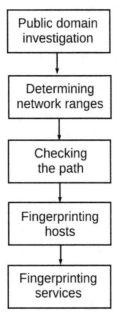

Figure 22: External penetration test recon

It should start with a public domain investigation aimed at finding all data pertaining to the test targets. Indeed, in our humble opinion any security assessment must begin from thorough public domain data gathering. The difference between the audit types can only shift the focus of such investigation, directing it more towards technical or human issues. When the assessment is technical, pay special attention to any questions from the auditee system administrators posted to various troubleshooting forums. In general, find all relevant public discussions in which they participate. These can reveal the wealth of information ranging from their skill level and specific interests to chunks of, or even the whole configuration files. Some of them may not be properly sanitised. In a similar manner, it is sometimes possible to discover fragments of code posted by the auditee developers to programming forums for a review from their colleagues. If the auditee's technical personnel participates in any online discussions and reviews of security methods and tools, these will provide valuable clues to safeguards and countermeasures deployed.

Some other interesting things you might incidentally bump into when searching the public domain for technical data pertaining to the target are:

- Their sites listed in a some googledork's (vulnerable sites that can be discovered simply by using Google) collection.

- Their sites that should be listed in a googledork's collection as they expose sensitive data or security weaknesses to general public.

- Their network addresses are blacklisted as sources of SPAM, malware, phishing, DDoS or other attacks.

- Records of previous target sites defacements.

- Phishing sites that emulate our target.

- Unauthorised web sites and other services run by the auditee's employees.

- Employees' e-mails and other contact details.

- Peculiarities of third parties that provide technical services to the auditee, security services included.

After you are done with the public domain investigation, determine the auditee network ranges (if not already provided). Investigate the paths to these networks. When doing so, use public looking glasses and related sites in addition to the standard tracerouting tools. If a massive network has only a single path to the Internet, or is connected through a single tier 3 provider, label it as a susceptibility to distributed denial-of-service attacks (DDoS). In fact, redundant connections to different ISPs should belong to different BGP AS paths to ensure proper resilience to provider shortfalls and DDoS attacks.

Continue with enumerating and fingerprinting separate systems on the analysed networks. Determine live systems by a combination of several methods rather than a simple ping. Consult the OSSTMM for a long check-list of system properties an auditor should try to determine. The major properties include OS type, version and patch level, system uptime, IPIDs and TCP sequence numbers. These must be listed in the assessment report. Scan for open ports using all portscanning methods at hand. Start from the less conspicuous ones, end with the noisy full connect scans. Use the source ports like 20 and 53 that are typically permitted by gateway access lists. Take into account the fact, that there are 0 to 65535 TCP and the same amount of UDP ports per system. Not scanning all of them might miss vulnerable services and even installed backdoors. To the contrary, trying to hit all ports of all systems on a large network can take more time than you have to perform the entire assessment. In particular, this applies to UDP scans that can be excruciatingly slow. Thus, even such simple and basic task as portscanning can require good judgement and experience to be performed in an effective way.

The last reconnaissance stage of a typical external penetration test is to fingerprint specific services you have discovered. A common recommendation is to never trust the service banners. Use a fingerprinting tool that sends probing input and analyses the responses it triggers. Use more than one such tool. If they do not produce definite results, probe the questionable services manually employing various packet crafting utilities. Match the port number, the service response, and all network protocols this response can indicate. A protocol scan can be helpful; besides, it may identify protocols unnecessarily exposed to the outside world and assist in OS fingerprinting. Always check and map port forwarding rules using TCP tracerouting, packet sequence numbers, timestamps and other means. The ports that appear to be open on a single host can be actually forwarded to many servers behind the gateway. In contrast, multiple network nodes that look separate during preliminary scans can be virtual machines hosted on a single platform. This must be verified.

So goes penetration testing reconnaissance 101. But is there more to it?

Collect all the data you have gathered together. Draw a diagram of the investigated network(s). Place all relevant information against every analysed system on the diagram. What is missing? What is unclear? Where the fog of war still lurks? Recheck and retest where necessary to eliminate its remnants. Don't be fanatical about it. If, after several serious attempts, you are still unable to identify a specific service with sufficient precision, the chances are the attackers will fail to do it too. Correct the diagram. Create a bird's-eye view of the tested networks and systems in your head. Then try to think out of the box. Did you discover any VPN-related services? There must be VPN users out there. Do the conditions of the audit agreement allow including them in the testing scope? If yes, is it possible to determine their network, and even physical addresses? Are there any other trusted sites and remote access means that can be used to circumvent perimeter defences? Did the scans indicate the presence of a dial-in gateway or VOIP services? If it is deployed and running, perhaps good old wardialing and VOIP security testing are valid options. Do you see a node that looks like a wireless access point? Is wireless security testing in scope?

Finally, after you have harvested, compiled and analysed the recon data from different angles and sides, review the network diagram, as well as separate systems and services information one more time. Recreate the bird's-eye view. Is there anything that looks strange or falls out of pattern? Revisit *Figure 21*. Sit back and contemplate the likely centres of gravity the reconnaissance phase has uncovered. Try to identify, describe and prioritise them following the strategic exploitation cycle. Draw an attack tree or plan, if that helps. When you feel confident, select the most appropriate exploitation methodologies and prepare all relevant tools. We find this approach to be far more effective than simply trying to exploit all potential flaws one by one in a time of discovery or alphabetical order.

Social engineering recon

Social engineering-related reconnaissance is as old as the very notions of conflict and warfare are. In his famous *Art of War*, Sun Tzu wrote: *'Whenever you want to attack an army, besiege a city, or kill a person, first you must know the identities of their defending generals, their associates, their visitors, their gatekeepers, and their chamberlains, so have your spies find out'*. Information about key opponent personnel can be used to win the battle before it starts by employing deception, misinformation and subterfuge. More often than not, a social engineering recon would follow the sequence shown in *Figure 23*.

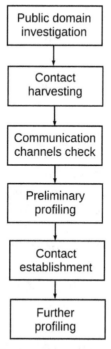

Figure 23: Social engineering recon

The OSSTMM template suggests gathering at least the following data on potential social engineering targets:

- Employee names and positions
- Employee place in hierarchy
- Employee personal pages
- Employee best contact methods
- Employee hobbies
- Employee Internet traces
- Employee opinions expressed
- Employee friends and relatives
- Employee history (including work history)

- Employee character traits
- Employee values and priorities
- Employee social habits
- Employee speech and speaking patterns
- Employee gestures and manners

What is missing from this list are the possible relationships the person has to the objectives of the social engineering assessment. Does this person have access to data, premises or systems a social engineer is interested in? How privileged is this access? How often does it take place (rarely, frequently, on a day-to-day basis)? Alternatively, does he or she know someone who has what the social engineer needs? How do they communicate? What are their relationships and level of trust? In other words, how useful is the potential target of the test for its designated aims?

A great variety of sources can be employed to harvest information about the target company employees and their connections. For instance, social networks, forums and blogs are social engineers best friends, instant messengers and chat rooms coming close second. We heard a fable about a retired old school employee of one of the most powerful intelligence agencies, who was shown a highly popular social network by his friend. After browsing it for a while, he exclaimed in total amusement: '*And they write and post it all themselves . . . voluntarily and for free?*' And now we also have Instagram . . . In the not so recent past, obtaining personal information – in particular the data that allows you to create someone's detailed psychological profile and contacts map – required significant effort. At times, it was even paid for in hard cash. It was necessary to observe people in different environments, approach them with care, and use various psychological tricks and techniques that sway them to expose personality traits, contacts, fragments of biography and what have you. For a variety of reasons, describing which would take a book on its own, modern folk extensively expose themselves to the public domain on their own accord. Even more, they do it regularly, elaborately, and sometimes in a great depth. This makes social engineering recon a much easier task.

We need to deliver a strong word of caution, however. When posting to open resources, people tend to exaggerate or plainly brag. Just as some doctor their photographs to look more attractive and appealing, they can alter any displayed personal information in a similar way. For instance, they can overstate their position or overall status in the company, or pretend to have access and rights they don't. Or claim to know someone important very well, while they have actually seen that person once and from a great distance. People often lie online because they think that only strangers who are very unlikely to discover the truth are watching. Unwittingly or deliberately, they provide plentiful mis- or disinformation. You can also find a variety of information about your potential targets posted by others. Naturally, it would be filtered through these posters opinions and views. Defamatory information is particularly interesting. It may or may not be true, but *it clearly indicates an ongoing conflict.* So, take all data you harvest online with a bit of salt. There is always a *misinformation noise* to deal with. Also, remember that the public information goldmine does not cancel more traditional approaches to social engineering that usually involve telephone and personal contact.

The channels through which a social engineer can obtain personal information about people could be rather unorthodox. For example, a search of peer-to-peer networks can reveal a wealth of information about their user. What does this person download or upload? Is it somehow security-relevant or related? At all accounts, it is likely to reveal personal interests, inclinations and hobbies. Does the auditee have shared public services or similar resources? Which files are uploaded there, and by whom? What's in there? The metadata of documents obtained from the auditee by different means can provide useful information as well. It can uncover who wrote and edited these documents, what was edited, when it was done, and who had the final word.

The very same channels employed in gathering information about the employees are frequently used to communicate with them during the social engineering attack. In general, the communication can be done via

- e-mail (mind the mail lists).
- instant messengers and chat rooms.
- blogs and social networks.
- topical message boards and professional forums.
- video and audio conferencing.
- telephone conversations and SMS.
- in person.
- through a *trusted* third party (the 'informant').
- via written letters and documents (seldom in modern social engineering practice, but has its advantages, for example it creates an impression of formality).

As *Figure 23* states, many of these channels need to be checked to ensure that they allow effective communication with the target. Is the person prolific on that social network or forum? There is little point in trying to reach someone through a resource they visit once in a few months. Does the target use the selected communication channel at home or in the office? Can it be utilised or supervised by someone else? If the identity of social engineer is going to be forged or concealed during communications over the chosen channel, can the target somehow uncover it?

Prior to commencing active contact with social engineering targets, do preliminary profiling on the basis of information obtained from the public sources and other people. In a more traditional approach, the targets can also be physically observed without attracting their or their associates' attention. The preliminary profiling should centre on the most feasible means of establishing and maintaining the contact. For instance, it should assist in selecting the most appropriate *contact avenues*. These can include, but are not limited to:

- *the need to receive assistance* (present yourself as a skilled troubleshooter or someone who can get what the target wants).

- *the need to provide assistance* as a part of assigned professional duties, or to reinforce self-esteem (pretend that you desperately need it).

- *the need to cooperate* (project oneself as someone with whom the cooperation looks fruitful).

- *common ground* (emerge as someone who strongly shares opinions, values, inclinations, interests and hobbies with the target. If possible, also claim that you are facing similar difficulties or opposition to generate sympathy).

- *part of the routine* (appear as someone expected in a due course, or in the regular course of business, and you won't raise any eyebrows. This is the common way of penetrating physical premises security.).

Note, that these contact avenues can be related to both professional and private activities of individuals. Besides, they can be combined to achieve the best result.

Do not perform the 'strategic analysis' of weaknesses and centres of gravity yet. The actual contact with the target may introduce significant correctives to the picture a social engineer has already started to create. The reality could be quite different from what people write about themselves or what is said about them by others. Besides, a personal contact, or even a telephone conversation will provide plentiful non-verbal information that cannot be obtained otherwise. Unless we are talking about a one-time contact assignment like bypassing physical premises controls, the first contact (or even the few initial contacts) is usually non-aggressive and non-committal. Otherwise, it can reveal the social engineer's intent and trigger unnecessary suspicions. It is still more of a reconnaissance than the actual attack, as *Figure 23* attests.

Only when the sufficient volume of information about the targets is obtained from the public sources, other people, and by communicating with the targets themselves, the 'strategic analysis' can be done. First, try to dispel the fog of war by eliminating clear misinformation. In this process of elimination think why and how it appeared in the first place. Can it be a sign of a weakness? *People frequently lie to conceal something a social engineer can use.* Then, if applicable, build a 'human diagram' showing connections between the auditee personnel involved. Label it. Create profiles of key persons where necessary. Who knows what? Who has relevant access privileges and where? Who can be reached through whom? Which connections are stronger or weaker? Are there any personality traits or specific facts that clearly strike the eye? What about apparent human weaknesses that can be exploited (we will address some of these in the next section of this chapter)? In a given situation, how is it possible to reduce suspicion, conceal your intentions and build the necessary level of trust?

Generate the bird's-eye view. Contemplate the likely centres of gravity the reconnaissance phase has uncovered. Try to identify, describe and prioritise them following the strategic exploitation cycle. What can be the schwerpunkt(s), nebenpunkte and systempunkts of the human network you need to assess? How about the separate key person(s)? The individual human *situation and psyche* can be effectively subjected to the strategic exploitation cycle of *Figure 21*. Hereupon, you should be able to execute social engineering tests in a more accurate and efficient way.

Internal technical assessment recon

Internal penetration tests are significantly different from their external counterparts. The main distinction that affects the reconnaissance phase operations and sequence is auditors having access to the internal network traffic flows. Thus, they should be analysed in a great detail prior to performing further scans of separate systems. In essence, this means that additional investigations shown on *Figure 24* are necessary.

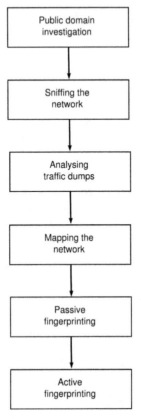

Figure 24: Internal penetration test recon

Depending on the conditions of the assessment, the auditors might have network diagrams and schemes supplied by auditee contacts prior to the tests. This will make the audit closer to a grey box variety. If this is the case, analyse these diagrams to determine the likely centres of gravity. Perhaps, you can also gather some helpful data by searching public resources in a way similar to doing it for external audits. The auditors should aspire to connect their laptops or other testing equipment as close to the potential centres of gravity as possible. In contrast, if the assessment is fully black box, it might be possible to persuade the auditees to provide different connection ports after all network mapping is done and likely centres of gravity are identified.

Start testing from sniffing the network(s) at a variety of accessible points. In a grey box test the auditors should be allowed to use special monitoring ports or VLANs for traffic interception. Sniff for 30-something minutes, as several critical infrastructure protocols use the half an hour interval to send regular updates you would want to catch. Keep in mind that the traffic dumps are going to be large – have sufficient available space at hand. Then perform an in-depth analysis of all collected data using your favourite sniffer's regular expressions and appropriate custom scripts. In the majority of cases, you can already build preliminary network maps based on the results of this dissection. Frequently, it is also possible to identify security weaknesses or even outright vulnerabilities of network protocols settings. Keep an eye open for any activities that clearly contradict the auditee security policies, like peer-to-peer and illicit sites traffic.

The collected traffic dumps can also be used to perform passive fingerprinting of separate hosts. For a non-technical reader, passive fingerprinting refers to determining the character of systems and their services without sending any data to them. It is the least intrusive fingerprinting approach that will not set off any intrusion detection alarms. Alternatively, passive fingerprinting can be done on a live traffic in the process of sniffing. After all these internal audit-specific reconnaissance procedures are performed, the assessors can continue with the traditional active scans. These are done in exactly the same manner as described when discussing systems and services enumeration and fingerprinting in external penetration tests.

Wireless penetration tests recon phase is similar to its internal black box assessment counterpart, although there are a few peculiarities that warrant granting it a distinct sequence scheme (*Figure 25*).

Figure 25: Wireless penetration test recon

Initially, do a wireless survey of the area to determine:

- how far the network signal spreads.
- other wireless networks and devices presence.
- sources of radio interference.

This shall assist in estimating the potential attackers position, discovering rogue devices and troubleshooting wireless connectivity. Do a thorough analysis of wireless traffic dumps. Even if the data traffic is encrypted, the management and control frames are not. They can provide plentiful data about the evaluated networks, like the encryption, authentication and quality of service (QoS) mechanisms in use. Are there any abnormal frames, or abnormal quantities of some specific frame type? Which network misconfigurations or weaknesses do they indicate? By looking at wireless network cards addresses in the harvested packet dumps you can usually tell their vendors. It is even possible to guess some of the running encrypted infrastructure protocols, if the specific multicast MAC (media access control) addresses they use are seen, and the intervals between packets sent to these addresses are clearly defined.

List all wireless access points. Flag those that fall out of the observed configuration and manufacturer pattern as misconfigured or rogue. How many clients are associated to all access points you have discovered? Do they roam? Are they wireless nodes or wired hosts sending traffic to the wireless network? Is the wireless network really separate from the internal wireless LAN as the policy claims? Do employees use (lower security level) guest wireless instead of the well-protected corporate wireless LAN for their comfort? Are network administrators aware of this issue? Do all wireless hosts appear to use the same encryption and authentication means? If not, what could be an explanation for the discrepancies observed? Are there any client devices that are not associated and actively scan for available wireless networks? Are they likely to belong to the auditee employees? Which networks do they search for? Do they leak any other interesting data you can ferret out? All these considerations are 802.11 standard-based. When assessing other types of wireless networks, however, a similar approach can be applied.

Just like with the external penetration and social engineering tests, finish their internal and wireless recon counterparts with assembling the grand view, rechecking unclear facts, drawing appropriate schemes and performing the strategic analysis as per *Figure 21*. Since the reconnaissance in application security testing goes in parallel with the actual vulnerability search, it will be reviewed in the upcoming section of this chapter when application assessments are addressed.

On evaluating vulnerabilities and gaps

'Invincibility is a matter of self-defence; vulnerability is simply a matter of having gaps.' – Wang Xi

Armed with the reconnaissance data and its thorough analysis, the auditors can begin determining vulnerabilities and gaps. A passive security assessment will typically stop at producing a list of potential flaws generated by an automatic scanning tool, hence the vulnerability scanning. Its social engineering counterpart will throw a pre-defined set of basic attacks at its targets and evaluate their outcome. An active security assessment, whether technical or human, will carry on with exploiting the discovered vulnerabilities until the assessment time or exploitation possibilities are exhausted. To emphasise the nature of active security assessments one more time: *'we must try to see ourselves through our enemy's eyes in order to identify our own vulnerabilities that he may attack and to anticipate what he will try to do so that we can counteract him'*. (MCDP 1 *Warfighting*).

Technical vulnerability discovery process

A typical vulnerability search in external penetration testing is summarised in *Figure 26*.

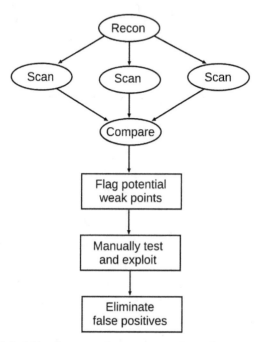

Figure 26: 101 of external pen test vulnerability discovery

The three repeated "Scan" entries on the scheme symbolise utilising more than a single vulnerability scanning tool. The more vulnerability scanners the auditors use – the better. Binding oneself to a single vulnerability scanner is a cardinal sin that goes beyond the vendor dependence. In our humble opinion, even the passive security scanning should employ several vulnerability scanners at once. These important tools are not the same, and one scanner can discover gaps the others do not detect. Some vulnerability scanners are highly specialised to address certain vulnerability classes and types. For instance, there are web application and database scanning tools that do more profound work on uncovering such vulnerabilities than their general purpose siblings. Specialised scanners must be used where applicable. In the case of web applications security scanning, this probably amounts to more than 90% of all modern external penetration tests.

Compare the scan results of all vulnerability discovery tools you have employed. Where do they match? Where do they differ? How large are these differences? What can explain them? Mark all potential weaknesses and gaps. The vulnerabilities shown by several security scanners at once make the most obvious candidates. If something is unclear, or you suspect that at some point scanning was interrupted by connectivity or other problems, rescan. Then you can subject the detected issues to the strategic analysis cycle, just as you did during the reconnaissance phase. Indeed, vulnerability scanning can be viewed as a 'battlefield recon', or recon-in-depth. After all of the priorities are sorted, begin manual exploitation of the uncovered flaws in a logically defined order of importance. This will eliminate false positives and hopefully provide a foothold for further exploitation. Such is the bird's-eye view of the vulnerability discovery process.

Figure 27 presents a more in-depth perspective of the same.

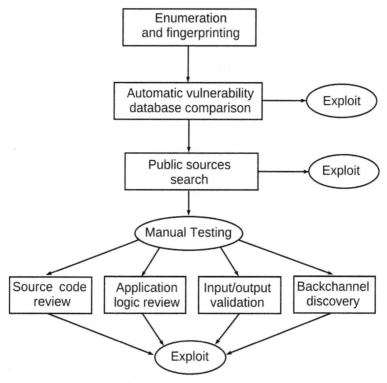

Figure 27: Vulnerability discovery explained

The first stage of exploitation is trying to break in at the conclusion of vulnerability scanning. There are vulnerability scanning tools that also perform automated exploitation. In our practice, they were efficient at doing so only when used in internal security audits. This is a classical consequence of the Maginot line mentality: behind the hardened network perimeter lies a soft, vulnerable underbelly. Defence-in-depth is clearly out of question. Overall, if a system can be broken into by vulnerability scanning results alone or even by automated tool exploitation, its security level is abhorrent. If this happens during an external test, it is plain disastrous. Stop the assessment, call the auditee contacts, explain the situation and wait until the flaw is fixed to continue.

The second stage of exploitation is trying to break in after investigating all available sources relevant to the suspected vulnerability. These often provide important clues to how the issue can be successfully exploited. You can look at other similar vulnerabilities to gain the needed insight. At times, a public exploit is available for the same issue, but is applicable to a different service version or platform on which it is running. The auditors can then modify this exploit to accommodate for the differences. Nowadays, easy to use utilities designed to do just that are freely available online – just check out the capabilities of the most recent Metasploit framework release. Thus, one does not have to be a dedicated programmer to accomplish this task. Generally, if a system can be broken into at this stage, it is vulnerable to medium skill level opponents who have sufficient determination to do some research.

The third stage of exploitation is trying to gain access using detailed manual testing. More often than not it involves breaking the software application involved, and may be even developing new exploit code from scratch. Hence, *Figure 27* provides an application testing example as a part of this phase. However, intelligent password guessing based on custom lists generated for the specific situation on the basis of recon data would also amount to less sophisticated manual testing. The same applies to hand-crafting malicious packets in customised network protocols security tests. If a system or network can be broken into at this stage, it is vulnerable to skilled and determined assailants only and threats not falling under the categories of 'advanced' and 'persistent' can be safely discarded.

On application security testing methods

The four modules of hands-on application security assessment shown on the *Figure 27* are by no means all-inclusive, but they are commonly applied. A general and rather basic check-list of application security tests is provided by the OSSTMM. The OWASP Testing Guide is a great free resource on performing in-depth web applications security tests. Numerous approaches and techniques it describes are evidently workable beyond web application audits only. Some of the authentication mechanisms verification, buffer overflow and denial of service tests provide good examples of these. We do not feel the need to repeat the recommendations of OSSTMM, OWASP and other relevant guides in this book. They are widely available and are regularly updated. With the next update some of the information these sources supply will inevitably become obsolete. Nevertheless, a few words about the general application testing methodologies listed on *Figure 27* should be said.

Source code reviews are probably the most traditional way of assessing application security. There are multiple automated utilities and tools designed to assist in them. At the end of the day, however, it all comes to the skills and 'try to break everything we can break' mindset of the programmers performing the review. The problem, as stated earlier in the book, is that often the source code of the application is proprietary and not available for analysis. At the same time, employing reverse engineering techniques to reveal the application structure and weak points is likely to be illegal. This, of course, won't stop malicious hackers to use them in vulnerability discovery. To counter it, source code security reviews by proprietary software vendors should be supplemented with reverse engineering tests. The latter can be done by an authorised specialist third party.

Application logic analysis is instrumental in any relevant security assessments. It has a very strong element of recon. First, the application must be understood. Study all available documentation, such as manuals, requirements, functional specifications and use (or breach!) cases. Learn the application workflows, business and operations logic, user roles, privileges and access rights, acceptable and unacceptable use scenarios. Contemplate the application dependencies, any files it creates, modifies or deletes, communication protocols it employs (if networked), the environment in which it operates. When all these matters become crystal clear, determine and analyse the centres of gravity and the likely security threats. Again, the strategic exploitation cycle (*Figure 21*) can come handy. Finally, design and execute appropriate logical tests.

Application input/output validation is probably the most common contemporary method utilised in black and grey box assessments. Its logic is very simple. Supply a variety of expected and unexpected input and analyse the output using application and system logs, debuggers, network sniffers, or other suitable means. The application might crash or otherwise misbehave, indicating a potentially exploitable flaw. In essence, this is the 'if then else' or 'fiddle until it smashes' approach incarnate. As such, it could discover the target systempunkts. If a thousand crashes results from a single flaw, it is a schwerpunkt, systempunkt or both. When properly automated, this methodology is referred to as 'fuzzing'. Due to the aforementioned facts, fuzzing production systems is not a brilliant idea. This type of application security evaluation is better done against a testing setup.

Fuzzing comes in two main varieties. *Mutation fuzzing* is the dumber 'everything but the kitchen sink' type. Flip the bits, add or subtract them, and throw the resulting data at the application *attack surface*. *Generation fuzzing* is far more creative. Learn about the application logic, protocol and file formats it accepts, and so on. In a nutshell, do a decent recon. Then select, modify or create a fuzzer tool that will take this vital information into account when producing the input for the tests. As a result, their performance and effectiveness will be optimised. A promising avenue is *evolutionary fuzzing* that combines both approaches in a sequence. To be considered truly evolutionary, a fuzzer should start as a mutation tool and employ artificial intelligence to teach itself generation methodologies. Nevertheless, no matter how sophisticated the fuzzing technique could be, the supreme art is not in producing the needed inputg – it is in detecting the errors caused by this input and determining which vulnerabilities such faults signify and how to exploit them by crash output (such as core dump files) and/or debugger output analysis.

It is interesting to note that the logic and elements of the fuzzing approach can be applied to different areas of information security outside hands-on software testing. When discussing security assessments of processes using the access management example, we have already used a fuzzing-like methodology to analyse this sample process. There are many things you can fuzz. It can even apply to security policies, standards, guidelines and other relevant documentation. Envision how applicable their statements, rules and recommendations could be in a variety of changing conditions. Which alterations of the environment, whether business, operational, technical or human, will make them irrelevant or flawed? Are these situations likely? If yes, is it possible to implement sufficient resilience to them in the existing security documentation and processes? If no, but the possibility still exists and can be catastrophic, is it accounted for in business continuity and disaster recovery plans?

By subjecting people to batteries of different tests and analysing their output, a psychologist effectively fuzzes human consciousness and mind. This allows the auditor to establish personality problems and traits, predict and even modify human reactions and behaviour. But is it not what a social engineer wants, alas with a more sinister end goal? So, generation fuzzing or even, to a certain extent, mild evolutionary fuzzing can be utilised to reach social engineering aims. Indeed, the tests used by professional psychologists provide a great example of the generation fuzzing input. Think what could be their social engineering equivalents. Borrow the psychologists' tricks to make people talk and gain their trust. Carefully probe the auditee employees and their relationships, fiddling until the exploitable human weaknesses become evident.

The last application security methodology of *Figure 27* is checking for backchannels or backdoors left by its developers. In companies that actively do in-house software development, we typically check whether such cases are defined as information security incidents and are appropriately covered in the incident response plan. As with other incident types that involve human wrongdoings, it is highly advisable to split these into 'erroneous' (a backchannel has been forgotten by mistake) and 'deliberate' categories. Discovering backchannels and backdoors in applications can be done by various means, the simplest being looking for and analysing plaintext strings within the application binaries. Or it can also be done by applying various login methods to the application attack surface. Common sense dictates that if a backdoor is present, it will be eventually discovered and abused by someone else than the developers who did not remove it. It also raises doubts about the developer's true intent. Could it be deliberate rather than simply forgetting about a temporary feature created for testing purposes? Hence, investigate it properly to exclude any such possibility. Note, that the backchannels could be present in any close source software, from web applications to device drivers. Thus, searching for them is relevant for literally any system security checks. We can recall a few examples of entire operating systems having in-built administrative backdoor accounts left by their creators for whatever the reasons could be.

As web application security testing is of paramount importance in modern technical security assessments, we would like to end this section with a brief checklist of the applicable approaches split into major categories of:

Authentication assessment

- Brute-force password guessing and grinding access points in the application.
- Bypass authentication system with spoofed tokens, credentials and replay attacks.
- Determine and bypass the application logic to protect authenticated sessions.
- Identification of limitations of access control within the application.

Session management evaluation

- Determine session management procedures and strategies.
- Guess the session ID sequence and format.
- Determine if the session ID is maintained with the IP address information.
- Gather sensitive information via man-in-the-middle attacks.
- Inject excess/bogus information with session-hijacking techniques.
- Replay gathered information back to gain spoofed access.

Input and output validation

- Find the limitations of the defined variables and protocols.
- Use long character strings to find stack and heap overflow conditions.
- Append and join commands in the input strings of the applications.
- Test for SQL injection flaws of database-interacting web applications.
- Examine XSS and CSRF conditions and their potential impact.
- Evaluate unauthorised directory/file access possibilities with path/directory.
- Use URL-encoded strings to bypass input validation mechanisms.

- Establish variables and cookies manipulation risks.
- Manipulate and fuzz different protocol variables.
- Test error handling mechanisms.
- Retrieve data stored in cookies, temporary files and other application objects.
- Harvest valuable information from the application cache.

Information leakage

- Analyse information in hidden field variables, temp files, comments and web pages.
- Examine the information contained in other application parts.

Both the auditee and the auditors should consult this list to ensure that nothing in their (web) application tests is amiss, unless it has been explicitly decided not to be used for sound reasons (such as fuzzing against production environments).Assessing network protocols security flaws

Similarly to the recon phase, vulnerability discovery and exploitation in internal penetration testing includes an additional preliminary stage centred on network protocols security. Its sequence is reflected in *Figure 28.*

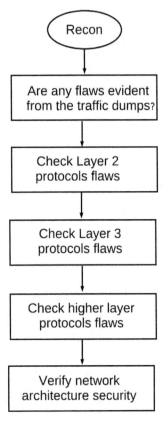

Figure 28: Protocols vulnerability testing

During reconnaissance, you collected plentiful samples of network traffic. Analyse them searching for the obvious flaws like important infrastructure or management protocols lacking strong authentication (or having any authentication at all). Also look for any login credentials sent in cleartext, SNMP (Simple Network Management Protocol) RW (read-write) communities included. Then perform active checks which would involve crafting custom packets to exploit the detected security weaknesses. The

rtrtrtrt

end results of effective network protocols exploitation could be:

- diverting traffic to the attacker's host for interception and modification.
- successful man-in-the-middle and session hijacking attacks.
- bypassing the existing network segmentation boundaries and separation of data streams.
- gaining access to network appliances and other systems via insecure management protocols.
- system-specific or network-wide denial of service.

Thus, this type of security evaluation is likely to cause severe availability problems for separate systems or even the whole network. At the same time, it is not realistic to mirror the entire internal network for security testing purposes. So, thorough network protocols security verification should be done during the off-hours, such as on weekends.

To keep the protocols testing structured and organised, *Figure 28* suggests performing it in a bottom-up fashion. Start with the OSI model Layer 2, or data link protocols security. Assess whether the spanning tree can be abused, VLAN boundaries can be circumvented, 802.1x-based authentication can be cracked and so on. Then, test security of the OSI Layer 3. In practice, this usually means assessing vulnerabilities of routing and gateway redundancy protocols often lacking appropriate authentication. In *Hacking Exposed: Cisco Networks*, we covered the relevant Layer 2 and 3 testing methods in detail. Despite the time passed since, they still hold relevant for the modern networks and there is no point to address them here in detail. Finally, check security of higher layer protocols, centring on the management ones. Using SNMP versions below 3 is still common, and so is employing insecure Telnet, FTP and HTTP for management logins and sensitive data transfers. Sensitive e-mails are often sent unencrypted and can be captured. At times it is even possible to capture a network appliance or VOIP phone configuration file sent, however scanning the network for TFTP servers and then trying to grab configuration files by their default names proves to be more fruitful.. These are typical security weaknesses that can be easily exploited by insiders.

A few words should be said about the 'traditional' network attacks like switch CAM (content addressable memory) table flooding and ARP (address resolution protocol) spoofing. By their very nature all IP networks are susceptible to these old attacks. A similar issue exists with higher layer protocols like DHCP and DNS. ARP and DNS spoofing against standalone systems can be used to assist in other man-in-the-middle attacks resilience testing. For example, it comes handy in SSL/TLS vulnerability evaluation. At the same time, launching CAM flooding or DHCP spoofing attacks will severely disrupt connectivity to prove quite the obvious. Thus, such tests are not compulsory. They should be applied in agreement with the auditee only if the real need exists. By the "real need" we mean assessing the deployed countermeasures that thwart such attacks.

The last stage of the network protocols security assessment is gathering all tests results together and generating the overall network security state view. The latter should reflect all uncovered vulnerabilities and possible relationships between them. Are they incidental misconfigurations that can be easily corrected? Or could it be that the network architecture itself is fundamentally flawed and all of the security problems you are seeing are only the tip of the iceberg? On several occasions we had to recommend the auditee to rebuild large network segments or undergo significant equipment upgrades. When these important matters are thoroughly evaluated and addressed, the auditors can continue with systems and services exploitation in a manner identical with the external penetration tests.

Wireless vulnerability assessments are expectedly akin to their internal audit counterparts. Even the vulnerability subsets of both can intersect. Reasonably common wireless-specific security gaps the auditors should look for include:

- flaws of authentication mechanisms and protocols.
- weaknesses of network discovery and association mechanisms (in wireless client security testing).
- rogue or obsolete devices that provide excellent wireless entry points.
- lack of secure separation between wireless and wired networks.
- device drivers vulnerable to buffer overflow attacks (rare, but possible).
- high susceptibility to Layer 2 denial-of-service attacks.

When talking about the latter, it makes no sense to evaluate denial of service conditions no one can protect against. A radio signal can be jammed, and that's that. In contrast, all DoS threats that have valid countermeasures (such as 802.11w) must be assessed. By the way, when performing wireless security testing and actively poking at the network, observe whether a wireless IPS will manifest itself. If the active defence is on, it might try to kick the auditors off. Analyse all packets the IPS sends. What is possible to tell about it? Can it be tricked? Or even have known vulnerabilities?

A brief on human vulnerabilities

What about social engineering? Social engineering vulnerability checks are highly situational and flexible. Typically, they require plenty of improvisation and are hard to systematise and methodise. Nevertheless, it is feasible to list major "human vulnerabilities" that can be exploited to gain access to data, systems, networks and premises. An attempt to summarise them is presented in *Table 4*.

Table 4: Common human security flaws

Human weakness	Notes
Lack of security awareness	It can be revealed by rather simple tests. Spoofed "click on this link", "open the attachment", or "please change your password" e-mails are textbook examples. Sometimes, people just don't think about such things and do it mechanically, especially if it fits into their routine.
Naivete	Tread carefully, especially if dealing with other security specialists. It could easily be a disguise. All truly intelligent people have learned the old trick of playing the fool. However, there are people out there who still think that "such a nice guy could not be a scammer", no matter the blatant facts and tell-tale signs.
Dissatisfaction and disaffection	Disaffected employees are obvious targets. At times, they can look to pass sensitive data to outsiders themselves. Boredom and lack of interest in the surroundings are signs of disaffection. They diminish vigilance and suspicion. Dissatisfaction often results from rigid command, misplacement, work and peer pressure.
Desperation	Desperate people can often provide great boons for little help or simple human compassion.

Conflicts	Both sides of a conflict tend to leak valuable information when slagging off their foe. By taking sides or expressing sympathy for one side's cause you can gain immediate trust since 'an enemy of my enemy is my friend'.
Overblown ego	Napoleonic ambitions, galaxy-sized ego and overblown self-esteem have been exploited with ease since ancient times. Flattery is the key. Furthermore, overconfidence decreases vigilance: after all "how could a genius like me fall for a silly trick?"
Obsessions	Obsessions can be shared to build rapport and gain trust. Even a little satisfaction of someone's personal (or work-related) obsession can bring hefty rewards. Obsessions often contribute to tunnel vision and wishful thinking, which decrease vigilance and make targets less sceptical about relevant propositions.
Fears	Fear of being dismissed, held responsible or being socially denigrated opens many gates. A typical "we have found a virus on your system, please install our virus removal tool" scareware exploits fears of being hacked. A social engineer can play disaffected customer, partner, or even the (sizeable) employer's management representative to abuse fears of being held responsible.

Notice that many of the weaknesses listed in the *Table 4* are closely related to contact avenues outlined in the recon section. Exploiting them is these contact avenues carried forward and amplified. For instance, the need to receive assistance, the need to cooperate and common ground can be efficiently combined to exploit both human conflicts and obsessions. The need to provide assistance and common ground go well towards the overblown ego. Replace common ground by the part of the routine and the approach becomes suitable for playing the work responsibility fears.

Furthermore, a great deal of social engineering vulnerabilities are related to processes and procedures, rather than actual human weaknesses. A classic example is the lack of proper identity verification within the access management process. Insufficient employee background checks and vetting procedures generate multiple gaps social engineers can exploit, and so do bad employee termination practices. Lack of communication between company departments, branches or teams, as well as with partners, customers and suppliers can allow effective impostor attacks. Skilled social engineers will weave together a variety of human and process weaknesses and gaps to develop the most fruitful approach to accomplishing their tasks. When the appropriate use of relevant technologies (client-side attacks, spear phishing, keyloggers, interception and surveillance tools, etc.) is added to the concoction, they can become virtually unstoppable.

We shall provide a simple example of a successful 'mixed' social engineering attack executed against one of our customers in the course of a relatively recent security audit. A well-crafted fake web page was set up right before Christmas claiming to be set up by the customer's HR department. The page offered to answer a variety of typical questions related to work conditions and satisfaction in exchange for entering a draw for a few latest iPads as the management's Christmas courtesy. After clicking through a sufficiently long list of questions to both look realistic and hook the target's attention, the next page opened. It simply asked the user to input the employee account credentials to be entered into the draw – how else would HR find out who won? Not to mention, it all looked neat company style (SET (Social Engineering Toolkit) framework allows anyone to clone any website in seconds), and was, of course, protected via HTTPS to enhance users' confidence. A mass mail-shot was fired, directed at the company employees (HR department excluded!) with a Christmas card, link to the page, and invitation to help HR in exchange for participating in the draw. The employee mail addresses were previously collected via a flaw in the mail server, but you can just as well get them all from Linkedin and other social networks. All of this amounts to spear phishing. After the sixth manager of the company entered his valid login credentials the test was called off by the customer. It could have been carried to its final conclusion, of course, including delivering (heavily backdoored) iPads to the 'winners'! That's what the corporate spies with some spare resources at hand would have done.

The tactical exploitation cycle

For now, we assume that by applying technical- or human-centric approaches discussed, the auditors have managed to uncover and exploit a few important vulnerabilities. At this point, many information security assessments would stop. The halt could be justified by specific limits imposed on the audit scope by its contract conditions. Otherwise, it amounts to breaching the defence line without following up the advantage. From the military strategy viewpoint it is a major, egregious mistake. Ideally, the exploitation must continue, penetrating the remaining defences deeper and deeper until all valid opportunities are exhausted. It should follow a cyclic pattern as shown in *Figure 29*.

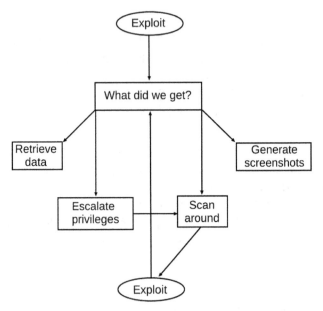

Figure 29: The tactical exploitation cycle

After the initial breach is achieved, look around and analyse its consequences. Where did we get? What did we get? What information can we now retrieve? Is it sensitive? Does it provide any clear opportunities for further attacks? If the information samples obtained are interesting, retrieve them. They should be submitted to the auditee together with the final assessment report, all confidentiality preserved. If the audit is technical, generate illustrative screenshots of the accessed data and broken systems interfaces. Proving the actual significance of all uncovered vulnerabilities to the auditee (management) is just as important as getting in.

Is there a need to escalate privileges? Study the accessed system well. Which other security flaws can be identified? Attempt the escalation. Scan all surrounding systems and sniff the network. If it is a social engineering attack, think what else can be gained from the person who fell prey to it, unless the alarms were triggered and it is time to retreat. Can this person's trust and access rights (if obtained) be used to social engineer other interlinked employees? Execute the strategic analysis (*Figure 21*) against the newly acquired targets, data and opportunities, if you feel the need. Or, at least, spin the full OODA loop with proper 'OO' to begin with. Then perform further tests. Exploit all potential vulnerabilities and gaps. Repeat the *Figure 29* cycle.

Real-life adversaries are unlikely to halt when they have achieved the primary foothold unless they are scared away. They will expand it by pushing forward, abusing connectivity and trust the exploited systems or people possess. The risks presented by a vulnerability are not limited to the immediate exposure, corruption or loss of sensitive data it allows. They also include all the opportunities that the exploited flaw opens up. Is it a barren cul-de-sac, or does it lead directly to the treasure chests? Can it cause any additional deterioration of the auditee defences? What if, by not exploiting it any further, the auditors have missed a critical systempunkt, as they did not initiate a cascade of events that can follow the initial breach? Understanding these matters is absolutely essential in estimating genuine security risks. Without evaluating them, the risk assessment will be incomplete.

The operational art of vulnerability assessment

'General Arroyo told him that the Federal army, whose officers had studied in the French Military Academy, were waiting to engage them in formal combat, where they knew all the rules and the guerillas didn't. "They

are like virgins," said the young Mexican general, hard and dark as a glazed pot. "They want to follow the rules. I want to make them."' – Carlos Fuentes, *The Old Gringo*

We began this chapter by observing the strategic matters. Then the discussion inevitably slipped into the more tactical realm down to technical testing checklists and overall methodologies. It is time to take a step back and stand in between. This allows to contemplate on subjects that frequently go amiss, becoming the source of common errors that plague numerous information security assessments. One such important subject is whether the auditors should seek to approach their targets laterally, frontally, or both. Sometimes, they are given a precise list of targets that must be tested. On other occasions, however, the scope of a black box assessment is not clearly defined. The aim is to clarify the borders of the auditee's *information security zone* and get in by any possible means.

Front, flank, simple, complex

Recall the external reconnaissance section discourse on discovering lateral exploitation paths like remote trusted users and sites, or out-of-band channels of access. If these are present, were should they be on the assessment's priority list? Logically, the answer has to depend on the ease with which such lateral elements can be discovered. If they are easy to find, they should be tested together with the obvious network perimeter hosts. If it takes quite an effort to detect them, their assessment can be postponed. Nevertheless, this approach does not take into account indiscriminate attacks. For instance, a trusted remote network can be infected with a worm which will then spread to the target net. Or, a wardriver can find insecure wireless network in a telecommuter's home and use it as a foothold to penetrate the corporate LAN. At the end of the day, a laptop providing VPN connectivity to internal corporate networks can be stolen or lost, and VPN access may not be immediately blocked, leaving a window of opportunity for potential attackers. It can also be given to a 'trusted' third party for repairs in an emergency situation without informing the company IT helpdesk. This may be especially applicable to BYOD computers. These scenarios are far from being unrealistic.

The solution we propose is reflected in *Figure 30.*

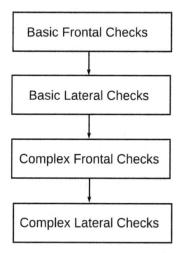

Figure 30: Frontal versus lateral tests

First, assess the most obvious *attack surface* using the basic evaluation means. By "basic evaluation means" we imply:

- automated security scanning.
- non-specific dictionary attacks.
- spidering for sensitive data leaks.

- evaluating guest and anonymous logins.
- running simple social engineering checks.

There are security auditors who take great pride in their skills at discovering new vulnerabilities and writing zero-day exploits. This pride is entirely justified. At the same time, such experts can ignore checks for low-hanging fruit that look boring and uncreative. Indeed, they are. However, they also address the greatest risks the auditee company or organisation is facing. As Bruce Schneier pointed out, '*insecurity is the norm*'. *Figure 27* and the discussion it triggers attest that more sophisticated tests should stay lower in the priority list. The auditors should aspire to reach their objectives employing the simplest well-known methods before their advanced counterparts are called in. Take no shame in it. Even Sun Tzu proclaimed that '*in ancient times those known as good warriors prevailed when it was easy to prevail*'.

Next, apply similar basic checks to the potential lateral entry points, if present. This addresses the issue of indiscriminate or incidental attacks these points can be exposed to. Also, the attackers who failed to get across the front line of defence the easy way face a simple dilemma:

1. Find and exploit a new or unorthodox vulnerability of the frontal surface (easy recon, difficult attack); or
2. outflank it (harder recon, easy attack).

Guess which one many of them are going to select? Indeed, if the attackers are not skilled in novel vulnerabilities discovery and exploitation, they are left with a rather simple choice. Cao Cao, a dedicated disciple of Sun Tzu, supplied the following sound advice:

- *'Find out the subtle points over which it is easy to prevail, attack what can be overcome, do not attack what cannot be overcome.'*

- *'Appear where there is an opening and strike at a gap; avoid where they are guarding, hit where they are not expecting it.'*

This suggestion is clearly applicable to the aforementioned situation.

When you have finally arrived at the complex and demanding assessment methodologies, return to the frontal defences first. This corresponds to point 1 above: "easy recon, difficult attack". Even if this does not succeed, the only option left is "hard recon and hard attack", which is the final stage shown in *Figure 30*. In our experience, in the majority of cases successful penetration happens before it is reached.

The strategies of creating gaps

MCDP 1 *Warfighting* declares that *'whenever possible, we exploit existing gaps. Failing that, we create gaps'*. In the context of technical information security assessments, this astute statement can apply to two things:

1. Discovering and exploiting novel vulnerabilities (that evil zero-day).
2. Combining several non-critical vulnerabilities to achieve a much greater result (see the previous systempunkt descriptions).

In social engineering, creating gaps might correspond to:

1. bringing otherwise stable, reliable and apparently (information security-wise) flawless people out of balance.
2. disrupting the intended flow of a relevant security process, so that its friction exceeds the safety limits.

Alas, the systempunkt principle application, similar to the technical gap creation point 2 above can also apply.

'Gaps can be created through depth, and gaps can be created through breadth'. Creating gaps through depth means dedicated effort and research applied to a highly specific point. This is clearly at work when novel vulnerabilities are discovered and corresponding exploits are written. Hard manual testing, similar to the one shown in *Figure 27*, is absolutely required. In different situations it may also involve reverse engineering, applied cryptanalysis and other advanced attack means. For the auditors who do not possess such knowledge and skills, this avenue is completely closed. Automatic vulnerability scanning cannot bring them any further than *Figure 30*'s second stage. Hence, the natural limitations of this method. Notice that the similar depth-centric approach can be utilised in social engineering. If enough directed effort and wit are expended, anyone can be placed in a staged tricky Catch 22 situation in which people typically become vulnerable. If the human weaknesses listed in *Table 4* are not manifested, some of them can be successfully cultivated given sufficient time.

Creating gaps through breadth frequently means using the *combined arms* approach. We have already touched it when addressing social engineering vulnerability evaluation. Mix technical and social engineering means. Fiddle with applications, services, systems, network protocols, operations, processes and people simultaneously and from various angles. Recall that the minor weaknesses that can create a greater flaw can belong to different applications, systems, networks, people, processes, classes, types or entire levels of abstraction. The sample systempunkt scenario we have employed when outlining this vital concept consisted of the following elements:

- flaws of a network switch configuration (technical, network appliance);

- permitting features of the gateway or firewall (technical, network appliance);

- a service that uses weak authentication mechanism (technical, service);

- weak login credentials (human, policy or guideline).

Thus, it can serve as a reasonable illustration of utilising *combined arms*. Basic social engineering could have been used to assist in guessing the login credentials or obtaining the network scheme from the system administrator. Indeed, a single over-the-shoulder glance at the scheme would have sufficed.

A powerful mix-and-match technique that can apply to breadth, but also depth-centric ways of creating security gaps is merging what is considered as orthodox and unorthodox. As Sun Tzu wrote, '*making the armies able to take on opponents without being defeated is a matter of unorthodox and orthodox methods*'. In truth, this is more of a psychological exercise for the auditors to enable strategic vision and train lateral ways of thinking. Wardialing was orthodox in the past and is unorthodox now. About a decade ago, wireless hacking was viewed as unorthodox. For a social engineer, using an RFID hack to gain unauthorised premises entry is unorthodox. For now, at least. In contrast, to a purely technical hacker common social engineering methods can be non-trivial. *'Various people have different explanations of what is orthodox and what is unorthodox. Orthodoxy and unorthodoxy are not fixed, but are like a cycle.'* (Ho Yanxi)

As an illustration, consider that a plain frontal attack against a firewall, or a social engineering attempt aimed at the company CISO can bear fruits. For the proponents of a 'smart' lateral approach this is blasphemy. Yet, we have discovered industry standard firewall security flaws in the past, and in one of the internal pen tests the first account to fall was that of a compliance officer who also played the role of the CISO of the auditee. *'Striking an open gap does not only mean where the opponent has no defence.'* (Chen Hao) Besides, the scope of penetration tests often includes (and should do so!) the assessment of various countermeasures and safeguards. If these are not evaluated in sufficient depth, they can become the sources of false sense of security, or even the bearers of fatal gaps. At the same time, information security audits are the perfect time to put one's monitoring, intrusion detection, logging and alarm systems and the corresponding processes on test. The real assailants would not debrief on their techniques, go with your team through the relevant logs, or tell when exactly the attack begins.

Review the following scenario we call a 'clock trick':

1. All systems clocks on the network are synchronised with a central time server. This is a good practice.
2. This server gets its time from reliable sources on the Internet. This is also highly recommended.
3. The NTP (network time protocol), however, is not authenticated. This would be classified as a minor security flaw.

4. The access lists do not block access to the NTP service from unauthorised sources. This is a minor security weakness.

A wily attacker floods the time service with incorrect updates. The 'echo' of these updates spreads across the entire network, altering all systems time. The hacker checks that the trick is successful by verifying systems uptime with a basic scan. What could be the outcome?

1. As the time of systems is now altered, security updates can fail. The licenses of antivirus or other protective software may now be officially expired. It stops working properly.

2. The timestamps of logs are now incorrect, making the logs useless, especially in legal terms. Who would take such *laterally tampered* logs as a proof?

The first ramification means that malware can now be pushed through, or potentially vulnerable services remain unpatched. The second allows the assailants to use more intrusive, aggressive and effective attack means (like application fuzzing or login credentials brute-forcing) without fear of persecution. This can enable discovery or even creation of new gaps through depth. All of it is achieved via two minor security flaws using rather simple methods. On its own, it is a typical nebenpunkte that softens the opponents defences. If the overall attack succeeds, and the 'clock trick' has clearly contributed to this success, it becomes a part of a systempunkt. Is it really orthodox or unorthodox? This depends on the point of view. By the way, externally exposed unauthenticated NTP service can be easily running on the otherwise secure firewall!

To summarise this vital discourse on a strategic note:

- *'Creating gaps through depth is the schwerpunkt principle at work'.*
- *'Creating gaps through breadth is the systempunkt principle at work'.*
- *'Merging both principles together is the pinnacle of exploitation science and art'.*

In real life situations it is also possible to create gaps *through time*. Wait and observe for long enough, and due to inevitable *fluctuations of friction* a security gap can surface. The passive 'good things come to those who wait' approach, however, is not highly feasible for information security audits which have timetables, schedules and deadlines. Nevertheless, it can still be used by dedicated, focused assailants.

We would like to end this key chapter with a lengthy excerpt from MCDP 1 *Warfighting*. It provides a perfect extraneous independent summary to many of the issues we have just discussed. Indeed, there is little in it for the 'substitution exercise', and nothing for us to add.

- *'When identification of enemy critical vulnerabilities is particularly difficult, the commander may have no choice but to exploit any and all vulnerabilities until action uncovers a decisive opportunity. By exploiting opportunities, we create in increasing numbers more opportunities for exploitation'.*

Furthermore,

- *'We should try to understand the enemy system in terms of a relatively few centers of gravity or critical vulnerabilities because this allows us to focus our own efforts. The more we can narrow it down, the more easily we can focus. However, we should recognize that most enemy systems will not have a single center of gravity on which everything else depends, or if they do, that center of gravity will be well protected. It will often be necessary to attack several lesser centers of gravity or critical vulnerabilities simultaneously or in sequence to have the desired effect. A critical vulnerability is a pathway to attacking a center of gravity. Both have the same underlying purpose: to target our actions in such a way as to have the greatest effect on the enemy'.*

CHAPTER 6: SYNTHETIC EVALUATION OF RISKS

*'What is required of an officer is a certain power of discrimination, which only knowledge of men and things and good judgement can give. **The law of probability must be his guide.**'* – Carl von Clausewitz

Discovering and evaluating vulnerabilities and gaps without the thorough analysis of risks they introduce is as good as doing recon without using its results. In fact, for the risk analysis phase all previous security audit stages are nothing more than the necessary reconnaissance. One of the fundamental principles of *chapter 1* states that *'information security assessment always operates with probabilities'*. Gauging these probabilities is a fine science and art that has to be fully mastered by at least a single member of the auditing team. It is absolutely essential for success of both the assessment and its follow-up acts. For the latter, the evaluation of risks represents the 'OO' in its overall OODA loop.

Numerous information security-specific risk assessment methodologies, standards and frameworks exist. The most commonly referenced examples are probably:

- ISO27005 and ISO31000.
- NIST Special Publication 800-30 *Risk Management Guide for Information Technology Systems*.
- OCTAVE (Operationally Critical Threat, Asset, and Vulnerability Evaluation) from SEI (Software Engineering Institute) and CERT (Computer Emergency Response Team).
- FRAP (Facilitated Risk Assessment Process) by Peltier et al.

SRMD (Security Risk Management Discipline) from Microsoft. Knowing these and other relevant published standards, methodologies and guidelines can come in handy when performing risk evaluation phase of an information security assessment. However, trying to absorb all available sources on methods and techniques of weighting and prioritising information security risks could easily lead to confusion. Reviewing many such publications creates a strong impression that anyone who has dedicated enough time to the subject eventually came up with their own specific risk assessment methodology to suit their needs, which was consequently given a fancy abbreviation name. Below we do exactly the same, alas with no fancy abbreviation attached.

In adherence with the general approach professed in this book, we divide the evaluation of risks into three levels: strategic, operational and tactical. The tactical plane refers to analysing risks introduced by separate vulnerabilities and gaps. The strategic level refers to assessing the overall auditee risk posture, which is a *non-linear sum* of its separate components. The operational level connects the other two by dissecting possible links between different security risks and risk types, addressing the whole affected processes, and transcending the boundaries between what is perceived as technical, human, process and policy flaws. When all three levels work in harmony and concert, a realistic picture of various risks faced by the auditee company or organisation can be established. Hence, what we call the synthetic evaluation of information security risks and its core element – the synthetic risk analysis.

On applicable epistemology of risk

'Take calculated risks. That is quite different from being rash.' – Gen. George S. Patton

In all its complexity, the assessment of risks is but a part of a much larger and all-encompassing risk management process. The split of this process between the security audit and its after-effects is nothing more than the division between *risk evaluation* and *risk control* (*Figure 31*).

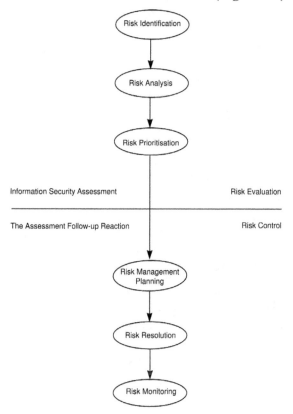

Figure 31: Risk management process and information security assessments

In this chapter, we are mainly concerned with the upper risk evaluation half of the scheme. Which practical approaches to it could be the most feasible for information security auditors? Are there any complications and traps they should be aware of?

First of all, there is a need to select a suitable definition of what is actually assessed. There are numerous ways of defining information security risk. Usually they come down to explaining some variety of the *risk severity = (probability of the event) x (impact of the event)* formula. A definition of risk as provided by the NIST Special Publication 800-30 is:

- *'Risk is a function of the likelihood of a given threat-source's exercising a particular potential vulnerability, and the resulting impact of that adverse event on the organization'.*

Thus, a risk is estimated by how likely a security incident is to occur and how severe its aftermath would be. Interestingly, the ISO27000:2012 definition of risk (which is to be taken as one for ISO27001:2013 in accordance to its section 3 Terms and definitions) is very different, being effectively based upon the concept of friction widely discussed in this book. Namely, ISO27000 states that risk is the "effect of uncertainty on objectives", hence the risk might also have positive effects! While it's good to put such an emphasis on friction, we are going to be conservative and utilise the NIST definition or risk (similar to definition in the old ISO27001:2005) as highly applicable for this discussion's purpose.

Risk, uncertainty and ugly Black Swans

A sensitive issue is distinguishing between risk and uncertainty proper, as sometimes they are mistaken for each other. The Boston Consulting Group Strategy Institute's book *Clausewitz on Strategy* provides a perfect summary that deals with this problem:

- *'American economist Frank H. Knight (1885–1972), who is considered to be among the most influential economic thinkers of the twentieth century and is a founder of the Chicago School of Economics, broke new ground by distinguishing between risk, where outcomes can be identified and their probabilities gauged, and uncertainty proper, where outcomes and their probabilities elude analysis. Risk can be insured; uncertainty cannot. In his seminal work, "Risk, Uncertainty, and Profit" (Boston: Riverside Press, 1921), he attributed entrepreneurial profit to successful engagement with uncertainty proper'.*

In practical terms, *there are certain limits by which a security audit can diminish the auditee friction.* After all, as one of the cornerstone *chapter 1* statements declares, *an information security assessment is never complete.* However, not all of the limitations are related to the expected restrictions imposed upon audits by budget, time, or the assessor's skills and tools. One of the key factors that contribute to friction is pure chance. No security audit can eliminate the possibility of its intervention. Nonetheless, *the auditors can address auditee capabilities of adapting to chance.* For instance, they can do it by pointing out risks related to insufficient redundancy and resilience measures implemented. In ISO27001 audits, security aspects of business continuity and disaster recovery have to be addressed (Annex A 17). Elements of the incident response and its overall effectiveness (Annex A 16) are also highly relevant for handling the unpredictable. Thus, apart from reducing *self-induced friction*, thorough information security assessments can actually assist with the *"successful engagement with uncertainty proper"*.

An interesting spin-off of this discourse on uncertainty and risk is dealing with the so-called '*Black Swan events*'. The term comes from the popular book by Nassim Nicholas Taleb, *The Black Swan: The Impact of the Highly Improbable*. A Black Swan event is considered to possess the following characteristics:

- It is highly unpredictable.
- It has a massive impact.
- It is rationalised to look more predictable afterwards.

To quote Taleb, '*before the discovery of Australia, people in the Old World were convinced that all swans were white, an unassailable belief as it seemed completely confirmed by empirical evidence. The sighting of the first black swan might have been an interesting surprise for a few ornithologists (and others extremely concerned with the coloring of birds), but that is not where the significance of the story lies. It illustrates a severe limitation to our learning from observations or experience and the fragility of our knowledge. One single observation can invalidate a general statement derived from millennia of confirmatory sightings of millions of white swans. All you need is one single (and, I am told, quite ugly) black bird*'.

In technical information security, a completely novel and highly effective way of exploitation or totally overlooked giant gap in abundant implementation are examples of

Black Swan events. Note that there could also be beneficial Black Swans in the shape of discovering potent unorthodox defensive means. Zero-day vulnerabilities and exploits could be Black Swans. The Morris worm surely was. The majority of current 'zero-day birds' belong to the shades of grey. It is often possible to predict a zero-day or, at least, be wary of the heightened probability of its emergence. The threat of buffer overflows was outlined back in 1972, sixteen years prior to the earliest documented use of a malicious buffer overflow. 'Bloatware' (bloated and bulky software) and highly complex network protocols are more likely to be insecure: complexity breeds potentially vulnerable points, in particular of a systempunkt type, and increases the *attack surface*. Besides, it is possible to look at security history of the investigated application or other target to draw useful forecasts. There are known network services that were hit by a zero-day, patched, then hit afresh, patched again and so forth. Although historical records could be deceptive. Sometimes people repeat the same mistakes over and over again. But some learn a lot from them, and do it well. The same applies to social engineering and human security issues.

How can information security assessments and their risk evaluation phase address the Black Swan problem? If the auditors discover a novel vulnerability or method of attack before the bad guys do, our bird is painted snow-white. This was referred to as "getting inside the opponent's OODA loop" earlier in this book. Notice that the *mutation fuzzing* is a direct hands-on approach to tackling the Black Swan. By applying unexpected and outright random input, this type of testing can produce similarly unexpected outcome. When its results are analysed, and corresponding potential risks are gauged, the bird changes its colour.

These are some of the tactical means applicable to dealing with the Black Swan issue. What about their strategic counterparts?

In his principal work, Nassim Taleb has suggested that humans are prone to concentrate on specifics when they should focus on generalities. This trend strongly aggravates vulnerability to Black Swan events. By uncovering and addressing *strategic level risks*, such as those introduced by lack of defence-in-depth, or prevalence of the 'autocratic control and drill-machine approach', or other relevant anti-patterns security audits evaluate adaptability. Which, according to military strategists from Sun Tzu to John Boyd, is the proper answer to uncertainty. The absence of strategic failures will not prevent assailants from *creating a gap* employing a Black Swan attack. It will enable robust *containment* of the attack's impact, however, as well as effective incident response and recovery reactions. In Taleb's own words, '*you are exposed to the improbable only if you let it control you*'. This shall conclude the brief uncertainty, the unknown and harmful unpredictability interlude.

On suitable risk analysis methodologies

The next step is to choose a general risk analysis approach. Risk analysis methods can be quantitative or qualitative. The quantitative variety strives to assign independently objective monetary values to different objects of the risk evaluation and to the estimates of the potential loss. In contrast, qualitative risk analysis is typically scenario-based. Information security assessments address, or even emulate active and passive security incident scenarios and their outcomes. Thus, the data they produce fits the qualitative, rather than quantitative approach. Besides, even the in-house security auditor teams are usually not supplied with sufficient details regarding their targets monetary values. Together with the previous observations on the role of intangibles and difficulties in estimating the value of information, this tilts the balance towards employing the qualitative risk analysis means. At the same time, *the results of such qualitative evaluation should be presented in a quantified way*. This helps to prioritise weighted risks and clearly explain their significance (or lack of thereof) within the security assessment report, so that the corrective actions can be also prioritised.

Then we need to select the parameters convenient for estimating risks in accordance with the aforementioned risk definition and the corresponding formula. Which is, to remind you, *risk severity = (probability of the event) x (impact of the event)*. What the auditors could see from the results of the performed tests are:

1. various security weaknesses, vulnerabilities and gaps, and how easy or difficult is to discover and exploit them;
2. the consequences of such exploitation (exposure of sensitive data, gaining unauthorised access, disrupting availability, etc.);
3. the efficacy of the auditee's defences.

The data that contributes to assessing the impact (mainly point 2 of the above) is more tangible, reliable and objective as compared to its probability gauging counterparts. It could be hard to evaluate the overall end effects of a successful security breach. It is not difficult to spot where and which level of access was obtained, however, and what kind of information was disclosed or otherwise compromised. Or, to detect any significant service or network availability disruptions. Thus, weighting the vulnerability impact is the easier half. The next section of this chapter will provide examples of numerous parameters that can be used for this important task.

Measuring the probability of the event can be tricky. If the auditors are looking at *passive* incidents only, relevant security history statistics come very handy. Unfortunately, such statistical data is frequently unavailable. Does your company or organisation keep track of all accidental sensitive data losses and their frequency? What about availability shortfalls? However, it is the *active* security incidents that make the matter truly complicated.

As discussed in the Introduction, they involve the clash of wills. It is possible to contemplate different attacker types and their traits, and make reasonable guesses about the opponents one is more likely to encounter. This could be advantageous when doing preliminary planning for an upcoming security audit, as discussed in *chapter 4* when covering threat profiles. Nevertheless, trying to predict motivations, aims and means of complete strangers (or even someone you think you know) can easily become an unrewarding business. At the end of the day, it is nothing more than creative guesswork. Estimating the likelihood of attacks on such shaky grounds during the risk evaluation phase of an audit is clearly far-fetched. The security assessment is expected to decrease the fog of war covering its targets and their close surroundings. Away from the assessment scope the dense fog persists. As the ancient Chinese strategist Du Mu pointed out, '*you can only know if your own strength is sufficient to overcome an opponent; you cannot force the opponent to slack off to your advantage*'.

Thus, a different approach should be adapted instead. Assume that sooner or later the attack will take place. Then, estimate the likelihood of its *success* by gauging points 1 and 3 of above listed assessment results conclusions. That is, the ease of vulnerability discovery and exploitation combined with feasibility of bypassing the deployed controls. In practice, this comes down to estimating attacker skills necessary to find and abuse the discovered vulnerabilities, security weaknesses and gaps. If the skill and effort bar is high, the probability of successful attack is low, and vice versa. This is a simple, yet highly effective method of dealing with the attack likelihood issue.

The final set of parameters that cannot be ignored when assessing security risks relates to the rectifying action. The situation in which a workable and reliable remedy for the evaluated vulnerability is readily available is dramatically different from its opposite. The absence, inapplicability or demanding costs or complexity of the fix significantly increase the risk the vulnerability presents. Thus, the basic formula for evaluating per-vulnerability risk in hands-on security assessment practice would be:

- *Risk severity = f(vulnerability impact, attacker effort/skill required, suitable remedy availability)*

Armed with this knowledge, the auditors can now commence the synthetic analysis of risks described in detail in the remaining sections of this chapter. Its results will allow effective prioritisation of risks that harmonises future corrective acts.

On treatment of information security risks

Various activities that address the evaluated risks, also referred to as risk treatments, are divided into four major categories:

1. Avoidance, or complete elimination of risk. This is desirable, but rarely applicable in practice outside disabling what is not needed anyway. If you don't use a feature, system or service the related risks are gone. If it is there at the first place, however, it is probably required for business operations.

2. Reduction, or mitigation of risk. This is the most sensible and commonly utilised approach of dealing with risks. Patch the hole. Replace the component by its more secure equivalent. Introduce appropriate safeguards. Improve security of processes. Tighten policies, standards and guidelines. Provide relevant security training. ISO31000:2009 suggests three major avenues of risk reduction, namely reducing the risk source, changing its likelihood or consequences. Some risk will inevitably remain, but presumably at a much lower level. According to ISO27001:2013, this residual risk must be signed off by its respective owner.

3. Transfer. Risks can be outsourced or insured against. For example, an appropriate SLA or MSA with a third party like hosting, data storage, Cloud or SaaS provider can transfer some risks to such an entity. Currently, insurance against information security-specific risks is still uncommon with exception of few US states. As time passes, this situation is likely to change.

4. Retention, or risk acceptance. Sometimes a risk can be retained. This happens when it occupies the very bottom of the priority list, or its mitigation can introduce more problems than the original risk itself. Risk retention can be accompanied by suitable budgeting arrangements that cover the estimated acceptable loss. The key to effective risk retention is having a clearly defined and well-managed list of acceptable risks in the company. It might

make sense to have several such lists, for instance 'technical' and 'non-technical' acceptable risks.

Risk acceptance is the most controversial and arguable point on the list. Many security specialists feel uncomfortable with retaining even the minimal security risks, which they perceive as inaction. It is almost like being silenced or pushed down by financial or political considerations. It offends the perfectionist attitude. However, accepting risks on the basis of their detailed assessment by experts is not the same as ignoring them. MCDP 1 *Warfighting* made a great observation highly relevant to this subject:

- *'By its nature, uncertainty invariably involves the estimation and acceptance of risk . . . Risk is equally common to action and inaction. Risk may be related to gain; greater potential gain often requires greater risk. However, we should clearly understand that the acceptance of risk does not equate to the imprudent willingness to gamble the entire likelihood of success on a single improbable event'.*

Note the correlation of the last statement with the 'Black Swan intermezzo'. The excerpt above also underlines that acceptance of risks is not a gamble. It should never become one. In his bestseller, *The 33 Strategies of War*, Robert Greene draws a clear line between gambling and taking measured risks:

- *'Both cases involve an action with only a chance of success, a chance that is heightened by acting with boldness. The difference is that with a risk, if you lose, you can recover: your reputation will suffer no long-term damage, your resources will not be depleted, and you can return to your original position with acceptable losses.*

With a gamble, on the other hand, defeat can lead to a slew of problems that are likely to spiral out of control'.

When the logic of both *Warfighting* and Robert Greene discourses is combined, the consequent conclusion can be derived:

- *'When the acceptance of risk is gauged, not the likelihood of the event, but its actual impact should be favoured as the basis for the final decision'.*

The impact is more straightforward to judge. It is predominantly intrinsic to the auditee. In contrast, the probability depends on a multitude of external factors concealed by the ever-present fog of war.

Envision a high attacker skill, high impact technical vulnerability that requires in-depth analysis of the target with subsequent creation of exploit code in order to be abused. For now, its exploitation appears to be unlikely, thus strongly reducing the associated risk. However, there is no guarantee that the exploit would not be released tomorrow. Or that the relevant exploitation technique would not be sufficiently simplified. Are you going to gamble leaving such a vulnerability unfixed? The human factor security bears its own burden of the risk acceptance issue. A highly trusted and loyal person holds keys to confidential information and privileged access. This is acceptable risk, but tomorrow the situation might change. For instance, this person may suffer a mental breakdown that opens opportunities for successful social engineering attacks. A common sense answer is 'trust, but monitor'. As soon as any reasons for suspicion appear, remove the trust.

When evaluating risks and contemplating appropriate risk treatments, the concepts we have borrowed from military science can offer vital insights. Spin the strategic exploitation cycle (*Figure 21*) the last time feeding into it all security testing results at hand. Ideally, at this assessment stage all centres of gravity should be identified, studied and categorised. If breaching the determined schwerpunkt or systempunkt is possible but requires high attacker effort and skill, not defending it any further is a gamble. This can apply to the above examples of the critical vulnerability which is hard to exploit, or highly trusted and loyal employee that should still be monitored. However, if the risk is not:

- related to any established centres of gravity,
- evidently a part of a systempunkt, or
- a useful nebenpunkte,

it can be safely retained in order to dedicate effort and time to more critical security issues.

Analysing individual vulnerability risks

> *'So the rule of military operations is not to count on opponents not coming, but to rely on having ways of dealing with them; not to count on opponents not attacking, but to rely on having what cannot be attacked.'* – Sun Tzu

Risks introduced by separate vulnerabilities and gaps are the building blocks of the entire information security risk state of the auditee. If one of the blocks is defective or goes amiss, the whole structure might collapse. The devil is in the details. Precise measurement of risks for every assessed security weakness, vulnerability or gap is the key to successful risk evaluation phase of any information security audit. Yet, we are employing the qualitative and not quantitative method. How is it possible to maximise its precision? The likely answer is take into account as many details as you can while keeping in mind their relevance and criticality for the specific situation.

Relevant vulnerability categories

Prior to reviewing practical assessment of vulnerabilities' impact and their likelihood of exploitation, it is sensible to revisit their classifications. There are many ways of categorising security flaws of various natures. Not all of them are suitable for evaluating risks these vulnerabilities present. Thus, only the pertinent taxonomies that closely reflect our previous discussions will be examined.

A handy methodology is to sort vulnerabilities by their specific discovery means. In accordance with the general assessment categories, it is possible to split all security issues into *uncovered by black, grey or white box testing*. All flaws detected and exploited during black box tests can be abused by anyone. If the test is internal, the "anyone" amounts to any insider. Their grey box equivalents require an additional exploitation step – getting the necessary unprivileged access. Vulnerabilities that can be uncovered via white box assessments only are usually the hardest to detect and abuse.

It is also feasible to classify vulnerabilities as discovered via:

- frontal recon and exploitation.
- lateral recon and exploitation.
- the combination of both approaches.

Revisit *Figure 30* and the corresponding discourse if you feel the need to refresh your memory. Vulnerabilities that require lateral reconnaissance and exploitation means are usually more difficult to attack, although some peculiar exceptions do exist.

Besides, it is useful to categorise vulnerabilities as *discovered by intrusive or non-intrusive techniques.* Intrusive methods are more likely to trigger alarms. In social engineering, it corresponds to arousing suspicion, doubt and mistrust. In technical attacks, it corresponds to setting off intrusion detection, monitoring and prevention systems. Intrusive technical testing is also likely to cause denial of service conditions that can prevent further exploitation. To summarise, vulnerabilities that demand the intrusive approach are harder to exploit, especially if appropriate safeguards are in place.

Finally, note how accessible the technical vulnerability is. It could be:

- remote.
- local – network.
- local – system or application.

Remote vulnerabilities can be reached from any position in the world providing that connectivity exists. Local – network vulnerabilities are accessible from the same network. Local system or application vulnerabilities require some form of unprivileged access to the target system or application. In social engineering, it is possible to create an equivalent classification by looking at communication channels that were employed to reach the assessment goal. Did it require personal contact, telephone conversations, or were the online communications sufficient? Also, did one-time contact suffice, or were multiple contacts with the target(s) necessary?

Gauging attacker skill

The classifications outlined above clearly relate to the exploitation likelihood rather than the vulnerability impact. If you look at them more closely, it will become apparent that the pivotal point is, indeed, the attacker's skill and respective effort. How do they get a foothold to enable grey box tests? How do they outflank strong frontal defences and discover what is hidden? How do they employ highly effective, but intrusive techniques without crashing (or scaring away) the target and sounding the alarm bells? How do they reach the soft vulnerable underbelly?

When discussing the tactics of assessing vulnerabilities and gaps, we have noted that security problems discovered earlier in the audit process tend to be less skill-intensive. *Figure 27* was used as the illustration of the three typical exploitation stages which correspond to gradual increase of required attacker proficiency and effort. In a nutshell, this divides technical attacker skill levels according to the testing methods employed:

- Low level – automated scanning only.
- Medium level – semi-automated testing.
- High level – manual testing.

Shifting further to the next 'operational' section of *chapter 5*, it is reasonable to draw a similar categorisation on the basis of ability to utilise security gaps:

- Low level – exploiting well-known gaps.
- Medium level – exploiting little-known gaps.
- High level – creating gaps at will.

The attacker skill level classification we use in actual penetration testing reports is represented in the *Table 5*.

Table 5: Categorising technical attacker skills

Skill level	Description
User	The *User* skill level attack can be easily performed employing well-known techniques and 'canned' tools that are freely available on the Internet. No specialist knowledge of the attacked application, system or network protocol is needed.
Administrator	The *Administrator* skill level attack usually requires using several methods and tools in a specific sequence, or employing a sophisticated attack tool with complex command line syntax. Good knowledge of the targeted application's logic, or system's structure, configuration and commands, or network protocol's operations and formats is necessary.
Expert	The *Expert* skill level attack typically requires writing a new hacking tool from scratch or heavily modifying existing tools to address a specific vulnerability. Discovering novel security flaws and attack techniques, producing zero-day exploits, performing reverse engineering or cryptanalysis belong to this skill level.

The "administrator" designation in the table reflects the fact that, at this particular level, attackers should be able to manage what they are able to breach. Or, at least, possess the same degree of competence system or network administrators they confront do. Note that more often than not passive security incidents could be judged as having an attacker skill level of "User". Picking up what was incidentally exposed anyway should not require a high degree of labour or proficiency.

Social engineering is a highly fluid and agile sphere of action where the levels of attacker effort and skill are harder to formalise. The following classification similar to its technical counterpart above can be used as a model for further pondering:

1. Amateur. Just like its technical equivalent, the 'script kiddie', an amateur social engineer relies upon application of simple and well-known methods en masse. The ruling principle is 'you are unlikely to kill two birds with one stone, but throwing a million stones will smash a sitting duck or two'.

2. Conman. At this level social engineers can employ inventive or cunning attack plots consisting of several coordinated moves. They can also make active use of the nebenpunkte concept. Unlike the amateurs who mainly operate online, a conman attack could involve telephone conversations and personal contacts.

3. Spy-master. Highly skilled social engineers can handle complex far reaching schemes that involve numerous people, connections and communication channels. They are able to create gaps in apparently well-protected lines of defence. The analogy supplied by modern chaos theory is the one of the strange attractor influencing complex dynamic systems via a variety of variables while being difficult to take notice of.

Highly skilled social engineers are also more likely to apply the interdisciplinary approach by utilising suitable technical means to assist in the human factor exploitation.

The descriptions in the *Table 5* were attuned to reflect the diverse attacker skill-related categories we have previously discussed. However, they could not fully absorb all relevant taxonomies and factors. For instance, the table does not explicitly state whether the lateral approach had to be taken, or if highly intrusive techniques have been successfully used. The criteria that did not fit into the table can still be utilised as modifiers when the decision on assigning the attacker skill level to the evaluated vulnerability is made. This can be of great assistance when making this decision is not straightforward. In other words, when in doubt, check them out. As for the listed accessibility categories, we routinely reference whether a vulnerability is local, local-network or remote in a separate line of its description.

Weighting vulnerability impact

There are plentiful classifications that directly pertain to gauging vulnerability impact. Successful exploitation of a security flaw carries a multitude of tangible and intangible negative repercussions. These effects can be thoroughly categorised so that the actual impact can be measured with a good degree of certainty.

Vulnerability impact can be estimated in monetary terms, causing:

- high loss.
- medium loss.
- minimal or no loss.

As compared to quantitative risk analysis calculations, such estimates are highly subjective. They would depend on what is perceived as high, medium or minimal loss by the auditee. Which is something third party auditors are unlikely to be well-familiar with. Thus, it is rarely used. In some specific cases, however, like trade secret or customer database exposure, being fined a fixed sum for legislation non-compliance, or losing a specific customer contract, monetary considerations may become predominant. This is even more true when the impact of vulnerability on the availability of services is judged for online traders, casinos or betting shops.

Since everything is a part of some process or, more likely, several processes at once, the impact can be weighted by its process-oriented effects. It can:

• disrupt a process (or a few processes),

• impair a process (or a few processes), or

• have minimal or no process-related effects.

This categorisation strongly depends on the criticality of the affected processes for the auditee business operations. Which is again lies beyond the auditor team competence in numerous, but not all cases.

A common and evidently fruitful way of gauging vulnerability impact is by looking at the effects the security breach has on the CIA triad:

1. Confidentiality
   • Exposure of highly confidential data.
   • Exposure of confidential but not critical data.
   • Exposure of private non-confidential data.
   • No sensitive data disclosure.

2. Integrity
   • Modification of highly confidential data.
   • Modification of confidential but not highly critical data.

- Modification of private non-confidential data.
- No sensitive data alterations.
3. Availability
    - Severe disruption of availability.
    - Tolerable reduction of availability.
    - No or minimal effects on availability.

To remove any doubts, the auditors can contact the auditee while being engrossed in the process of risk evaluation and ask to provide the existing data classification standards, policies and guidelines. Responding to such a request in a positive and rapid manner is clearly in the auditee's interest. However, there are numerous cases when the auditee does not have data classification, or it is not properly implemented, or the data accessed is exempt from this classification and is difficult to label (for example, binary files, system images or media content).

Technical vulnerabilities impact can be easily weighted by the levels of unauthorised access to systems and applications their successful exploitation provides. These reduce to:

- highly privileged access (root, administrator, etc.).
- unprivileged user access .
- no or negligible unauthorised access.

The same classification can apply to some of the social engineering-related security flaws. When physical premises access is the social engineering test's aim, a similar approach can be used by categorising criticality of the penetrated premises.

The military science concepts that saw heavy use in this work could be also used to estimate the impact of assessed vulnerabilities, security weaknesses and gaps. In more general terms, a security issue can:

- belong to a centre of gravity.
- lead to a centre of gravity.
- be unrelated to a centre of gravity.

Coming down to the strategic contemplations of specific critical points, the analysed issue can constitute, or be inseparable from:

- a schwerpunkt.
- a (part of a) systempunkt.
- a nebenpunkte.
- none of the above.

The most critical vulnerabilities, weaknesses and gaps pertain to determined schwerpunkts or systempunkts. When reflecting on the decisive moments of military conflict, Clausewitz wrote that *'no battle is decided in a single moment, although in every battle there are moments of great importance, which chiefly bring about the result. The loss of a battle is, therefore, a gradual falling of the scale. But there is in every combat a point of time when it may be regarded as decided, in such a way that the renewal of the fight would be a new battle, not a continuation of the old one.'* Think which particular flaws "chiefly brought about" the security assessment result and at which point of time and specific testing sequence it was decided. These are the *key vulnerabilities* that have the highest impact.

In fact, even the FUD game described in the Introduction might be utilised to contemplate the most intangible, psychological or moral effects a security breach can produce. As previously discussed, it may end up with the following outcomes:

- Attacker wins the FUD game.
- A draw-like condition (which casually favours the defender).
- Defender wins the FUD game.

Would the successful exploitation of a vulnerability push the auditee's friction to the point of causing disorder, disarray or even panic? When performing the security assessment, watch all auditee reactions with utmost attention. You might get a call with agitated voice on the other end saying something like: "Oh, my God! Our critical database has new entries saying 'Penetrated by Bob the security tester. We can modify all stored data at will'. What should we do? Do we have to stop all tests ASAP and try to close the hole, whatever it is?" If an actual malicious database attack took place, guess who would become the undisputed FUD game champion? Whose will would be shattered in the never-ending attacker-defender conflict of wills?

This brings into the spotlight a rather subjective, but nonetheless potentially handy way of judging vulnerability impact by gauging it against the expected assailant goals. As a result of the specific vulnerability exploitation, the attacker aims can be:

- fully realised.
- partially achieved.
- not reached.

A decent preliminary threat model can make at least some of the attacker goals predictable, for example, 'gain access to the credit card database' or 'abuse the shopping card application to reduce prices of goods'.

Table 6 provides an example of the vulnerability impact classification we use when performing analysis of risks in the course of penetration tests.

Table 6: Categorising vulnerability impact

Impact level	Description
Severe	The *Severe* impact level vulnerability usually leads to full takeover of the targeted system or critical application and/or exposure of sensitive information to attackers. Malicious hackers can use this vulnerability in order to gain privileged access to the system, copy, alter or delete sensitive data, or capture and modify confidential or otherwise security-critical information passing through communication channels.
Considerable	The *Considerable* impact level vulnerability typically allows limited unauthorised access to data, application, service, system or network. Attackers can utilise this flaw in order to gain unprivileged user-level access to non-critical data. Denial-of-service (DoS) attacks usually belong to this category, since they do not provide access to systems or confidential data, but can severely disrupt service or network operations. However, if the availability of affected resources is business-critical (online trading, betting, news services, SaaS, etc.) the impact of DoS can be classified as *Severe*.

Limited	The *Limited* impact level vulnerability commonly leads to non-critical alterations in system behaviour and/or non-sensitive information disclosure to attackers. It is often considered opportunistic, thus requiring a specific set of circumstances in order for attackers to benefit from it. A typical example of a low-level vulnerability is leaking additional information about networks or systems, which allows attackers to map network topology or server directory structure with precision. Low-impact vulnerabilities are often auxiliary to their medium- and high-impact counterparts, and are abused by assailants to increase their attacks' efficacy or stealth.

It is founded on the most subjective and tangible (from the auditor's point of view!) repercussions related to the CIA triad and levels of unauthorised access. Some conceptual strategic overtones are also present. Similarly to the case of evaluating an attacker's effort and skill, the rest of the relevant categories discussed can serve as applicable modifiers in the decision making process. A very similar classification can be developed for estimating the impact of social engineering attacks.

Contemplating the vulnerability remedy

The remaining element of our per vulnerability risk evaluation formula is the remedy. It might fully *eliminate or mitigate* the risk. It can be *complex, of average complexity, or simple*. The complexity of the fix is usually correlated with its costs in terms of money, time and effort spent. A remedy can also have different application scope. It can be *separate security flaw-specific or generic in nature.* In theory, the generic remedy is preferable, since it addresses many facets of the issue, or even multiple issues at once. It is also a good indicator that the root of the uncovered security problem has been firmly established. In practice, however, the combination of specific and generic remedial actions is often the most sensible approach. For instance, a vulnerable critical service must be patched ASAP (a specific remedy), while the entire patch management process and the corresponding guidelines and practices are appropriately improved (its generic counterpart).

The most important criterion in evaluating the corrective action is whether a suitable solution is readily available or not. *Table 7* represents our practical take on this issue.

Table 7: Categorising vulnerability remedies

Remedy	Description
Non-existent	There is no permanent or acceptable temporary fix for this vulnerability. Until an appropriate remedy is discovered and produced, the affected application, service, system or network protocol must be disabled or disconnected from the network to be replaced by a sufficiently secure alternative.
Temporary	The fix is indirect, does not mitigate the issue in full or address its real cause, and might partially impair functionality of the affected application, service, system, or network protocol.
Available	The adequate security fix is readily available from the system or application developer or vendor. Alternatively, the remedy involves easy-to-perform and straightforward changes of the affected target's configuration, like changing a weak user account password to a strong one.

An example of a temporary or partial remedy could be restricting access to a vulnerable service or application to highly trusted and monitored systems or users only. The risk is reduced, but as soon as the fully-fledged fix is available it must be applied. Since social engineering attacks rely upon basic principles known since ancient times, situations in which appropriate remedies are non-existent are seldom. The majority of human security issues can be solved with relevant training and mentoring. At times, however, all access of vulnerable persons to critical data and systems must be completely removed until suitable replacements are found. This corresponds to the temporary remedial action. Keep in mind that many social engineering-related headaches can be effectively addressed through technical, operational and policy means.

Defining vulnerability risk level

After the vulnerability impact, attacker skill and remedial action levels are assigned, a consolidated per-vulnerability risk value can be produced. *Table 8* demonstrates a possible way of generating this value for all assessed vulnerabilities, security weaknesses and gaps. This is the approach we currently use in routine security auditing practice.

Table 8: Per-vulnerability risk level estimation

Impact	Attacker skill	Remedy	Per-vulnerability risk level	
			Level	Description notes
Limited (+1)	Expert (+1)	Available (+1)	Low (= 3–5)	The risk is limited and easy to mitigate.

				Elimination of such flaws can be safely placed at the bottom of the remedial priority list. A possible exception is when other uncovered issues are at the same low level of risk and the impact of the particular flaw is estimated as 'Considerable'. Limited impact expert skill level flaws with no available fix (risk level 5) can be safely retained.
Considerable (+2)	Administrator (+2)	Temporary (+2)	Medium (= 5–7)	The actual risk often relies upon multiple factors, thus an individual judgement of Medium-risk issues is crucial. The

				differences between the lowest (5) and the highest (7) ends of the medium-risk interval can be highly significant: compare a limited impact expert attacker skill level flaw with no available fix (risk level 5) and severe impact user attacker level skill flaw with a readily available fix (risk level 7). It is evident which one has to be addressed first.
Severe (+3)	User (+3)	Non-existent (+3)	High (= 7–9)	The vulnerability presents a grave threat. It must be dealt with ASAP and by all means possible, even

				if the level of impact is judged as 'Considerable' rather than 'Severe'. If its elimination is going to involve disabling the affected application, service or system functions or network connectivity, it must still be done until this serious security issue is fully resolved.

The risk summary for individual vulnerabilities is quantified by simply adding up the points assigned to three major risk-defining criteria. By adding them up, it is possible to obtain the summary values ranging from 3 (the lowest level of risk) to 9 (the highest level of risk).

Notice that the borders between Low, Medium and High risk summary levels are "fuzzy": a vulnerability ranked as 5 can be labelled as low-risk or medium-risk, while a vulnerability ranked as 7 can be marked as medium or high. This is done on purpose and aims at providing the auditors additional manoeuvre space in judging the risks presented by the examined security issue. It can be done on the basis of personal experience and specific situation that pertains to the particular assessment. At this point, various *modifiers* we have outlined can be recalled to assist with the decision.

For example, a Severe impact (3) vulnerability that is easy to exploit ("User" attacker skill, 3), but is also very straightforward to fix ("Available" suitable remedy, 1) would sum up as risk level 7. It could be marked as presenting Medium risk if the auditee has proven rapid corrective actions and eliminates the flaw as soon as it is found and reported. Otherwise, the risk presented by such a vulnerability should be judged as High. In particular, this applies to situations where numerous uncovered security issues have 'available' remedies, indicating that the relevant mitigation procedures within the auditee are ineffective (if present at all). Thus, we have already arrived to the point when the *synthetic overall risk state* is taken into account.

Risks synthesis, summary and its breakdown

> '..war is an indivisible whole, the parts of which (the subordinate results) have no value except in their relation to this whole'. – Carl von Clausewitz

Synthesising all individual risks to create a summary that defines and explains the overall risk state provides numerous eloquent advantages. The majority of them originate from being able to:

1. generate, analyse and streamline the strategic view of the information security state for the auditee management.
2. deduce important details that cannot be seen without assembling the whole picture.

The first point enables creation of a risk reduction plan aimed at strategic organisation-wide risk treatment. This goes hand in hand with recommendations of the OCTAVE process's Phase 3: "Develop Security Strategy and Plans" using a common evaluation basis. Instead of merely selecting tactical responses to individual risks, OCTAVE risk assessment methodologies aim at establishing a protection strategy for the critical assets of the entire auditee company or organisation. Alas, the approaches to identifying critical assets we have previously described are different from the corresponding OCTAVE Phase 1 ("Build Asset-Based Threat Profiles). Besides, the OCTAVE process Phase 2 ("Identify Infrastructure Vulnerabilities") does not appear to go any further than automated vulnerability scanning. In addition, please note that ISO27001:2013 does not require binding risk evaluation to assets as the previous version of this standard did. This does not mean that you cannot do so, of course, especially if it works fine for your company or organisation.

As the strategic concepts-based illustration of the second point above, the process of producing the total summary of risks can assist in determining systempunkts. In fact, current risk assessment theories have a concept *similar, but not identical* to the systempunkt – the so-called *compound risks*. A compound risk is usually described as a '*dependent combination of risks*', and is considered to be one of the most troublesome issues of risk analysis. Textbook advice for dealing with the compound risk is to reduce it to a non-compound one where feasible. This echoes the centuries old recommendation of Clausewitz to curtail several determined centres of gravity to one. However, it is practically impossible to do with the systempunkt proper. The great Prussian strategist was totally unaware of this modern concept. The MCDP 1 *Warfighting* quote that closes the previous chapter outlines the current productive approach to the problem. To conclude:

- *'All systempunkts introduce compound risks. At the same time, not all compound risks have a systempunkt at their core.'*

In a nutshell, *summarising risks points out where the major risk areas are.* This can be done at many levels of abstraction. When applied to the CIA triad, the holistic evaluation of risks demonstrates which parts of the triad are most affected by the security issues uncovered. If used for the assessment of operations, it can show which processes are more unsafe or have evident security flaws. Consolidating risks is likely to pinpoint high-risk weak spots within the auditee ISMS organisation and structure. It can hint whether human, operational, policy or technical factors are the main contributors to the security risks faced by the entity. Comparing separate risks to the whole is a fundamental way of establishing their actual root sources. Is there a major strategic risk to which the tactical ones are evidently subordinate? On the basis of such a comparison, some individual risks might be re-assessed, with their remedial priorities altered as a result.

Risks faced by large components

Our notions of the synthetic risk evaluation and analysis refer to assembling, disassembling and analysing the total summary of risks. The general scheme of how it could be done is introduced in *Figure 32*.

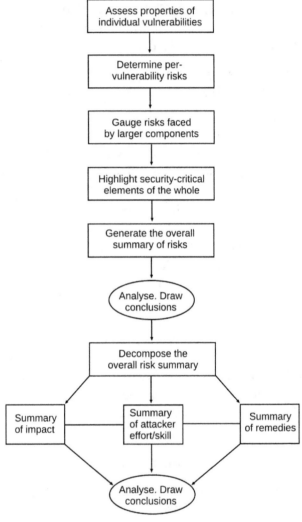

Figure 32: The process of synthetic risk evaluation

The first two stages depicted in *Figure 32* culminate at assigning per-vulnerability risk levels for all applicable security issues. These stages were already in the previous section in sufficient detail, important modifiers included.

Thus, we pick up the discourse from the third phase: *"gauge risks faced by larger components"*. This is the first stop at which risks introduced by individual vulnerabilities are summed up. An example of a typical 'larger component' in technical security assessments is a separate system. In software testing it can also mean a large part of a complex application, such as its core, back- or front-end. If a wide scope audit targets several networks at once, a separate network presents the next 'larger component' level as compared to its individual hosts. Yet, on a larger scale, it could be a routing domain up to the BGP Autonomous System. In human factor security evaluation, the larger component can refer to a group of people united by common characteristics and aims. It can be a specific project team, selected department's or branch's staff, customer account support or service line personnel and so forth. When operational security is reviewed, the larger component is typically a whole process – if assessing premises security, for instance, a building floor or a standalone building. In analysing security policies it would be a separate policy chapter. Depending on the size of the total, it could be feasible to split it into several components that co-exist in parallel or nested one within the other.

We shall use a simple *external* technical assessment example, in which the large component is a modest size network. Firstly, look at the individual systems. How many vulnerabilities does a system have? What are their assigned levels of risk? Are they strongly influenced by any specific modifiers? Which vulnerabilities or their combinations are the most critical for the system? *Then approach the network as a composite entity.* The bar chart in *Figure 33* shows risks faced by a small network that consists of six nodes only. If the assessment was internal, it would have also included any discovered network protocols-related risks.

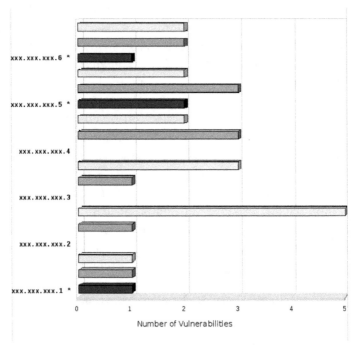

Figure 33: A technical example of risks distribution

The colour of the bars in *Figure 33* represents three levels of per-vulnerability risk from Low (light grey) to High (dark grey). Systems with network addresses ending in 2, 3 and 4 do not have any high-risk security issues. The other half of the sample network evidently does. Thus, the hosts with addresses ending in 1, 5 and 6 are marked with a star as *security-critical*. To define the criticality, we suggest employing the following criteria:

- *'The elements that have even a single high risk level vulnerability are security-critical'.*

- *'The elements with the number of medium risk vulnerabilities exceeding the amount of their Low risk siblings can be security-critical depending on these flaws impact'.*

System 4 of *Figure 33* could satisfy the second criterion, as it has two low- and three medium-risk vulnerabilities. It is not, however, labelled as security-critical on the chart. This indicates that none of the discovered medium-risk flaws have Severe impact whether on their own *or in combination.* Security problems embodied in systems 1, 5 and 6 introduce higher risks and must be addressed first when corrective actions are done.

Compound risks, systempunkts and attacker logic

At this stage of the synthetic risk evaluation we are likely to encounter the accursed compound risk/systempunkt issue. *Addressing it will require to bypass the boundaries of a single reviewed element, or even re-evaluate the scope and nature of the selected 'larger components'.* Revisit the systempunkt example in *chapter 5.* Earlier, we promised to supply non-network-centric illustrations of the same. Time has come to fulfil this promise. In the area of application security, a compound risk vulnerability can consist of:

1. improper input validation, plus
2. unsafe memory use, plus
3. ineffective memory protection, plus
4. violation of the least privilege principle.

Is it also a systempunkt? Point 4 above hints at 'yes', as gaining privileged access to the system constitutes a definite collapse of its defences and the vulnerability impact of

'Severe'. On a larger scale of things, though, the correct answer will depend on the role of the penetrated application and system, sensitivity and criticality of information it handles, and the sum of all repercussions of the breach. Thus, only a proper synthetic summary of risks, *knowing the whole risk state picture*, can provide the final answer.

Note that in a real life installation:

- input validation can be done by a different application module (it's front-end) or even a totally separate entity, such as the application layer firewall.

- memory protection can be also performed by an extrinsic entity, for example, the operating system or even in hardware.

- violation of the least privilege principle can be an error of configuration, with the only fault of the application itself in being insufficiently fool-proof.

Even in such a case, the individual risks presented by all *distributed* constituents of the vulnerability are still inseparable from its summary risk level. It doesn't matter whether these constituents belong to the same or different entities or parts.

However, *separate components of a compound risk can have highly uneven individual contributions to its whole*. Thus, it is feasible to prioritise them when the remedy is considered. We shall use a common client-side targeting attack example to illustrate this vital point. This time the sample compound risk vulnerability comprises the following factors:

1. A cross-site scripting (XSS) issue on a corporate website that allows the theft of users' login cookies if they click on a forged URL link.

2. The TRACE method enabled on the affected webserver. It can assist the cross-site scripting attack.
3. E-mail addresses of employees can be harvested. Thus, the forged malicious link can be sent to all or selected members of staff.
4. Some users lack security awareness and will click on the insidious link if the e-mail that contains it is sufficiently enticing

Part 1 of the described compound risk flaw pertains to the web application; part 2 to the web server hosting it; part 3 is an information leak that could either be allowed or violate the existing security policies; part 4 is a human security issue.

In relation to this specific risk, the cross-site scripting flaw is the most critical. Eliminate it, and the problem is gone. This is a good illustration of how the compound risk can be reduced to a non-compound equivalent in practice. The use of the TRACE method is the least important. Providing that other relevant issues are solved, it can be safely retained as a low risk level security weakness. The exposure of staff e-mail addresses is of great assistance to attackers. Nonetheless, in its absence a malicious link can still be sent via other available means, such as message boards, forums, social networks and instant messengers used by employees. Finally, lack of security awareness exhibited by some users is at least as important as the XSS itself, but does not lie at the very core of the sample compound risk. Increasing user awareness would reduce the risk without bringing about its complete avoidance, as removing the XSS issue will. Under other circumstances, however, and when reviewing a different attack type, the security awareness problem can introduce far more serious risks than the specific technical cross-site scripting flaw!

Is this sample compound risk a systempunkt? Again, the answer will depend on knowing more than the specifics of the complex vulnerability described. Who are the users whose accounts can be broken into and what are their roles, confidentiality levels and access rights? What would be the real consequences of the breach? What connections do the exposed targets have? Is their exploitation able to create a domino effect propagating along these links? For instance, could the potential attackers utilise the breached accounts to disseminate the malicious URL or malware within the organisation? Only the in-depth active security assessment is able to provide sufficient unbiased data on the basis of which any meaningful analysis of such compound risks can be performed.

The discussion of the compound risk example above highlights non-linearity of the strategic concepts when applied to the modern information security field.

- *'Part of a systempunkt in one attack can be a schwerpunkt or nebenpunkte of the other, and vice versa. The critical points and specific risks their exploitation creates can be independent, interlinked with a different connection strength, or even nested within each other'.*

If you encounter such a phenomenon when analysing the assessment results and summarising the risks, don't be surprised. When contemplating the corrective actions, take this complexity into account. Reducing a specific risk could diminish other risks. This is desired. Mitigating a specific risk may have no effect on any other risks. This is a typical view of risk reduction if the strategic considerations are totally ignored. Reducing a specific risk might even increase other risks. This can be predicted and avoided.

The compound risks issue raises another interesting subject. Whether the atomic or complex elements of summarised risks are selected, their choice is usually based upon the objective auditee structures and processes. The auditors typically split the risks faced by applications, systems, networks, groups of people, separate departments, defined operational units and processes, and so on. However, all examples of compound risks we have used are, in essence, reflections of the specific *processes of exploitation and structures, or scenarios of attack*. So, the compound risks emerge when these *offensive* processes and their elements *do not match* individual or large components of their targets as seen from the defender's viewpoint. *'This footprint mismatch is the real "extrinsic" compound risks source.'* Among other things, *'compound risks relate to exploiting differences and weaknesses of perception.'*

Instead of adapting to the opponent as suggested since the time of Sun Tzu, the defenders operate in accordance with their own structure, categories and logic. Gauge the risks faced by the network A, process B, data set C, or team D. Treat them in accordance with this *objective, yet ultimately perceived and not the solely unique division*. However, the assailants can reach beyond such separation as it might have no actual relevance to the arrangements of a complex attack. They have their own 'offensive' separation methods, as the given compound risk or systempunkt examples demonstrate. How do we counter them?

If the entire all-encompassing view of both the risks and the corresponding security state is synthesised first, we can then divide it the way we want. It is possible to split it into large and then individual components the traditional way. This is probably how the whole was assembled in the first place. Alternatively, *it can be divided using the attacker approach and logic*. This would possibly highlight potential compound risks and permit reducing them to the one or several key constituents that can be effectively mitigated or altogether removed. We would define it as the direct approach to the problem. Its indirect equivalent is treating wide scope strategic risks (like lack of employees secure awareness from the previous example) which is likely to reduce the compound risks by proxy. *'This means countering breadth with an even larger breadth, or even fighting fire with a greater flame'.* You can also compare it to the earlier passage on addressing the strategic risks in dealing with the Black Swan problem.

Total risk summary utilisation and dissection

When the risks of *all large components, their constituents and interconnecting links* are thoroughly reviewed, a formal total summary of risks can be successfully produced. This is, in essence, a short conclusion of the entire security assessment process directed at the auditee's senior management. As *Table 9* demonstrates, the criteria we advise employing for this task are more granular than those used when designating individual security-critical elements.

Table 9: Defining the overall security state

Security state	Criteria
Insecure	High risk level vulnerabilities are present.
Insufficiently secure	The amount of medium risk level vulnerabilities exceeds the number of low-risk flaws.
Sufficiently secure	The amount of low risk level vulnerabilities exceeds the number of medium-risk flaws.
Secure	Only low risk level vulnerabilities are discovered. They do not create a higher compound risk vulnerability if combined.

Draw a summary pie chart that presents the total percentage of high-, medium- and low-level risks to supplement the general security state conclusion. At this point, it is helpful to stop and review the entire operation of coming to it. What are they key findings of the assessment? Are they interrelated? What do they pertain to in terms of processes, the CIA triad, vulnerability classes and types, infrastructure or organisational elements, and so forth? List all critical findings and place any helpful explanatory commentaries and notes next to them. This will come in very handy when writing the assessment report.

The next step suggested in *Figure 32* is to split the summary of risks according to the chief three contributing factors. This will produce the general summaries of all vulnerabilities impacts, attacker effort/skill estimates, and suitable remedies availabilities. Generate the corresponding pie charts to demonstrate total percentages of vulnerabilities split by their impact, attacker skill and remedy levels.

Finally, analyse the results. Which per-vulnerability risk levels and their constituents predominate? How do the breakdowns of the three parameters match the overall risks summary? What can be said about these parameters' contribution to it? How do their distributions compare to each other? Which types and categories of impact are the uppermost? What about the suggested remedies? Are there any specific processes and areas with prevalent Severe impact, or User attacker skill, or Non-existent remedy level issues? How about their opposites? What could be the most likely explanations for answers to these and other relevant questions you can think of? Which information security elements would they apply to on the strategic, operational and tactical planes? In the next chapter, we will revisit such matters as the solid foundation for drawing the final conclusions to entire security assessments. For now, they shall remain as engaging food for thought.

Apart from being the source of essential data for the audit report conclusion, executive summary and accompanying debriefs, the process of the synthetic evaluation of risks generates numerous graphical representations. At the very least, it will produce:

- the overall risk summary pie chart.
- vulnerability impact level distribution pie chart.
- attacker skill level distribution pie chart.
- suitable remedy availability distribution pie chart.
- the component risk evaluation bar charts (similar to *Figure 33*).

Such schemes not only help to analyse and make sense of the assessment results, but are also easily understood by the auditee management representatives. Which is essential for the top-down endorsement of the audit, its follow-up corrective, and any future security assessments from the same auditor team. As stated by Napoleon himself, '*the first quality for a commander-in-chief is a cool head which receives a just impression of things; he should not allow himself to be confused by either good or bad news; the impressions which he receives successively or simultaneously in the course of a day should classify themselves in his mind in such a way as to occupy the place which they merit; because reason and judgement are the result of the comparison of various impressions taken into just consideration*'.

Thus, if you want dedicated support from the "commander-in-chief", it is best to offer the assessment results being already classified and prioritised on the basis of the respective summarised and individual risks. The language of risks is as universal as it is effective. Presenting the risks' sum, distribution and main contributing factors concisely and accompanied by visual aids goes a great way towards getting your point across.

CHAPTER 7: PRESENTING THE OUTCOME AND FOLLOW-UP ACTS

'The comprehensiveness of adaptive movement is limitless.' – Mei Yaochen

As emphasised in the closing part of the previous chapter, properly presenting information security assessment results is essential for the overall success. Which tangible outcome does the company or organisation expect from the security audit performed? First of all is the assessment report. Beyond this, the accompanying presentations and debriefs are likely to be requested. In addition, assistance from the auditors can be called for during the assessment follow-up. After all, the ones who have offered the remedial advice are expected to be the experts in all the suggested remedies. There is no point in recommending a solution you are not well-familiar with yourself.

Remember that even the most professional information security audits can be completely ruined by badly composed reports and an inability to present their content. Who cares about the astonishing results or prudent and far-sighted recommendations if they are not understood correctly, by the right people, and in a timely manner? A security assessment report that gathers dust with no actions on its recommendations ever done is not always the auditee's fault. Recall that the audit itself can be viewed as the 'OO' part of the strategic risk treatment OODA loop. If the Observation and Orientation are not properly performed, the Decision and Action can go terribly wrong or awry. The same applies to communicating the 'OO' findings to the decision makers. Damage the neurons that carry visual information to the brain, and the person can go blind despite having a hundred percent eyesight.

On structure and content of the assessment report

> *'As a general rule every one is more inclined to lend credence to the bad than the good.'* – Carl von Clausewitz

Information security assessment report must match competence, understanding, abilities and skills of all auditee professionals involved in the process of the assessment and its follow-up. In the majority of cases, the report will be reviewed by the CISO or equivalent, as well as the selected heads and appropriate members of all relevant departments or specialist teams. For instance, heads of risk management and compliance are expected to participate in studying and reacting to any information security audit outcome. However, there is always a chance that key content is going to be shown to senior management representatives. This is very likely to happen if the audit findings are considered as business-critical and/or require significant expenditure to mitigate the uncovered risks. These possibilities must be taken into account when assembling and composing various information security assessment reports.

The report audience and style

Since the competence areas of the aforementioned auditee specialists strongly differ, it is not possible to cater for everyone at the same time and place. Thus, there must be a clear division of the assessment report, at least into the management and focused specialist parts. Depending on the nature of the audit, the latter can be oriented at either technical or human resources professionals. If the security assessment is ISMS-centred, this division can be partially downplayed. Nonetheless, keep in mind that evaluating security policies, organisation and processes addresses strategic matters and will be reviewed at the top. The professional expertise and background of a CISO strongly differ from, for instance, their CIO or CTO equivalents, not to mention the CEO. Revisiting the discourse on the top-down approach and different levels of expertise in the second chapter of this book can provide insights which are highly applicable for the current subject.

Unlike the audit report, presentations and debriefs can, and should be arranged to match the specific audience type. Giving a technical presentation to the techs and management level debriefs to the appropriate managers is a good practice based on common sense. Trying to save time by giving a mixed audience presentation would have exactly the opposite effect. One fraction of the listeners would be bored and confused during the technical parts of the presentation, the other in the course of its management counterparts. The cumulative question time would become a complete mess. Avoiding such mishaps is beneficial for both the auditee and the auditors.

Both security assessment reports and any auxiliary presentation materials must be clear, accurate and readable. All difficult or unusual terms must be explained either within the text of the report or in a separate Glossary appendix. Usually, we do not utilise the glossary as it would mean mixing technical and non-technical terminology in a single section. The style of the report, presentations and debriefs must aspire to reflect the assessment's objectivity based upon the thorough synthetic analysis of risks. Scaremongering is a no-no, even when it might appear to be advantageous for the auditors in selling any additional services. Or even if the overall security state of the evaluated targets is determined to be 'insecure'. Calmly explain what the major risks are and in which priority they should be dealt with. Discuss with the auditee management what they may mean for their business. The aim of the assessment is to assist the auditee in gaining the upper hand in the FUD game, not inhibit their will or induce panic. As the epigraph to this section attests, people are inclined to lend more credence to the bad news anyway.

The style and structure of audit reports must be streamlined while taking into account all peculiarities of specific security assessment types. They should not be strongly distinct between the same assessment type reports submitted to different clients, or the same customer in the course of time. Since *'information security assessment must be a part of a continuous process'*, comparing the current and previous audit reports should not be clogged with unnecessary complications. This enables effective ongoing monitoring of the auditee security state. Typically, companies that provide security assessment services will have well-defined formats and prefabricated templates for all common audit type reports. These templates must be regularly reviewed to incorporate the necessary modifications driven by relevant technological, regulatory and other developments. We suggest at least an annual review of the audit report templates. Also, a dedicated template, and not a different customer's report should be used to produce the document in progress. This simple measure prevents revealing any customer details to a third party either by accident or via metadata.

A proposed conceptual structure of an information security assessment report based upon our live documents is outlined in *Figure 34*.

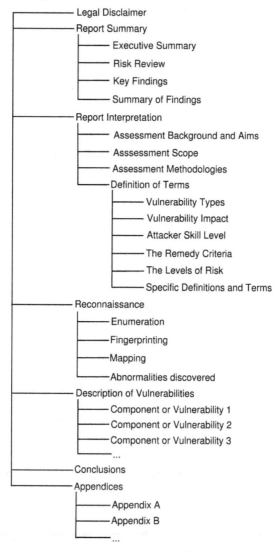

Figure 34: Suggested security audit report structure

It is important to begin the report with the appropriate legal disclaimer reflecting the security assessment's nature. The disclaimer should strongly emphasise that the audit and its recommendations do not provide hundred percent insurance against future security incidents, and the auditor company cannot be held responsible if they take place. This might appear to be a one-sided protection of the auditors against any negligence-related lawsuits, but such a statement also warns the auditee about the real state of affairs and prevents them from yielding to false sense of security on the basis of the assessment results. Besides, the disclaimer should underline high confidentiality and non-disclosure of the report's content.

The report summary

The summary of the assessment report is probably the part everyone is going to pay the most attention to. It is safe to expect that any non-specialist management representatives will only read the report's summary and totally ignore the rest. So it is this section of the entire document that will actually determine the top-down endorsement (or lack of thereof!) of the completed audit and corrective actions to follow. Thus, it must be composed in a highly concise way, using appropriate visual aids and language that will get all the described points across to the auditee's management. This is easier said than done, especially if the report is written by technical experts. To circumvent this problem, *Figure 34* suggests splitting the summary into four distinct sections.

The executive summary proper should be brief, simple and to the point, while avoiding any technical terminology whatsoever. It should not exceed a single page except in exceptional circumstances. Such situations might arise if the critical assessment findings are too numerous to be outlined in one page even in the most general and abridged terms. What is feasible to include within the executive summary? First of all, it must declare the overall security state level. Consult *Table 9* for its possible definitions. Then, it should briefly explain which business areas, specific departments, operations and processes, and so on are most affected by serious security issues. At this stage, utilising the CIA triad could come in handy. What confidential information can be exposed, modified or lost? Which important service's availability can be disrupted? What impact might it have in monetary terms or upon ongoing business processes, compliance and legal demands, the auditee's image, reputation and customer relations? The executive summary should never mention any specific vulnerabilities. It is there to highlight the general areas of critical risk.

The risk review section should present all estimated information security risks in a clear, easily understandable, management-oriented manner. It should illustrate the distribution of vulnerability risk levels to justify the overall security state rating declared in the executive summary. Afterwards, the breakdowns of risks by their levels of impact, attacker skill and suitable remedy availability, as well as by the affected *large or complex* components should be reviewed. This section of the report is where all the pie charts and diagrams created during the synthetic risk analysis should go, as described in *chapter 6*. Appropriate brief explanations and *strategic or operational level* conclusions derived from examining the summary of risks and its disassembly results should accompany every illustration.

The key findings section is the first part of the assessment report that addresses separate vulnerabilities, security weaknesses and gaps. Its aim is to list all security issues with a high level of risk and provide very short comments outlining their nature and impact. These commentaries should not go any further than "the SQL injection flaw allows unauthorised access to the customer database" or "a social engineering attack against the selected staff has exposed personal employee data". Note that "a security issue with high level of risk" can be a compound risk problem comprising multiple individual flaws. In such a case only the whole issue, and not its specific components should be covered in this part of the report.

The following 'summary of findings' section lists all discovered security problems giving only the vulnerability name, risk level and reference number. The latter usually corresponds to the section number of the specific vulnerability outline in the 'description of vulnerabilities' chapter of the report. It is best to present the summary of findings as a set of simple three-column tables. It is also advantageous to arrange these tables according to separate tested components, such as systems, networks, processes, departments or project teams. *Table 10* presents a simple instance of this approach.

However, if the components are too numerous (for example, systems in a large-scope technical internal audit), sorting the summary tables by vulnerability type is more practical. Frankly speaking, top management are unlikely to go through this final part of the report summary. On the other hand, it is comfortable to have a brief of all vulnerabilities in one place rather than skim through the entire description of vulnerabilities chapter. The readers of the report who are more technically inclined would appreciate it.

Table 10: A fragment of technical summary of findings

Summary of findings for host xxx.xxx.xxx.xx1:

Ref. N	Risk Level	Issue
6.1.1.	medium	HTTP – Cross Site Scripting vulnerability
6.1.2.	low	HTTP – HTTP TRACE method allowed
6.1.3.	low	HTTP/S – Disclosure of internal IP addresses, directories and files
6.1.4.	low	HTTPS – Weak cipher support
6.1.5.	low	HTTP/S – Test applications remain on the production server
6.1.6.	low	HTTP – Internet Printing Protocol (IPP) is enabled but not used

Summary of findings for host xxx.xxx.xxx.xx2:

Ref. N	Risk Level	Issue
6.2.1.	medium	ISAKMP - Aggressive mode with pre-shared key in use
6.2.2.	medium	ISAKMP – Weak cipher selection

The report interpretation chapter

The 'report interpretation' chapter aims to provide clear statements of the assessment scope and background. What exactly was tested? What were the main reasons for the audit? Is it a part of a continuous process building up upon results of the previous tests? It should also specify the assessment methodologies and techniques used. The auditee must know what they are paying for. They need to estimate how well the approaches that were employed correspond to their specialists' expectations. This might assist the auditee in judging the quality of the assessments, but, more importantly, it can also prevent false sense of security from creeping in.

In technical security assessment reports, outlining the methods does not mean going into a great detail down to the lists of used tools, configurations and commands. However, the report must state whether the audit is black, grey or white box, or if the intrusive or non-intrusive techniques were employed. It should note if multiple scanning tools were used in parallel and manual tests were performed. Any specific evaluation approaches towards assessing various safeguards must be outlined. Were the firewall access lists and filtering rules tested? How about egress filtering in the internal audits? Did the auditors assess centralised SPAM and malware filters, or intrusion detection and protection mechanisms?

For instance, a fragment from our current penetration testing reports elaborates that '*during the whole process of scanning we continuously verify that there are no interruptions in the assessed network functionality. The "noisiness" of the attack is gradually increased, thus testing the efficiency of the IDS/IPS, while also bringing the assessment closer to emulation of a determined Black Hat hacker behaviour. First, the services are tested for known vulnerabilities using slow-pace, cautious scanning. Only then any "noisy" fuzzing to search for new or unknown security flaws is performed.*'

Another relevant excerpt deals with discovery of novel vulnerabilities, stating that '*if such flaws are found, or a "purely theoretical" vulnerability is detected, a proof of concept exploit code might be written, applied and provided in the report Appendices and/or in the encrypted electronic format. Such code will not be made available to the public domain, unless explicitly authorised by the customer company or organisation.*'

It is also vital to declare what was *not* tested during the security audit for a variety of situational reasons. To continue with the external penetration test report example, *'no attempts were made to access the targeted systems physically, or by means of wireless-based, or social engineering attacks. No deep evaluation of resilience to various denial-of-service (DoS) attacks and poisoning of the external service caches has been performed during the tests in order to avoid serious interference with online business operations of the auditee. However, a few non-generic DoS issues have been discovered and reported.'* More often than not, the audit scope, objectives and hands-on methodologies are absolutely inseparable.

Finally, the 'report interpretation' chapter must provide precise definitions for all specific categories and terms used within the entire document. For instance, in *Figure 34* it covers all the levels and criteria of risk described in *chapter 6* of this book since this risk evaluation approach is presumed. As for any other explanations that should be included, they will strongly depend on the nature of the assessment. For instance, in technical audit reports we casually include tables that define categories of IPID and TCP sequence numbers randomness.

The bulk of the report

The 'reconnaissance' chapter of the report should present all the recon data in a structured clear manner. *Figure 34* represents it as split into Enumeration, Fingerprinting, Mapping and Discovered Abnormalities parts. In this division, the Enumeration corresponds to the overall listing of all uncovered targets and determination of their basic characteristics and types. The Fingerprinting goes further into details exploring a variety of separate target traits and their peculiarities. Mapping brings the recon information together in an attempt to generate the all-encompassing view of the entire 'attack surface'. Finally, the Discovered Abnormalities section should describe all deviations from the intended functions and standards spotted during the recon phase. Such oddities do not constitute vulnerabilities proper, or even security weaknesses. However, they can negatively affect the auditee operations and should be taken into account.

Continuing the previous discussion thread, in penetration testing reports the Enumeration section should cover networks, systems and their characteristics like the address ranges, domain names, packet paths, OSs, system uptime and so on. The Fingerprinting part should describe separate services and, where applicable, network protocols. The Mapping should bring all this data together by presenting applicable infrastructure diagrams. Such schemes show how the assessed networks and systems are seen through the external or internal attacker's eyes. In black box application security testing, schemes demonstrating the overall application structure, logic and data flows can be provided instead, if possible.

Finally, the Abnormalities section is dedicated to the discovered misconfigurations that do not present direct security threats. Nevertheless, as Dan Kaminsky pointed out years ago, '*network security and network stability are two sides of the same coin*'. A system or network that does not operate properly is harder to defend. For instance, such behavioural oddities can generate plentiful false alarms that can decrease intrusion detection and monitoring efficiency. If the flood of false alarms is relentless, it can render these important security functions useless. At the end of the day, deviations in applications, services, systems and networks operations contribute to the overall *self-induced friction*. The aim of any security assessment is to reduce it as much as one can.

The 'vulnerability description' chapter lists and outlines all the discovered security flaws, weaknesses and gaps. As previously discussed, depending on the scope of the audit this can be done in a per-component or per-vulnerability type order. A description of separate vulnerability we typically provide includes:

1. Vulnerability type
2. Vulnerability impact
3. Attacker skill level needed to exploit this flaw
4. Suitable remedy availability
5. Level of risk
6. Technical (or 'social') vulnerability description
7. Outline of the proposed remedial solution

Note that both points 6 and 7 should be sufficiently detailed to explain the vulnerability and its suggested remedies' nature and hands-on utilisation. They should not be too elaborate and extensive, however, especially if it means highly unequal distribution of attention and report space between different vulnerabilities that belong to the same level of risk. If a long detailed description of a specific security flaw and its elimination is clearly needed, it is better to move it into a dedicated appendix to the report. Any proof-of-concept code, screenshots, data samples and other evidence of the vulnerability exploitation should also go into this appendix. The vulnerability description should simply reference the appendix with such data.

The 'conclusions' chapter is akin to the report summary in bringing together important discoveries of the audit. Unlike the summary, however, the conclusions can be as technical as necessary, so that all the uncovered security issues are properly addressed. Nonetheless, it frequently tends to deal with them on strategic and operational, rather than tactical planes. The subject of drawing appropriate conclusions is of such utmost importance that the next section of this chapter is entirely dedicated to these critical matters.

Finally, the appendices to the report might include:

- 'crude' output of scanning and exploitation tools, or social engineering communications records where needed and considered as helpful for the auditee.

- representative evidence of successful exploitation, such as screenshots, lists of cracked passwords, retrieved sensitive data and so forth (see *Figure 29* and the corresponding discussion for more details).

- extensive highly technical descriptions of specific security issues and their remedies.

- exploit code.

- Other data deemed as important that does not quite fit the proposed assessment report format.

Some of the information listed above is highly confidential by its very nature. We wholeheartedly suggest that it should be submitted to a trusted auditee representative in person or in the encrypted form. The auditor's security policy must also cover retention of such data. It is best to delete it in a secure manner as soon as the assessment is over. If there is a need to preserve this information until the next planned assessment or for any other reasons, however, it must be protected by strong encryption and stored on dedicated secure systems only.

On drawing conclusions

*'The superior efficacy belongs not to the **means** but to the **end**, and we are only comparing the effect of one realised aim with the other.'* – Carl von Clausewitz

The general conclusions to the security assessment performed belong to both the report summary (primarily, its executive summary and risk review sections) and the conclusions. We shall start reviewing suitable and example approaches to drawing the assessment conclusions from the report summary part.

Explaining the overall security state

The first all-encompassing characteristic encountered in the report summary is the estimate of the overall security state. When discussing it, list the number of vulnerabilities that contributed to it and underline their general effects. A corresponding example excerpt from one of the assessment reports risk review is: *'The overall security state is judged as "insecure" since four high risk level vulnerabilities were identified. Three of these vulnerabilities allow remote access to highly confidential data. The fourth can be abused to launch attacks against third parties, thus creating potential legal and PR problems. There are also eleven medium risk level flaws, which is close to the number of their low risk counterparts (fifteen). Such a state of affairs is clearly unacceptable and requires urgent intervention.'*

More often than not, the 'insecure' state means that the target is vulnerable to both the determined and 'sweeping' automated attacks. The results of the breach are expected to correspond to the Severe impact level. The 'insufficiently secure' state indicates that there is more resilience to low-skill automatic attack approach, but the determined assailants are very likely to get what they want. The anticipated predominant impact of the attacks is Considerable or Severe. If the state is determined as 'sufficiently secure', the auditee company or organisation is still susceptible to a few medium risk level issues, which are likely to require significant skill and effort expenditure on the attacker's side. Take care to note the true extent of these issues' impact. As previously discussed, retaining a hard to exploit but Severe impact flaw is closer to a gamble rather than a thoughtful risk treatment approach. 'sufficiently secure' is not 'secure': these are different security risk categories!

Even if the overall state is evaluated as 'secure', it is not a reason to sit back and slack. First of all, this is the current security state, which can dramatically change tomorrow. Thus, an entity considered 'secure' on the basis of an audit should concentrate on security processes and controls that relate to change control. Besides, the auditee's professionals should clearly understand scope, depth and limitations of the assessment, as its final judgement is valid within these confines only. This is why the 'report interpretation' chapter and its descriptions of methods and techniques used are so important.

Elaborating on breakdown of risks

The next stage is concluding the breakdown of the overall risks summary. Check which impact, attacker skill and suitable remedy availability levels are predominant (if any). Gauge them against each other taking into account whether per-vulnerability risk estimates apply to the same or different security flaws. For instance, are Severe impact, User level and Non-existent suitable remedy vulnerabilities more common than Severe impact flaws that are easy to fix and hard to abuse? Or is it the other way? At this stage, a fine judgement of the specific circumstance is clearly needed. We strongly warn against 'assembly line stamping' of standard 'canned' conclusions based on the summarised risk criteria without taking into account all the peculiarities of the given audit findings. Nonetheless, some general breakdown-based inferences can be applicable to a variety of situations.

More often than not, the prevalence of Severe impact vulnerabilities indicates absence of proper defences-in-depth that could otherwise delimit the repercussions. This commonly signifies existence of major strategic flaws pertaining to infrastructure, application, process and overall ISMS design. Suitable examples may include situations in which:

- the breach of a vulnerable application provides highly privileged access to the system. It could have been contained by sandboxing or virtualisation, kernel level or other countermeasures, and adherence to the least privilege principle.

- the exploitation of a system gives direct access to highly confidential data. It could have been contained by using strong encryption; access to a DMZ server or corporate wireless LAN allows to breach the internal wired LAN. It could have been contained by secure network separation.

- highly confidential data was accessed because it was stored too close to the network perimeter (e.g. on publicly accessible servers), or on mobile computers. Alternatively, a social engineering attack has succeeded since far too many employees had access to confidential information. It could have been prevented by policies and their implementation mechanisms effectively controlling dissemination of the auditee's sensitive data.

A sample vulnerability impact distribution excerpt from one of the audit reports states that *'the presence of seven Severe impact vulnerabilities clearly points at the general lack of proper defence-in-depth architecture and highly flawed elements of the ISMS design. Five of these vulnerabilities are due to weak authentication credentials and methods, or weak file and directory permissions. This demonstrates serious problems with access control and password policies and guidelines, and/or their practical implementation. These problems are further underlined by the discovery that unprivileged user accounts and internal, but not confidential or highly confidential, information can also be remotely accessed, as indicated by existence of eleven related Considerable risk level flaws.'*

Prevalence of User skill level vulnerabilities typically points at low security awareness of the involved personnel, or low overall knowledge of applied information security. In relation to technical issues, it might signify the absence of a proper test environment with new insecure roll-outs being directly deployed to production and exposed to untrusted networks. In general, the skill level of defenders mirrors its estimated would-be attackers counterpart. So, if the majority of vulnerability skill level estimates are 'Expert', the auditee's professionals surely know their trade.

Human user skill level flaws commonly indicate total lack of appropriate security awareness training. This is clearly a policy or process fault. Technical User skill level vulnerabilities usually belong three major categories:

*   Easy-to-guess passwords (no proper password policies, guidelines or their enforcement).

*   Password-unprotected resources or unnecessary data disclosure due to weak or inappropriate permissions (no proper access control policies, guidelines or their enforcement, or weak data classification guidelines and controls).

*   Plaintext transmission of sensitive information (no data encryption policies or their implementation).

A sample attacker skill distribution conclusions excerpt from a black box penetration test report elaborates that *'nearly equal distribution of this level estimates indicates highly uneven approach to security of all tested systems and services. Effective centralised security management solutions and related policies and procedures are clearly lacking. Most likely, different systems and applications are handled by several system administrators with large IT security skill gaps between them. If a single person is responsible for maintenance of the assessed network, than his or her knowledge of hands-on IT security is sufficient in some specific areas only. Alternatively, several tested systems and services are viewed as less critical and thus ignored. However, the results of penetration tests demonstrate that if applied to this particular situation such an approach has already caused serious security issues, like the high risk level vulnerabilities described in this report.'* Further communications with the auditee pinpointed which of the anticipated reasons were the actual causes of the nearly equal distribution of the attacker skill level estimates observed.

The predominance of the Available suitable remedy flaws strongly indicates absence or serious gaps of vulnerability management policies, guidelines and procedures, or their working implementations. Slow or inadequate reactions from responsible staff counterbalance all the benefits of a solution being immediately and widely available. Thus, when the summary of per-vulnerability risks is finally reviewed, the borderline risk level values of *Table 8* should shift towards the increase. Appropriate technical examples might include situations, in which:

- some, but not all systems run obsolete and vulnerable services (no centralised automated patching and upgrade system in place, or its scope of application is limited).

- recommendations of previous security assessments are ignored (security audit mismanagement, also a vulnerability management shortfall).

- the fix is a configuration change and its distribution is highly uneven (weak centralised configuration management).

Abundant easy-to-eliminate human security flaws go hand in hand with the corresponding User skill level estimates. They demonstrate gross personnel mismanagement, lack of appropriate security training included. Quite often such mismanagement also involves misplacement: people who have divided allegiances, are security unaware, incompetent, negligent or naturally naive must not have any access to critical data and systems.

A relevant excerpt from one of our technical security audit reports points out that '*the fact that the appropriate remedies are readily available for all the uncovered vulnerabilities except two, but are not actually applied, demonstrates the absence or total disregard of effective systems and software security maintenance and change control policies and procedures. If these were in place and properly followed, our consultants would have discovered only two vulnerabilities instead of twelve. Alternatively, if the awareness of many gaps uncovered by this assessment already exists, the reaction of the tested IT infrastructure management to serious security issues is unacceptably slow.*'

It is not difficult to invert the aforementioned observations and examples, so that the opposite 'secure' conditions and situations can be concluded. However, we prefer to support the discourse from the 'negative' point of view. After all, '*advantages and disadvantages are interdependent – first know the disadvantages, then you know the advantages*' (Li Quan). It is finding the middle ground and inferring the results which pertain to the overall prevalence of medium-level risks that is the most difficult. This task is highly situational and usually demands taking into account large numbers of specific factors. Fortunately, more often than, not splitting the summary of risks into the integral components of impact, skill and remedy shows whether the situation tilts towards one of the extremes. This is also the reason behind our use of four and not three general security state categories, as shown in *Table 9*.

Further insights can be gained from concluding the estimated risks faced by separate large components. To refresh the reader's memory, depending on the nature and scope of the audit, these components could be:

- company branches, business units, departments, or service lines.
- project teams or other groups of employees.
- different types of premises.
- networks, systems or complex application modules.
- complete processes.
- sets of policies, standards and guidelines.

At this stage, it is vital to look for evident *risk patterns*. How uneven is the distribution of evaluated risks between different assessed components? Which large or complex components present higher risk? Why is it so? What lies in common between them on strategic, operational and tactical levels? Who has direct responsibility for their design, management, maintenance and information security? Is it the same members of staff, or employees sharing common background and previous training (or lack of thereof)? Are there any third parties involved? Are there also any apparent patterns of vulnerability distribution that clearly relate to their specific characteristics, classes and types? What are these patterns and how can they be explained? Answering these questions not only provides important elements for concluding the review of risks, but can also assist at establishing the actual causes of uncovered security flaws, weaknesses and gaps. Which is a subject we aspire to cover in the conclusions chapter of the report.

Depending on the volume of the security assessment discoveries, the conclusions chapter casually occupies one to three report pages. Its content is highly condensed and intense. The topics we might typically discuss in this chapter are:

- scenarios of attacks that exploit the evaluated security flaws on their own, or in specific sequences and combinations[3].

- security weaknesses that do not qualify as full-blown vulnerabilities and cannot be included in the vulnerability description chapter.

- examinations of critical vulnerabilities causes, sources and roots.

- descriptions of strategic and operational level security issues that became apparent from the results of 'tactical' testing.

- more general and generic (as compared to their specific per-vulnerability counterparts) remedial recommendations.

- risk treatment suggestions outlining what can be eliminated, reduced, retained or transferred.

- risk treatment prioritisation.

- suggestions regarding any future security/corrective actions monitoring and testing in relation to the existing and planned auditee security programs.

Analysing attack scenarios and trees

The attack scenarios form the essence of the qualitative risk assessment methodology and provide practical foundations for the estimated overall security state. Furthermore,

---

[3] If too numerous or extensive, the scenarios of attacks could form a separate chapter of the assessment report, placed between the description of vulnerabilities and the conclusions.

evaluating and reviewing these scenarios is an effective way to address present compound risks and systempunkt issues. Inevitably, it will include *'dividing any existing compound risks and complex security flaws into separate elements using the attacker separation approach and logic'*. The limitations of the description of vulnerabilities report chapter dictate that it can only cover standalone problems without the analysis of any possible connections in between. The conclusions chapter that follows provides an excellent opportunity to outline how potential assailants can combine them to reach the desired aims. *'The attack scenarios transform static descriptions of the uncovered vulnerabilities into dynamic, fluid, situational schemes.'* Afterwards, critical links in these schemes can be accurately identified. Such links correspond to gaps, closing which can completely *'ruin the flow of the attack, break the tactical exploitation cycle, or uproot the entire attack tree'*. Elimination of these security flaws should be at the top of the suggested corrective actions priority list.

It is advantageous to categorise the suggested scenarios in accordance with attacker effort and skill needed to execute them with success. To do so, contemplate where, how and how far the assailants can get if only the user (or amateur) skill vulnerabilities are utilised. Then add the administrator (or conman) level vulnerabilities into the concoction. Finally, supplement it with expert (or spy-master) security flaws. How different are the attack scenarios corresponding to the three estimated skill levels? Do they resonate well with the low, medium and high level risks uncovered? Which skill category scenarios contribute the most to the determined overall security state? Needless to say, when it comes to treatment of risks, the priority should be given to preventing the attack scenarios which do not require a high level of dedication and expertise from the opponent. However, there might be cases in which it is preferable to stave off high risk, severe impact and demanding skills scenarios first, as their easier-to-do counterparts are far less threatening. A related issue of deciding on the retention of risks while gauging their impact versus attacker skill level was already discussed in the previous chapter of this book.

Another feasible way of evaluating scenarios of attack is by looking at them from the specific threat, or estimated likely attacker's aims perspective. Taking into account all the discovered vulnerabilities, security weaknesses and gaps – is it possible to materialise the threat and achieve such goals? For instance, what needs to be done to obtain the trade secret, access personal data, or steal the customer database? How many steps would it take? What will these steps involve? Which uncovered security flaws will the assailants have to exploit and in which sequence does it have to be done? When these questions are answered, it becomes possible to estimate the level of attacker effort and skill required to reach the specific aim. Then, the conclusions outlining such an incident's likelihood, as well as the specific risk reduction plans can be deduced.

While analysing sophisticated attack scenarios that involve sequential exploitation of several security gaps, draw the corresponding attack trees or maps. You will find them incredibly helpful, and may even include such illustrations in the conclusions of the audit report or in a dedicated appendix. Security issues which are close to the attack tree roots or create its embranchments are likely to cancel the entire scenario or eliminate its vital parts if eradicated. If you prevent the initial breach that allows the entire attack scheme to proceed, the problem is solved. On the other hand, eliminating vulnerabilities that lead directly to the centres of gravity while being well behind the attack surface is a far-sighted approach that lies at the core of defence-in-depth. *'Thus, the most critical elements of the attack tree are likely to be encountered where it starts and ends, rather than in the middle.'*

From a strategic viewpoint, the structure and flow of a complex attack have their own centres of gravity, represented by these vital points of the attack tree or map. It is even possible to categorise them as schwerpunkts, nebenpunkte and systempunkts, as per *Figure 21*. Centres of gravity of the attack and exploitation process could also be reduced to a few key points and prioritised to assist the corrective actions. Then they can be effectively counterattacked by closing gaps that allow these critical attack elements to exist. Correct priorities are crucial. They enable addressing the whole issue presented by the attack scenario as soon as possible, thus getting inside the assailant's OODA loop. So, even the craftiest attack plots can be thwarted by utilising accurate scenario-based analysis of thorough security assessment results. This is the pinnacle of the defender's art, founded upon employing the attacker's perspective and mindset. It goes hand in hand with the classic notion of winning the battle well before it starts.

When examining attack scenarios or going through checklists in a more formal assessment, security flaws that do not constitute a vulnerability per se become apparent. For instance, the auditors may discover that there is no data leakage prevention or any egress traffic filtering at all where it clearly should be in place. Or that the use of instant messengers, social and peer-to-peer networks by employees is excessive and may be violating the auditee's acceptable use policies, not to mention open avenues for social engineering attacks and malware infections. Or, perhaps, highly confidential information is not strongly encrypted. All such problems clearly underline lack of appropriate security controls. They emphasise the distinction between what allows the attack (vulnerabilities) and what does not stop it when it should (absent or inappropriate countermeasures and safeguards).

The assessment report of a dedicated internal white box audit is expected to have separate sections that list and describe these issues. In black box assessments, however, their discovery is secondary to the evaluation of vulnerabilities. Quite often, insufficiency of specific controls becomes apparent only when the testing results are analysed and conclusions are produced. "The IPS should have blocked this attack." "The firewall should have not allowed such packets through." "The identity verification process must have stopped this social engineering attempt cold." These statements are not independent, but present inseparable parts of the examined scenarios of attack. The earlier examples in this book also demonstrate that inadequacies of controls frequently constitute components of a systempunkt. This provides sound reasons to outline important security weaknesses of the kind in the conclusions chapter of the report and in relation to the relevant attack scenarios or complex flaws. This approach helps to conclude which insufficiencies of the auditee's controls contribute the most to the ascertained overall security state.

Using vulnerability origin investigations

When pondering the place of a specific security problem in the general scheme of things, it is possible to determine its original source, as well as the true extent of its impact. The auditors should ask themselves the following questions:

- Which specific processes the vulnerable element is a part of?

- Which flaws in these processes could lead to this and similar security issues?

- Which security policies, standards and guidelines clearly relate to the uncovered problem?

- Which flaws in these documents, or their practical implementation and enforcement, could lead to this and similar security issues?

- Who are the people responsible for the design, management and security of the vulnerable element?

- What are their wrongdoings and why would anyone commit such errors or misdeeds?

- Do any answers to the questions above fall into or form a specific, distinct pattern?

More often than many security professionals realise, even the most peculiar vulnerabilities have several contributing source factors that can belong to completely different realms (*Figure 35*).

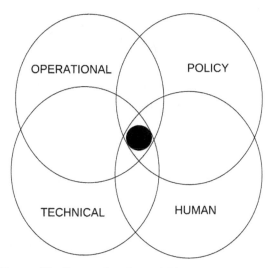

Figure 35: General vulnerability source factors

Numerous information security issues come to existence only if these factors are combined, as the intersection of the areas at the "black security hole" in the centre of *Figure 35* demonstrates. However, their contribution towards the flaw is typically uneven. Gauging this contribution correctly and determining which factors came first can be a very difficult task. Is it human resources mismanagement, inappropriate policies, inaccurate guidelines, lack of knowledge, controls, attention or time? Is it a third-party vendor's fault? Or, maybe, a different and more secure solution should have been selected at the first place? User attacker skill vulnerabilities are commonly a result of sheer human incompetence or negligence. Nonetheless, it is not always clear who and at which level of corporate or organisational hierarchy should bear the actual blame. In the majority of real-life situations it would be placed on subordinates by the management. If the true source of the problem has little to do with these subordinates' actions, however, it will persist, or similar security issues will appear. Finding a scapegoat does not make you more secure, and the attackers could not care less.

Figure 36 is a version of *Figure 35* redrawn in a traditional top-down hierarchical manner.

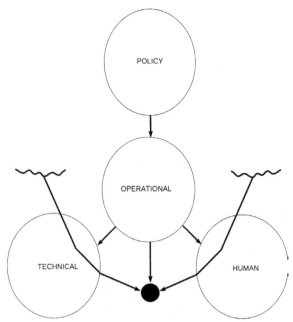

Figure 36: A top-down view of vulnerability origins

In accordance to this figure, strategic policy-level faults negatively affect larger scale operations and processes. The problem is then propagated downstream to technical and personnel levels, eventually producing a vulnerability. When discussing the influence of top level policies on the actual combat, Carl von Clausewitz noted that '*when people speak, as they often do, of the prejudicial influence of policy on the conduct of a war, they say in reality something very different to what they intend. It is not this influence but the policy itself which should be found fault with. If policy is right, that is, if it succeeds in hitting the object, then it can only act on the war in its sense, with advantage also; and if this influence of policy causes a divergence from the object, the cause is only to be looked for in a mistaken policy.*' He has summarised this issue by stating '*it is only when policy promises itself a wrong effect from certain military means and measures, an effect opposed to their nature, that it can exercise a prejudicial effect on war by the course it prescribes*'. Replacing "military" with "technology means" or "human resources measures", and "war" with "information security" in the above quote produces an accurate picture of common policy faults. In addition, the "influence of policy" can be referring to its upholding processes and operations, thus generating a scheme very similar to *Figure 36*.

More often than not, investigating the initial source of a major security problem can pinpoint relevant operational-level weaknesses. Consider how many security flaws are produced by poor processes of access and change control, employee background and qualifications verification, configuration or vulnerability management, software development life cycle, and so forth. Such operational inadequacies can result from:

1. *'defective strategic security programs, plans, standards, policies, and so on.'*
2. *'negligence in implementing and maintaining the proper ones.'*
3. *'a combination of 1 and 2.'*

The auditors should review all relevant documentation and processes to distinguish between these reasons. This amounts to an ISO27001-style ISMS audit. When searching for the vulnerability cause in a black box technical or social engineering assessment, however, it is frequently impossible to determine whether it is a wrong security policy, standard or program, or a correct one that was not properly implemented and enforced. This should be reflected in the report's conclusions, alerting the auditee team and letting them discover the truth themselves.

What if the origins of a vulnerability cannot be established, even though the assessment has supplied reasonably accurate data to do so? In our observations, such situations usually apply to either technical or human security issues. Hence, two arrows that cross into these areas from the external "great unknown" on *Figure 36*. If the skill level required to exploit the "unknown source vulnerability" is very high, then it is a likely case of a dedicated ingenious attack creating a gap in otherwise sufficient defences. What if it isn't? What if an easy-to-exploit vulnerability, yet unknown or of unclear origins, is discovered? There could be two feasible explanations for such an event. The first is the interference of pure chance. Even the most well-protected systems and security-conscious people are not invincible to accidental faults and errors. In such occasions, the flaw completely falls out of pattern of an otherwise secure entity. Thus, it is reasonably straightforward to determine and attribute it to friction.

The second possibility is sometimes observed in technical information security when an idiosyncratic, totally unexpected zero-day vulnerability is discovered. This is followed by quick release of an easy-to-use exploit (or a worm!) using such a flaw before suitable countermeasures are available. It is likely that the very first '419' spam mails or other unaccustomed social engineering attempts had a similar impact. Such situations closely mirror medical epidemiology. When a totally novel virulent organism is encountered by its first human hosts with zero immunity to this threat, a lethal pandemic could occur. The Black Death and smallpox attest to that with gloomy perfection. In essence, these events clearly fall under the Black Swan category.

We have already discussed dealing with chance and the obnoxious black birds via employing rapid adaptability and effective containment based upon sound defence-in-depth. If the entity is properly protected, unexpected errors and novel means of attack can degrade its estimated overall security state to 'insufficiently secure'. However, they should not make it 'insecure'. For instance, assailants might obtain highly confidential data utilising a zero-day exploit only to discover that it is strongly encrypted and cracking the key would take a million years or so. At the same time, the monitoring system generates alarms that trigger appropriate incident response and recovery actions. When the audit report conclusions related to this subject are produced, it is reasonable to elaborate that the vulnerability which allowed the breach exists due to error of chance, or cannot be effectively protected against at the moment. It is not a result of any systematic security fault, whether strategic, operational or tactical, policy, process, technology or human. Then, the conclusions should address the observed containment measures sufficiency (or lack of thereof).

Formulating the strategic conclusions

Drawing the deductions on strategic, high level issues uncovered by security testing is probably the highest point of the conclusions chapter and its key input to the executive summary of the report. This subject was already touched upon when investigations of vulnerability origins have been outlined. Other major hands-on assessment elements that provide strong contribution towards its strategic conclusions are:

- generation and dissection of the summary of risks.
- recognition and analysis of likely attack scenarios.
- discernment of patterns formed by vulnerabilities, security weaknesses and gaps.
- comparing the outcome of the current and previous security assessments.

If the security audit itself is directed at evaluation of policies, standards, procedures, processes and so on, its whole conclusions are already dedicated to strategic (or at least operational) matters. Alternatively, different smaller scale ISMS reviews can accompany technical or social engineering tests or, indeed, be triggered by them. In the latter case, they constitute a critical component of the follow-up corrective action. '*Where possible, the outcome of hands-on tests should be correlated with the existing security documentation, processes, programs and plans.*'

Scenarios of attacks, character and distribution of risks and their underlying security flaws provide potent indicators of high-level areas plagued by strategic faults. As an example, a single access control vulnerability can be safely attributed to friction. A dozen such flaws signify that access control policies are absent, inappropriate or completely neglected. If these gaps are evenly distributed, this is clearly the case. If they tend to concentrate within a single department or team, however, most likely the relevant policies are there, but specific responsible personnel are unable or unwilling to implement or enforce them.

Furthermore, compare the distribution of risks and corresponding types of security flaws between different systems (e.g. servers, workstations, network appliances) or employee positions and roles. Then do the same for the relevant operations and processes. Are there apparent gaps peculiar to any of the selected categories? What about the attack scenarios? Some elements and processes will be more engaged in their execution. Can it be due to weaknesses of relevant policies, guidelines, standards and programs? Which particular areas of the above are more likely to be involved? Generate conclusions stating that a certain group of employees, class of systems, or a particular process are proven to be susceptible to a specific attack approach or vulnerability type. Supplement them with an educated guesswork explaining why it could be so.

The conclusions of the report could also elaborate on the high-level issues nature rather than just the spheres affected. This is where our observations of various general strategic deficiencies can become helpful. They start as early as the introduction, where the pitfalls of prevalent cataclysmic approach to information security are outlined. Many of the strategic flaws can be deduced from the *chapter 1* fundamentals or outlined in its further discussions of aggressive defence and counter-offence. Finally, *chapter 2* is fully dedicated to such issues. Now it is a good time to revisit it. If you are a human resources or technical security specialist who found the second chapter to be of a little relevance for your everyday work, perhaps this ongoing discourse will change your mind. We shall briefly review typical security strategy blunders to assist in forming relevant conclusions of the assessment report.

It cannot be overemphasised, that all information security plans and their implementation must correspond to business aims, operations, models and processes. Lack of such correlation can be manifested on lower levels by major usability versus security conflicts, important business infrastructure elements, information and processes being inadequately protected, impact of significant business changes on security being totally ignored, and so on. Information security auditors should notice such an apparent discord and comment on it in the report's executive summary and conclusions.

Effective information security programs must be present and carried out to a full completion unless some dramatic shift of circumstances occurs. Then a documented readjustment must take place. They should be continuous without any major interruptions, reinforced by a strong vision, and centred upon clear mission statements and goals as potent rallying points. Successive, regular security assessments can determine whether this is the case. In fact, they are a form of monitoring the ongoing security programs via evaluating their practical outcomes. An abrupt degradation of the auditee's overall security state signals an important security program failure. Analysing specific factors that have contributed to such degradation can pinpoint which security programme or programme element has failed, and where. Besides, regular security audits can comment on the risk treatment tempo. Remember that we need to get ahead of the opposition. Persistently sluggish organisation-wide reaction to uncovered security issues is a major strategic problem in itself. Incomplete or insufficient reaction is a fault of security programmes that deal with risks and vulnerabilities management.

Failures of strategic security programmes and processes can be explained by bad planning and organisation, and resulting separate components desynchronise. The desynchronisation might originate from lack of, or ineffective vertical and horizontal communications between departments, teams and separate employees. We have already covered this subject in the second chapter: revisit *Figure 7* and its corresponding discourse, then contemplate the sections dedicated to the top-down approach and its shortfalls. A thorough ISMS audit must detect and analyse such problems. Its conclusions should elaborate what is disorganised, desynchronised or amiss (again, *Figure 7* should help). Even the tactical level, however, hands-on assessments can indicate the presence of these strategic faults. Why such a discrepancy between security risks faced by different large components exists? Is it related to the same or different processes? Were the results of the audit communicated to all members of stuff that should be involved in their review and corrective actions? How and by whom the assessment was handled? What about follow-up reactions to the previous audit? If its specific technical recommendations were followed, but their policy and other security management counterparts weren't, why is it so? An opposite situation is also possible. Search for the likely explanations at all levels: they must go into the report conclusions.

Lack of effective communication and organisation-wide propagation of the same security flaw with clear internal strategic origins are potential signs of what we have dubbed "the autocratic control and drill-machine approach". Another good indicator is mitigating tactical, but not operational or strategic vulnerabilities, weaknesses and gaps uncovered by the previous audit. The bottom was not heard by the top and bears all the responsibility and blame. Hence, they do what they can within their specific roles' limitations. This issue is difficult to reflect in the assessment conclusions and can be uncomfortable for many. Nevertheless, if it is detected, it must be described.

The next large set of strategic security faults can be grouped under the banner of unbalanced, or inordinate defences. The general term we have used to underline such situations is the Maginot line mentality. Of course, it is not feasible to state "you demonstrate a typical Maginot line mentality" in the assessment report's conclusions. They are more likely to elaborate that "the uneven defences coupled with insufficient defence-in-depth means are apparent". Or, perhaps, that "the listed information security elements are overemphasised at the expense of the following equally important areas, which creates exploitable security gaps". Lack of defence-in-depth is a very common representation of the problem. However, the perimeter line defences can also suffer from it. This tends to happen because '*the boundaries of the information security zone are not properly understood*'.

There could be a variety of reasons behind the unbalanced state of defences, reflected through strategic, operational and tactical planes. It could be a belief in some sort of a panacea, whether technical, human or operational, that should instantly resolve the lion's share of information security headaches. The shiny box with flashing lights mindset and its modern-day application and service equivalents outlined in the second chapter of this book are common instances of it. The narrow compliance-centric approach described in the same chapter can also be the source of the issue. If the areas or methodologies not covered by specific regulatory or compliance requirements are ignored in order to dedicate all effort to satisfying these demands, they will remain, or become vulnerable. To summarise, practically all situations in which we have encountered the unbalanced defences involved gross misunderstanding of information security fundamentals by the responsible management. This makes this issue strategic by its very nature. Evidently, the real lines of defence of any level and type cannot represent a homogeneous monolith. However, their unevenness must be based upon calculated analysis and treatment of risks, not misconceptions and lack of knowledge!

Finally, organisation-wide deficiency or poor quality of appropriate security documentation also constitutes a strategic flaw that must be noted in the assessment report conclusions. Not documenting information security intent, directives, standards, processes, procedures, methodologies and means signifies crass deficit of consistency and is a glaring form of negligence. At the end of the day, security documentation of any kind is an important (formal) mode of communication. As emphasised several times in this book, lack of effective communication could lead to formation or retention of gaps, and is a security weakness per se.

Determining the character of strategic faults is a more complex business than, for instance, pinpointing that the change control process is unsafe or proper in-house secure software development guidelines should be introduced. In the majority of cases, a thorough internal security audit which includes detailed ISMS review is required. However, the above discussion highlights that at times the presence and nature of such problems can be effectively deduced by analysing results of specific technical or human security tests. The earlier schemes in *Figures 8* and *9* provide general illustrations of such assessments' contribution towards accomplishing this intricate task.

On audit recommendations and follow-up reaction

'The essence of the problem is to select a promising course of action with an acceptable degree of risk and to do it more quickly than our foe.' – MCDP 1 *Warfighting*

The suggestions on treating all uncovered risks can appear in several parts of the assessment report. Advice on specific remediation of separate security flaws must constitute a part of the vulnerability description. More general and strategic recommendations, as well as any suggestions on dealing with complex vulnerabilities and compound risks, should go into the conclusions. Treatment of security weaknesses and gaps that do not make a fully-blown vulnerability on their own could be also described there, especially if they are related to compound risks or play significant role in any of the attack scenarios. Just like the scenarios part, if the general remedial advice is too extensive, it might form a chapter of its own that finishes the report. Alternatively, lengthy descriptions of mitigating specific security issues can be included in a separate dedicated appendix.

In technical and social engineering assessment reports, all per-vulnerability remedies are tactical and typically do not correlate with each other. Their descriptions must be brief, but very precise. If a configuration change is needed, a suggested configuration line should be supplied. If it is a question of patching or update, a secure version of the application or patch must be stated. In social engineering reports, what should be corrected first to prevent the specific attack against the given target has to be outlined. Recommendations like "provide security awareness training for finance department personnel" are far too general and should go into the conclusions. Wider scope technical suggestions, such as "consider installing an application layer firewall" or "consider deploying a DLP (data leak prevention) system" should be treated in a similar manner, as they address multiple vulnerabilities at once.

Delivering a risk reduction plan

Whether the assessment is directed at an ISMS, people or technology, its strategic recommendations should include a basic risk reduction plan. This is the approach advocated by the OCTAVE methodology. It constitutes an integral part of the OCTAVE risk evaluation Phase 3. This plan must be priority-centred. Time is essential: it is better to eliminate the most critical vulnerabilities right now than all uncovered security flaws in a few weeks. To prioritise remedies for risks belonging to the same level, review these risks constituents. While all high-risk problems must be dealt with ASAP, those that are easier to abuse and fix should have higher priority than their harder-to-exploit-or-eradicate counterparts. If doubts remain, revisit the descriptions of various modifiers in the per-vulnerability risk evaluation section of the previous chapter. For a specific situation, taking into account one or a few of these modifiers can prove helpful.

Ideally, a risk reduction plan should aspire to eliminate the actual sources of risks and address multiple issues at once. This commonly means correcting strategic, or at least operational shortfalls. However, dealing with such high-level issues can take a rather extensive period of time while being both effort and resource-consuming, and requiring extensive staff involvement. The detailed recommendations on how to do it can make the plan unnecessarily complex and even create confusion. Thus, subscribing to '*a good plan violently executed now is better than a perfect plan executed next week'* (a motto from MCDP 1 *Warfighting*) is a very sensible idea. So, what makes a good risk mitigation plan to include within a security assessment report?

Firstly, it should be concise. Then it should have clear priority and risk treatment sequence marking. Consider the following theoretical example of such a plan:

1. Eliminate high-risk vulnerabilities A and B.
2. Eliminate medium-risk vulnerabilities C and D.
3. Eliminate low-risk vulnerability E, since it can be used to enhance the exploitation of C and D.
4. Low-risk vulnerabilities F and G can be retained until more critical flaws are eradicated.
5. The set of security policies N is strongly related to vulnerabilities A, B, D and F. It is either flawed, or not properly implemented. Review N, its supporting documentation, and the implementation processes.
6. Introducing a security process X is expected to eliminate vulnerabilities A, B, C, D and F, as well as prevent any similar security issues in the future. Deploying safeguards Y and Z would have the same effects.
7. We suggest performing the next security audit of the same nature when all security problems described in this report are corrected.

The hypothetical vulnerability E is part of a compound risk. It is either a component of a systempunkt together with C and D, or constitutes a nebenpunkte in relation to them. Thus, it has a higher priority than F and G, in spite of formally belonging to the same per-vulnerability risk level. Point 5 of the sample plan is strategic in nature and can address multiple vulnerabilities at once. Point 6 could be a consequence of the previous point spanning into operational and tactical planes. By all means, it will require at least creating or amending the relevant guidelines upon the implementation.

Following the suggestions of 5 and 6 can do more than simultaneous *extirpation* of several serious flaws. It can prevent similar problems from happening thereafter. This is highly desirable. However, reviewing a set of security policies with all relevant downstream guidelines, manuals and procedures, as well as the actual processes is likely to be time-consuming. It is also evident that the solutions outlined in point 6 are not instantaneous and easy to deploy. Otherwise, taking into account the advantages they provide, these solutions would have had a higher preference than the specific tactical recommendations of points 1–4. In the example situation, the suggestions in point 6 would require additional planning, budget allocation, a pilot study, training for applicable personnel and so on. Meanwhile, the tactical remedies for all critical vulnerabilities must be applied ASAP according with the priorities set forth by the plan.

In the words of Clausewitz, '*if we quit the weak impressions of abstract ideas and descend to the region of practical life, then it is evident that a bold, courageous, resolute enemy will not let us have time for wide-reaching skilful combinations, and it is just against such a one we should require skill the most. By this it appears to us that the advantage of simple and direct results over those that are complicated is conclusively shown*'. According to John Boyd, strategic OODA loops spin slower than their tactical counterparts. We need to get inside the opponent's OODAs in order to win. In fact, many attackers do not have any strategies whatsoever. Possessing something the attackers don't have gives the defenders a strong advantage in the long run. Nevertheless, it is absolutely necessary to defeat the immediate adversaries on the tactical plane first.

- An important element of the sample plan point 6 is suggesting two different solutions, thus giving the auditee some choice and manoeuvre space. Whenever valid comparable alternatives exist, they should be suggested side by side. The differences between them should be briefly outlined, which could be done in the appropriate report appendix, or even during a post-audit presentation or debrief. This is one of the reasons why vendor-independent auditors ought to be preferred. Even if one remedy provides more advantages, or addresses the problem better from the auditor's viewpoint, the auditee's selection can be influenced by a plethora of factors. These can include:
- budget considerations.
- company politics and vendor preferences.
- internally available skills.
- estimated implementation time and effort.
- regulatory and compliance issues.
- compatibility with other elements, including those of partner companies or organisations.
- third party (e.g. service providers) relationships.

The auditors should explain why they think the suggested solution A is preferable to B and C, but the final word always belongs to the auditee's management. As a technical instance of such a situation, eradicating and preventing security flaws of a complex critical internally developed web application is better than deploying an application layer firewall in front of it. Doing so, however, could require a major overhaul of the existing software development cycle, extensive additional training, and even hiring a dedicated full-time software security specialist. This is a long process, which may not have sufficient funds allocated for it until the next accounting year begins. Meanwhile, a properly configured and maintained application layer firewall might well do the job while meeting the financial circumstance. It is also relatively quick to acquire and deploy, and can be an instant subscription service. PCI DSS requirement 6.6 offers a choice between the above described controls.

The final seventh point of the example plan advises performing a similar security audit after the reported flaws are eliminated. This highlights the role of information security assessments as a form of quality control. Every security audit should carry the seed of the next assessment within it. The previous section of this chapter argues that, apart from being an effective tool of security monitoring, regular auditing enables discovery of important strategic security issues which cannot be deduced otherwise. Nonetheless, security assessments might fall out of the planned schedule. Usually, this happens when demanded by change control procedures because major changes took place. It can also occur if an additional assessment constitutes a part of the follow-up reaction and its risk reduction plan. It could suggest verifying that all discovered critical flaws are fully rectified without additional risks being introduced. Such a recommendation typically applies to situations in which the overall security state is determined as 'insecure' and the problems are hard to eliminate.

Quite frequently, we suggest that the black box assessment should be followed with a logical grey box sequel. Or, that the external audit should be supplemented by further internal tests. This relates to evaluating defences-in-depth and discovering sources of security issues that are not clear from the current assessment's outcome. In a similar manner, the auditors might recommend that the specific technical, physical security or human security tests should come next after ISMS-centric reviews. Or vice versa. Whether to follow such an advice or not is, of course, up to the responsible auditee management.

Post-audit assistance and follow-up hurdles

Aside from the future scheduled or auxiliary assessments, after the report is submitted the auditors might participate in a variety of activities directly related to the accomplished tests or information security reviews. The most obvious ones are briefings and presentations, typically dedicated to:

- explaining to the auditee representatives all matters they find unclear in the report.
- giving a more technical or management-oriented overview of findings.
- discussing the recommended remedies and the risk reduction plan.

The latter might lead to a request for assistance from the assessors, who are often more experienced with the suggested solutions than the auditee's team. Or, at times, they can recommend a suitable third party that is a real expert on the matter. Any follow-up remediation work by the auditors is usually done for an additional charge, although it might be previously agreed to be a part of the expected service covered by the contract.

In our experience, the subject frequently brought up during such presentations and debriefs is deciding which risk treatments should be applied to the specific risks discovered. Which risks can be completely eradicated or partially reduced given the available resources, time and expertise? What about those that can be retained, and is it really safe? If any risks are transferred, then how could it be done, and to whom? To summarise, the auditee's team might not be sure regarding the precise course of the follow-up reactions and needs some help in making their decisions. This happens even when the risk reduction plan is to the point, and general suggestions on how to deal with various risks are provided within the report conclusions.

For a cautious mind, it is natural to verify all critical information one more time before any important decisions are made. When the volume of such information is high and its content is rather complex, it is easy to get stuck at the second O of the OODA loop. Besides, the auditee might have a different view of the situation, including the priority of some risks and their corresponding remedies, whether tactical or strategic. Before such differences between both sides are effectively resolved, the follow-up acts are unlikely to receive their go ahead. The auditors should aspire to understand financial, political and other factors that affect the other side. They should be ready to compromise, unless it would lead to retention, or increase the likelihood of emergence, of serious vulnerabilities and high level risks. The applicable wisdom from MCDP 1 *Warfighting* is '*as a basis for action, any decision is generally better than no decision*'.

There are several issues both the auditors and the auditee have to be careful with when solutions for the uncovered problems are considered and prioritised. One such dilemma is balancing the competing risks. In this book we are naturally concerned with information security risks and their reduction. However, a challenge might arise when acts directed at dealing with this important matter create other, security-unrelated risks at the same time. Then the risks collide, and the auditee is left at the crossroads, having to weight the competing risks against each other prior to deciding on the remedial and other security-enhancing measures and means.

The *resource-related risks* (budget, but also working hours, level of effort and resources of systems and networks) are the most commonly cited instance of risks that have to be gauged against their security counterparts. The subject was contemplated thousands of years ago, when the ancient Chinese strategist Mei Yaochen wrote that '*the more defences you induce your enemy to adopt, the more impoverished your enemy will be*'. On the technical side, there were times when introducing certain security measures, such as strong encryption, could put unacceptable strain on servers, workstations and network appliances. Nowadays, this issue still persists in relation to the security of embedded devices and RFIDs. Besides, even powerful servers can experience shortfalls of internally generated entropy. The entropy here refers to random numbers collected by an operating system or a specific application for use in cryptography. If it is depleted, the process of encrypting can become painfully slow and lead to serious service availability issues. To rectify this problem, the affected systems have to be upgraded, or external hardware sources of randomness acquired. If we are talking about a large scale installation, this could be quite costly. Is there a budget for it? This is a good example of technical details that are unlikely to be uncovered in the process of assessment, but should be taken into consideration when the suggested security solutions are reviewed.

Systems, services and applications usability can be viewed as a type of productivity-related resource. If the suggested controls reduce usability below a certain level acceptable for the auditee employees or customers, they become self-defeating. Thus, it is feasible to talk about competing *usability risks*. Note that such risks are relevant for operations and processes, not just technologies. If improving security of a process makes it too complicated with far too many complex steps for its users to go through, its usability risks can easily outweigh their security counterparts. Besides, sophisticated processes are more error-prone. The similar principles pertain to important security documentation, especially manuals and guidelines. As the end result, the auditee's friction goes up, which is completely the opposite of what a security assessment and its follow-up reactions should aspire to achieve. Again, the auditors can only guess which usability requirements are reasonable for the auditee, until this subject is brought up by post-assessment discussions.

Another competing risk that must frequently be considered when corrective actions are reviewed is the *risk of delay*. Here it refers to the downtime of systems, services, networks or processes due to treatment of security risks. It can cause productivity losses, employee and customer dissatisfaction, and other unpleasant effects. Essentially, *availability becomes the enemy of security instead of being its integral part*. The risk of delay is highly likely to arise if the evaluated vulnerabilities remedies are categorised as 'non-existent' or 'temporary', or are difficult to implement. It can be reduced by thorough pilot studies employing appropriate test environments. *'The more refined the processes and procedures of change control are, the lower the risk of delay.'* Take note that implementing strategic security improvements in practice can introduce significant delay risks. Since doing it is typically a lengthy gradual operation, however, good foresight and advanced planning can help a lot. For instance, important processes or parts of infrastructure can undergo major overhauls at the periods when it will put minimal strain on business, such as during the holiday seasons.

The last subject that needs to be considered in this section is the balance between different types of controls. As previously emphasised, effective solutions for security problems can lie within different areas. This is especially true when the roots of security flaws are eradicated. Resolving a technical issue can belong to the sphere of personnel management and involve training, disciplining, reassigning or hiring employees involved. Human security shortfalls can be addressed via technology, such as by deploying more effective authentication and monitoring systems, or improving existing channels of communication. Information security of various processes commonly includes both human and technological elements and can correct, or be corrected by them. When both per-vulnerability and more general or strategic remedies are taken into account, risk treatment recommendations provided within the majority of audit reports will affect several areas at the same time. The sample risk treatment plan we have reviewed can apply to both technical and social engineering vulnerabilities alike. It also covers security policies and their downstream documentation. No doubt, all corresponding processes will be also influenced.

It is vital that all areas that pertain to reduction of discovered risks receive due attention and effort. This is why it is so important that all of the auditee's relevant specialists participate – if not in the process of assessment, then at least in its follow-up actions. For example, if a social engineering-centric audit report suggests using specific technologies to rectify the evaluated problems, the corresponding technical specialists must be invited to review and contemplate its summary, recommendations and results. In a similar manner, if a technical assessment indicates a clear necessity of personnel management-related measures, participation of the Head of Human Resources or other appropriate HR department representatives is a must. Ignoring any risk treatment areas or concentrating on a single one at the expense of the others is an instance of the strategic unbalanced or uneven defences fault addressed in this chapter's previous section.

Overreliance on purely technical means is a very common error. On the one hand, *'those who cannot deploy their machines effectively are in trouble'*. (Du Mu) On the other hand, MCDP 1 *Warfighting* has a perfect summary of this approach's shortfalls:

- *'There are two dangers with respect to equipment: the overreliance on technology and the failure to make the most of technological capabilities. Better equipment is not the cure for all ills; doctrinal and tactical solutions to combat deficiencies must also be sought. Any advantages gained by technological advancement are only temporary for someone will always find a countermeasure, tactical or itself technological, which will lessen the impact of the technology. Additionally, we must not become so dependent on equipment that we can no longer function effectively when the equipment becomes inoperable.'*

When selecting technical remedies for any uncovered security flaws, the auditors should consider using existing systems and applications first, and consider deploying any additional safeguards second. Where appropriate, consideration ought to be given to what will happen if the suggested safeguard "becomes inoperable". '*Thus, the recommended security solutions should contain an element of redundancy.*' This principle might apply to non-technical recommendations just as well. The fact that the suggested technology-centric means cannot substitute their concurrent non-technical counterparts (or vice versa!) could be highlighted in the report conclusions.

Finally, whether the advised risk treatment means are technical, human, process or strategic, engage the auditee to find out which actions *that lead to elimination of high risk vulnerabilities* can be done right away. As the old boxing proverb states, "the fastest with the mostest is the bestest". By identifying and immediately using elements of remedial actions and solutions that are effective at preventing serious threats yet require little time to accomplish, the defenders can outrun their adversaries despite having complex large structures to protect. '*Some win through speed, even if they are clumsy.*' (Cao Cao) This constitutes the key method of getting inside the opponent's OODA loop.

CHAPTER 8: REVIEWING SECURITY ASSESSMENT FAILURES AND AUDITOR MANAGEMENT STRATEGIES

'The essence of strategy is not to carry out a brilliant plan that proceeds in steps; it is to put yourself in situations where you have more options than the enemy does.' – Robert Greene

Even if you studied and comprehended everything said in this, and other relevant sources on information security auditing, everything can still go terribly wrong. There are always some inevitable influences of chance, human error, technical fault and sudden environment change. Because of the latter, quite often both the auditee and the auditors have to make important decisions on the basis of insufficient information and in a very limited timeframe. This might lead to a variety of shortcomings on both sides, which can easily amplify their net negative effects when synchronised. As a result, a security audit or, even worse, successive series of security assessments could become a complete failure. To understand and know what needs to be done is one thing. To implement it properly is an entirely different matter. Especially, if it involves numerous people, complex processes, sophisticated technologies and unfavourable circumstances.

An information security assessment is unsuccessful when:

1. *'it does not address critical security issues of the auditee.'*
2. *'it fails to produce proper evaluation of individual risks and the overall information security risk state.'*

3. *'the follow-up reaction is insufficient, incorrect or simply absent.'*

In our observations, point 1 is more often the auditee's fault. This is the reason behind dedicating an entire chapter to pre-assessment planning and preparations, including the initial gap analysis. These are not straightforward, easy to perform tasks. The auditee team should not be ashamed to ask their auditors, or any other third party, to assist with the preliminary gap analysis if in doubt. Spending additional money for it saves a lot on the audit itself. It ensures that the right things will be done. Nevertheless, in any black box assignments that do not have a pre-defined set of targets (alas, they may have a desirable trophy) the responsibility of identifying and prioritising security issues is transferred to the auditors in full. Thus, it is a good option to consider if, for some reason, performing a decent pre-assessment gap analysis presents certain difficulties for the auditee.

Point 2 is usually blamed on the auditors, since this is what they are expected to deliver. In the majority of cases, such a reproach is entirely justified, unless there was clear lack of cooperation, or even obstruction on the auditee's part. This problem could stem from inaccurate pre-assessment planning, however, that could pick the right targets but err when it comes to preferences of relevant methodologies. A typical example is subscribing for basic vulnerability scanning when in-depth penetration testing is required. Or, if the black box approach is embarked upon where its grey, or even white box equivalents are far more appropriate. Also, it is worth revisiting the "audit the auditors" section of the forth chapter. Perhaps, if the auditors could not deliver a quality service, a different specialist team should have been scoped out in the first place.

In contrast, point 3 of the above is commonly viewed as the result of auditee carelessness, if not plain negligence and ignorance. However, if the auditors did not:

- clearly communicate testing approaches and results,
- accurately prioritise risks,
- suggest realistic effective remedies, and
- produce a workable risk reduction plan,

it is senseless to accuse the auditee in not acting upon the assessment discoveries with precision and vigour.

To conclude, depending on a specific situation, the actual responsibility for security assessment failures could be on either of the sides, or shared between both. The first four chapters of this book provided extensive coverage of the auditee perspective and some of the strategic fallacies they can fall prey to. In this chapter, the issues faced by the auditors will be accentuated to restore the balance.

On information security assessment follies

'The influence of theoretical principles upon real life is produced more through criticism than through doctrine, for as criticism is an application of abstract truth to real events.' – Carl von Clausewitz

A previous discourse has illustrated that dedicated attackers are able to create gaps by exploiting depth or breadth, or using a skilful combination of both approaches. Flawed information security strategies of the defenders could also produce gaps via insufficiencies related to depth (for instance, lack of suitable echeloned protection) and breadth (such as poor visibility of resources or desynchronisation of security processes and controls). In both cases, these shortfalls disrupt the balance of defences producing their unjustified unevenness. A flawless security strategy (if such thing is ever possible in practice!) compels the opponents to look for weaknesses of implementation. That is, if the adversaries cannot counter strategies, they are forced to attack tactics. The auditors can encounter, and should be prepared for, a variety of such situations while discerning information security issues on all applicable levels.

However, the organisation and performance of security assessments themselves are subject to very similar problems. It is fascinating to observe that the auditor's strategic follies often mirror those of the auditee! To remove any doubts, this discussion is not about information security issues faced by the auditors themselves. It is more akin to the reflections on 'weak points' of the attack structure and processes in the previous chapter's discourse on attack scenarios and trees. Security assessors have their share of strategic, operational and tactical failures that can turn any affected audit into a waste of resources, effort and time. We shall review them in a top-down order.

The fundamentals infringed

It is hard to provide a totally unbiased view of what security audit shortcomings could be. Especially, after outlining how, according to our estimations and experience, such assessments should be done. The first method that immediately springs into mind when looking at the issue at higher levels is to revisit the basic principles from the first chapter and see what can happen if they are violated. Where would it lead? Would it correspond to actual failures we have observed in the past, including, perhaps, some of our own faults? Would you recognise any familiar problems in

the following list of commentaries on the non-observance
of chapter one's fundamentals?

1. Breaking the first fundamental principle means not taking into account strategic circumstance of the assessment.

2. Its second counterpart also addresses important lower levels factors and conditions that cannot be ignored.

3. Violation of the third principle is reflected by failures to trigger appropriate corrective actions. As previously discussed, this could well be the auditor's fault.

4. The fourth 'incompleteness principle' brings up several critical subjects. One of them, the auditor's perfectionist attitude, was already discussed when this principle was outlined. It can be mirrored by 'false perfectionism': thinking and announcing that the accomplished assessment is impeccable and nothing else could be done. This is likely to instil a false sense of security in the auditee and is a blatant misunderstanding of the assessment's limitations and scope. Note that imperfections of a security assessment are reflected in the suggested legal disclaimer that should open the audit report.

5. Breaking the fifth 'continuity principle' destroys the assessment's value as a mighty security monitoring tool and eliminates possibilities to deduce several important strategic security issues, as illustrated in the previous chapter's discourse on producing audit conclusions.

6. Imbalance between the assessment tempo and depth signifies mismanagement and clear lack of planning on the auditor's side.

7. Narrow mechanistic perception of the audit scope and aims ensures that the sources and roots of many uncovered security issues will not be discerned.

8. Any security problem is somehow related to ISMS shortfalls. If these relations are not contemplated, the ISMS will remain deficient.

9. In a similar manner, if the actual sources of security flaws are not discovered and addressed, the audit is not fully accomplished, and its suggested corrective actions are incomplete.

10. If underlying strategic shortcomings are not discerned and rectified, any proposed tactical solutions will be no more than a temporary patch.

11. Without top-level initiative, a security audit would be a purely mechanical exercise at best. Any strategic-, or even operational-level advice will not be implemented. Or even heard.

12. Without the corresponding initiative at lower planes, the process of assessment will not be adequately supported, and its suggested remedies will not be properly implemented.

13. A failure of communicating the audit outcome to all auditee managers and specialists involved means that important areas addressed by the assessment will be misunderstood or ignored.

14. If the audit has produced sophisticated, confusing and difficult to accomplish recommendations and plans, it could easily turn into a useless exercise. Citing Clausewitz, *'far from making it our aim to gain upon the enemy by complicated plans, we must rather seek always to be beforehand with him just in the opposite direction'*. The assessment should shed light on the auditee's security state, not obscure it behind a hailstorm of ambivalent descriptions and vague terminology. Unless absolutely necessary to rectify

critical security flaws, any recommended risk reduction means should not make already complex processes and structures even more complicated.

15. A security audit properly executed, reported and explained has immense educational value for the auditee's professionals. This aspect of information security assessments is frequently underestimated.

16. The fact that descriptions of audit outcomes have to be clear does not mean its results are black-and-white. Failures of risk analysis that stem from unaccounted factors and underestimated complexity of the entire situation can easily lead to wrong conclusions and erroneous recommendations. The latter are particularly detrimental when it comes to remedial priorities in the risk reduction plan.

17. While it is better late than never, earlier is still better. If information security assessments are one of the very few effective ways to get ahead of the opposition and even negative chance, not utilising them as soon as favourable opportunities arise can lead to troubles in a longer run.

18. If security assessment conclusions and advice are clouded by any of the auditor's business or personal agendas, they may not reflect the actual auditee's security state and offer most appropriate and effective remedies and solutions.

19. If the assessors are somehow bound to auditee structures, systems, processes and so on, it would be hard for them to think outside of the box. Such auditors are unlikely to discern security problems and solutions that the auditee themselves cannot see.

Which, in essence, defeats the whole purpose of the assessment.

20. Breach of the security audit confidentiality is a grand disaster.

How many of the listed points clearly assign major blame to the auditee side? Point 5 is likely to do it, since the auditors are expected to be genuinely interested in providing regular services, if only for purely financial gain. Similar reasoning can apply to point 17. An assessment not done in a due time effectively responding to the auditee's request, however, can be a fault of the auditor's management of timetables and multiple customers relations. Points 11 and 12 are also more of an auditee problem, even though they might equally apply to managing the auditing team. Besides, security assessors should aspire to generate interest and initiative in the auditee to support their effort. This leaves us with 16 points out of 20 where the responsibility for failure is, to a large extent, on the auditor's side.

To provide a concise summary of the aforementioned and related issues, the major high level slips of security auditors frequently fall under the following categories:

- *Lack of strategic vision*

On the one hand, it applies to not being able to discern all factors and circumstances that apply to particular security assessments, their actual requirements, scopes, targets, expectations and aims. Besides, the auditor company or team must have a continuous strategic program of service improvement, of which all assessments are integral parts.

- *Desynchronisation*

An assessment can be out of synch with what the auditee actually needs or can afford. Desynchronisation can relate to targeted areas, depth, breadth, suitable risk reduction means, tempo and any specific (e.g. regulatory and compliance) needs and demands. There is also a potential problem of various audit processes being desynchronised within the assessor company or team.

- *Poor communication*

The problems of communication can negatively affect all interactions between the auditors and the auditee from the pre-assessment planning to post-report submission debriefs. It could also be an internal problem of the auditors, especially if the assessment involves specialists with different background, knowledge and skills.

- *Excessively formal approach*

When the approach to security auditing is too formal, it can easily become perfunctory. By reducing initiative and suppressing creativity, it can transform any presumably active security assessment to a purely passive set of tasks. However, even the passive information security audits can suffer from excessive formality. One has to be quite creative to generate quality checklists, or analyse results and produce high-level conclusions and recommendations for even the most standard and streamlined tests. Points 7, 8, 9, 10 and even 16 of the fundamental shortcomings listed above can be caused by the auditors being far too formal. In addition, unless the agreed conditions of the engagement strictly define all targets or even the testing methodologies to a minute detail, the auditors should not treat auditee suggestions as bona fide formalists. Recall the earlier *chapter 5* examinations of how different the critical points can be if viewed from the perspectives of the assessors and the assessed.

- *Bias, personal agendas and injurious politics*

These factors can lead to non-observance of practically any fundamental information security assessment principles we have reviewed. Violation of the very last principle for such reasons is particularly unsettling. They should never interfere with the assessment objectivity, veracity and effectiveness. If they do, sooner or later it will be discovered, disclosed and ruin the auditor's reputation. Disciplinary, legal, customer relations and other negative repercussions are highly likely to follow.

More often than not, these and other (e.g. skill- and organisation-related) problems are caused by incompetent assembling and management of the auditor team. This subject will receive its share of coverage in the next section. But, before that, various tactical and implementation security assessment shortcomings have to be contemplated in brief.

Bad tactics and poor tests

From a vertical perspective, tactical assessment errors often originate from strategic faults, like the ones we have just outlined. A horizontal view can be founded upon corresponding lover levels OODA loops being incomplete or improperly executed. This often suggests badly designed and orchestrated testing processes. The lowest plane at which security audit blunders take place relates to lack of specialist knowledge and skills. Of course, this problem does not materialise from thin air and signifies either insufficient or inappropriate training, mis-assignment, or poor personnel hiring practices.

8: Reviewing Security Assessment Failures and Auditor Management Strategies

In a tactical security assessment OODA the first O stands for recon. The consequences of improper reconnaissance are quite obvious: missing important targets and going after the wrong ones, or selecting inappropriate testing methodologies. Frequently, poor recon underlines lack of effective lateral approach. Metaphorically speaking, the auditors can spend days banging at the armoured front door while a window around the corner is wide open. In human security testing, there could be an obvious person who has what the social engineers want. However, that person is well aware of this fact, and is highly security conscious, vigilant and careful. At the same time, more vulnerable colleagues might have access to the very same trophy, even though it is not so apparent at first sight.

Selecting the wrong target by mistake can sometimes have negative legal consequences. Think what can happen if, during the test, a breach of data or systems occurs that was not authorised by the auditee and does not even belong to them. Or totally the wrong person is approached by a social engineer. We have heard of such blunders in relation to wireless security assessments, in particular their client-side evaluation parts. The auditors can hook up a wireless-enabled laptop to a rogue access point, breach its security, and then discover that this computer actually belongs to an employee of a different company or a business visitor. When wireless security tests are performed for an auditee that shares a large office building with other organisations, errors of this nature are highly likely and should be watched for.

Another common situation that clearly relates to this obnoxious issue is evaluating security of hosted services with resources shared between numerous client entities. The growing popularity of virtualisation, the Cloud and SaaS dictates that any assessments of such installations must be done with the utmost care and agreed in writing with such service providers. In these environments, it is very easy to target and affect another company's data, service, or entire virtual system by mistake. Besides, the last thing any security auditors would want is to accidentally bring down a critical application or element of infrastructure used by thousands of organisations, out of which only a single one is the actual auditee that authorised the tests. *'We strongly suggest employing the grey box approach when hosted multiuser environments are to have their security scrutinised.'* This, at least, should alleviate recon-related hardships.

Just like any stage of a process OODA loop, it is possible to get mired at the reconnaissance phase. In fact, this is a very common misadventure. Always allow sufficient time for the tests while splitting it between different assessment milestones and preserving the needed balance between them. Reconnaissance can take plenty of time, but it is rather predictable and can be thoroughly planned in advance. For instance, hands-on experience allows the auditors to estimate how long different portscans will take, or how quickly a sweeping social engineering mailshot is usually responded to. The same applies to physical security checks, for as long as the approximate scope and scale of the assessment are known. The only exception that makes such planning rather difficult is a fully black box assignment with their initially unclear range of targets.

The next O of our tactical OODA loop is orientation based upon reconnaissance results. At this critical testing process stage, appropriate targets, techniques and tools are opted for *and prioritised*. Unless we are talking about the specific case of mutation fuzzing, throwing everything but a kitchen sink at the targets is a very ineffective approach. It is also highly noisy and intrusive, which can cause a variety of troubles such as crashing evaluated systems and their monitoring safeguards. Unfortunately, many technical security assessors do just that by pressing the big 'select all' button of all-purpose vulnerability scanning tools without any regard to the target's nature estimated during the recon phase. On the other hand, good orientation allows you to decide which tests are the most suitable in a given situation, and which are clearly out of place and should be discarded. Then the priorities of carefully selected tests and their targets can be decided. This saves the auditors time and reduces unnecessary testing intrusiveness-related risks.

Proper orientation applies to assembling and analysing the whole picture, as well as examining its minute details. Inability to do the former means that the correlations between different elements of a complex evaluated target are not deduced. Further down the testing path, the same problem would inevitably apply to connecting together the uncovered vulnerabilities, security weaknesses and gaps. Thus, any systempunkt flaws will go amiss, proper attack scenario creation will become impossible, and both the analysis of risks and the assessment conclusions will heavily suffer.

In respect to considering the details, a good observation phase is expected to produce a massive amount of data. It is the orientation that assigns its separate bits with the implied levels of importance. If such assumptions are wrong, some weighty components of the evaluated target can be treated as insignificant and not worthy of any further checks. Personal convictions of the auditors can heavily interfere with orientation and result in detrimental misjudgements. For instance, it is possible to treat certain types of applications, systems, appliances, employee roles, and so

on as genuinely uninteresting, while in reality they might
hold the keys to a successful breach. Or become sources of
rather unpleasant passive security incidents. Hopefully, the
previous discourse on critical points and the strategic
exploitation cycle can assist in streamlining orientation and
avoiding common pitfalls that plague this stage of security
assessments OODA loops.

The soundness and accuracy of decisions could be equally
botched by specific preferences *and dependencies* of the
auditors. At the beginning of the fifth chapter we
highlighted that overreliance on a single general purpose
vulnerability discovery tool is a folly. In a similar manner,
it can apply to overreliance on a selected method, technique
or even a skill set. This type of problem can be summarised
under the banner of '*failures of adaptation*'. The so-called
'law of the instrument', or Maslow's hammer, states that '*if
all you have is a hammer, everything looks like a nail*'. We
can reformulate it as '*if all you can use very well is a
hammer, everything looks like a nail*'. In fact, the first part
can even be rephrased into '*if all you truly enjoy using . . .*'.
This shifts the accent from the instrument to specific skills
or personal preferences. Unfortunately, the surrounding
reality has a limited number of nails, some of which could
turn out to be screws under closer scrutiny. To aggravate
the issue, it also contains highly precious objects artfully
made of fine glass. Which is not particularly hammer-
friendly.

Common sense dictates that differing situations demand
dissimilar approaches. Thus, methodologies and techniques
have to be adapted to the audit circumstances and the
evaluated targets nature. Where necessary, new skills must
be learned and testing instruments suitably modified. Even
the purely passive security assessments presume accurate

selection and timely update of all appropriate checklists and corresponding automated toolsets. Nonetheless, we have observed plentiful violations of these basic tenets. For instance, on numerous occasions exactly the same procedures, methods and tools are applied to external and internal, black and grey box security tests. What are the reasons behind it? "We have acquired a great gimmick, so we have to use it." "We have honed this skill to perfection, so it must be applied." "It worked so well before, so why shouldn't it work now." However, everything has its time and place that can be accurately determined by using proper OO of the OODA loop.

Apart from various applications of Maslow's hammer, there could be other misjudgements that can negatively affect the auditor's decisions. For example, unjustified preference might be given to approaches considered orthodox, or unorthodox. As highlighted in the final section of the fifth chapter, at times simplistic and straightforward assessment techniques can be utterly neglected. Everyone knows that thou shalt not click on a suspicious URL link, right? Or, how secure passwords should be chosen – that's what the existing good password guideline is for. Of course, all users must have read this refined document and follow it to the point. Sometimes, a grand security problem lies on the very surface but ends up unnoticed. A far less critical issue is if complex evaluation methodologies or instruments are avoided because they are viewed as too sophisticated for likely attackers to use. However, are you sure that all potential adversaries share the same view?

Finally, if the OOD part of the loop is flawless, the act should be seamless and smooth. In practice, it is not always so. When we discard the inevitable interference of human error and technical fault (or anything else clearly falling under the general category of 'chance'), what remains is either lack of hands-on experience or plain negligence. The former will go away with training and time. The latter shall require some form of reprimanding or other disciplinary action. If such dereliction persists, however, it is also the auditor team management fault.

On assembling and managing the auditor team

'The subordinate agrees to make his actions serve his superior's intent in terms of what is to be accomplished, while the superior agrees to give his subordinate wide freedom to exercise his imagination and initiative in terms of how intent is to be realized.'
– Colonel John Boyd

The available sources that cover managing information security auditing teams are very limited and restricted to periodic or online publications. Perhaps, it is not considered an issue because such teams are usually somewhat limited in size. Or, when it comes to penetration testing or social engineering, it is expected that the group of testers consists of dedicated specialists driven, to a large extent, by sheer enthusiasm that provides cohesion and intent. At the same time, what we define as passive security assessment is often viewed as a mere mechanical routine. So, managing a team of such auditors is treated as business as usual and does not sufficiently differ from running a group of office clerks. Save, perhaps, for more in-depth background checks, since handling confidential customer data is inevitable. This might, or might not be the actual case. In our humble opinion, at least some elements of the auditor team's creation and management should be reviewed and highlighted.

On the assessment team ordnance

The composition of the auditor team is strongly determined by its mission and most likely assignments. The services offered can be highly specialised, for example, source code security auditing, selected standard compliance or physical security checks. In a very specific, narrow field of knowledge this could even be a one-man job. However, more often than not information security companies aspire towards the Jack-of-all-trades operating model, so that a wide variety of customer requests can be answered. The same applies to internal security auditor teams of large corporations, although these have a tendency to lean towards attracting experts in solutions form selected vendors commonly used by the enterprise. If the major overhaul of IT infrastructure occurs, such technical specialists can be re-trained or replaced.

A well-rounded Jack-of-all-trades security auditing team should at least have:

- *An application security specialist*

In the current technical environments and market conditions this is an absolute requirement. Skilful application security consultants are typically security-oriented programmers capable of performing some reverse engineering work and writing (or modifying) the needed testing utilities.

- *A network security engineer*

While this role is beneficial when running external technical assessments – for instance, in doing recon and evaluating security of remote access means – keep in mind that, for their internal counterparts, a good knowledge of network-centric security is a must. If there is no dedicated wireless security consultant in the team, a network security engineer must be able to handle these assignments as well. Another important area of testing that should be covered by these specialists is VOIP and virtual environments security assessments.

- *'An expert in common technical safeguards, such as firewalls, IPS/IDS, monitoring and authentication systems, and VPNs'*

In a very small team this role might be appropriately shared between the network security engineer and the application security specialist. Alas, it pays to have a dedicated full-time professional since the modern safeguards are both abundant and increasingly sophisticated. Notice that, apart from examining the safeguards, this specialist can play an important role when the advice on remedies and solutions for the uncovered security weaknesses, gaps and flaws is considered.

- *'A social engineer'*

Basic social engineering tests over the Internet or even telephone can be performed by other information security consultants. If human security evaluation assignments are complex and involve personal contact, however, it is advantageous to have several dedicated social engineers available. Perhaps they could be hired from a known and trusted pool on a temporary contract basis. The obvious problem with any visual or voice contact with regular testing targets is that the auditee's employees are likely to remember the social engineer and will not fall for his or her tricks again.

- *'An ISMS specialist also versed in the areas of risk assessment, regulations, compliance and applicable laws'*

Apart from executing security management-centric audits like documentation and processes reviews, or assisting with any audit-related compliance issues and needs, these professionals can be of a great value when estimating risks and producing conclusions of lover level assessment reports. In addition, they make perfect negotiators with auditee managers of all sorts, being able to speak their language and address their doubts and worries.

Thus, at the very minimum and if some of the listed critical roles are combined, a decent security auditing team must contain at least 3–4 full-time professionals highly skilled in the aforementioned areas. An individual person cannot absorb such different spheres of competence without sacrificing their level of comprehension, proficiency and depth. If the auditor team is quite large and has narrowly focused experts (such as full-time security compliance consultants, malware specialists, wireless security engineers, or dedicated vulnerability researchers) on board, shortfalls of effective communication between its members can become a rather demanding issue. Another obstacle that could easily arise is synchronising testing procedures, processes, and their end results. A designated role of experienced security audit team manager becomes a requirement for proper fulfilment of its purpose.

The discussion above is centred upon specialist competence and skill sets only. Nonetheless, there are more factors pertaining to the audit team structure *and function* that have to be taken into account. They relate to the auditors' natural cerebral capabilities and mindsets. Many years ago and in a place far away, one of the authors of this book played a popular team-based televised quiz game called the Brain Ring. The official rules of the Brain Ring were as follows:

- The questions must be composed in a way their answers could be guessed. Thus, it was not a direct knowledge/good memory exercise as the bulk of quiz games are.

- It was played team against another team or two. A team consisted of six people.
- After a start signal, whichever team presses the button first and provides the correct answer wins a point.
- Otherwise, the right answer must be provided within a minute.
- If no one gives the correct answer, the next question follows.
- The team that scores a pre-defined number of points first wins.

So, the game required its players to deduce the right answer in a reasonably large group and in the shortest time possible. It became apparent that, in order to gain the upper hand, the team must be structured and operate in a certain way (*Figure 37*).

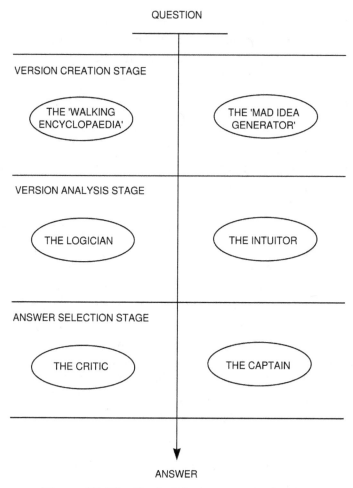

QUESTION

VERSION CREATION STAGE

THE 'WALKING ENCYCLOPAEDIA'

THE 'MAD IDEA GENERATOR'

VERSION ANALYSIS STAGE

THE LOGICIAN

THE INTUITOR

ANSWER SELECTION STAGE

THE CRITIC

THE CAPTAIN

ANSWER

Figure 37: The Brain Ring team organisation

The answer generation process is split into three phases. At the first stage, different versions of the answer are produced. If the relevant direct knowledge is available, the 'walking encyclopedia' player supplies the most likely answer. However, if this is not the case, this player can still give some information potentially related to the question subject. The main attribute of the walking encyclopedia is, thus, an extensive and powerful memory. In contrast, the 'mad idea generator' is the player with the highest level of creativity and lateral, or unorthodox thinking. They are the 'what if' person – the 'living fuzzer'. If no obvious version of a potentially correct answer is in the air, the mad idea generator can supply a wide variety of useful insights on what this answer might be. Obviously, such insights need further scrutiny. In fact, the walking encyclopedia is not flawless and could also err.

So, the next answer analysis stage kicks in. The players with the strongest logical reasoning and intuition in the team apply their capabilities to the outcome of the first phase. Besides, they can also deduce or viscerally discern the answer themselves, especially if this outcome is highly inconclusive. At the end of the second answer generation stage, a few relatively refined versions are likely to be produced. These are attacked by the critic – the most sceptical, incredulous and sober-minded member of the team. The critic finds flaws in the proposed answer variants and discards those that are clearly at fault. The final word belongs to the team captain. This player decides:

- which precise version of the answer will be given,
- how it will be formulated (badly worded answers can be rejected by the jury), and
- who will answer (this is important to fulfil the previous points).

The captain is usually the player who presses the button. He or she also oversees that the answer generation process runs smoothly and all members of the team have their say. It is the team manager, strategist and psychologist all in one breath. Typically, it was the captain that has assembled the team at the first place.

To complete this Brain Ring interlude, notice that:

- the answer generation process we have described takes seconds to accomplish (or a minute at its best if the other team is indecisive or wrong).

- it forms a perfect OODA loop with pressing the button and giving the answer for 'Act'. The aim of the game is to get inside the other team's OODA.

- the left and right sides of *Figure 37* roughly correspond to what psychologists onced viewed as left and right human brain functions.

There is a lot that could be learned from it. Take *Figure 37* and replace "question" with "the problem", and "answer" with "the remedy" or "the solution".

A very similar process with its stages and roles can be applied to many important information security assessment tasks, especially if handled by a group of professionals with similar areas and levels of expertise and skills. For example, it could be used when deciding upon audit tactics, gauging risks, producing assessment conclusions, contemplating suggested remedies and generating risk reduction plan. The described process is reusable, adaptable and flexible. As far as the auditor team goes, it might consist of three professionals only, or two dozen of them. Just like with the specialist skill sets, in a very small team an individual member can share several of the listed player roles. Its large counterpart might have a collective logician, intuit, mad idea generator (hence, the practice of group brainstorming) or critic. There could be several walking encyclopedias in respect to different spheres of competence. However, to preserve *the unity of command* there should be only one captain.

In his "Avoiding the snares of groupthink: the command and control strategy" chapter of *The 33 Strategies of War*, Robert Greene provides sound advice on building and managing effective teams attuned to rapid and adaptable complex tasks. By "groupthink", he refers to '*the irrationality of collective decision making*', stating that '*the need to find a compromise among all the different egos kills creativity. The group has a mind of its own, and that mind is cautious, slow to decide, unimaginative, and sometimes downright irrational*'. We are aware of other definitions and descriptions of the groupthink anti-pattern in various management-related publications, but for the purpose of this discourse they are of no concern.

Since every bird likes its own nest, when specialists with very different areas of in-depth expertise and skills are intermixed into a single group, the problem is aggravated by the necessity to compromise between professional views. Everyone would like to assign the highest priority and importance to their particular methods, targets and findings. Application security specialists will insist that the software flaws they have discovered should be addressed first in the report summary, conclusions, and the suggested risk reduction plan. Network security or social engineers might disagree. At the same time, an ISMS specialist could say '*all your discoveries are interesting and fine, but this is what the auditee really need in order to be compliant to <insert the standard or regulation here>, and the compliance audit is looming*'.

To give all members of the team their say, synchronise their approaches, operations and findings, produce well-founded prioritisation of risks, accurate assessment conclusions and apt risk reduction advice, a sole experienced and qualified 'final word authority' is necessary. Without such unity of command, chaos will inevitably reign. In the technical parlance, a situation of this kind is sometimes ironically referred to as the 'design by committee'. This term implies poor results of insufficiently unified vision and divided leadership in "let's get together and do the job that will please us all" projects. Remove the central OODA loop from the scheme depicted in *Figure 7* and contemplate likely repercussions. The auditors have their strategic processes too, even though they might not strictly conform to PDCA. As suggested by Robert Greene in relation to this highly critical issue, *'rely on the team you have assembled, but do not be its prisoner or give it undue influence'*.

Another advice he has provided is *'never choose a man merely by his glittering resume. Look beyond his skills to his psychological makeup'*. This statement can have various interpretations. For instance, it might relate to verifying personal background and any related undesirable traits like being particularly arrogant and conflict-prone, or unable to sustain serious commitments. Nonetheless, it might be also viewed in the light of the elaborated team-based solution-seeking process. Apart from the requisite focused specialist skills, do you think that the auditor team needs the walking encyclopedia or the mad idea generator? Would it be more advantageous to get a logician, or someone who can sense the situation well due to having rich previous experience? Or, may be the critic is rather indispensable to assure the accuracy of security audit results and their interpretations? Do you require an independent creative thinker to participate in active security assessments, or someone more meticulous and persistent to handle their large-scale passive counterparts' routine?

Note that these matters apply equally to hiring people and assigning already available professionals to perform specific tasks. In the latter case, keep in mind that, depending on the character of engagement, the discerned process roles can alternate. A walking encyclopedia in a particular area of expertise could make a great logician in a somewhat different field. The logician in one sphere of competence might make a perfect mad idea generator in the other. Where necessary, the captain may pull up the sleeves and do the job of a critic or intuit. Taking notice of such 'situational artefacts' and using them when similar circumstances arise the next time can tremendously expand capabilities of the auditor team.

Of serpents and eagles

What about more specific inclinations and traits of relevant professionals and any influence these might exert on running an effective information security assessor team? Much was said about the so-called hacker mindset. To summarise, it is usually described as the combination of unorthodox lateral thinking with the 'disassemble and/or reassemble everything' attitude. Previously, we have highlighted that this approach can be applicable to a wide selection of information security auditing engagements. It is entirely possible to be quite 'hackish' in analysing the ISMS. Conversely, hands-on technical or social engineering testing, commonly viewed as 'the hacker's playground', can be reduced to repetitive and methodical template chores. Notwithstanding, generating, correcting and modifying these templates could be quite a challenging and creative task. Thus, a hacker mindset is generally desirable for an information security auditor of any kind and should

be encouraged and looked for. When coupled with highly
focused specialisation, however, it can have interesting side
effects on the human mind.

For instance, such a combination frequently leads to what
can be labelled as 'tunnelled lateral thinking'. This mindset
is capable of generating rather ingenious ideas, but within
particular area limits only, and not without contamination
by Maslow's hammer law. Because of the former, the latter
influences and constrains are not realised, or are even
actively denied. Consequently, shrewd and hard-headed
tacticians who are not very responsive to outside advice
from anyone not matching their advanced degree of
specialist expertise are produced. These professionals
surely know their job and do it well. At the same time, they
do not like to be bothered by instructions and tend to treat
strategic level inferences and intents as big and impractical
words. This does not help in directing a highly skilled
security assessor team where this way of thinking is clearly
predominant. Which is often the case.

A popular notion regularly applied to handling a team of
software developers compares it to herding cats. If we have
attempted to write an article about managing a group of
hardcore information security testing experts, we would
probably entitle it "How to herd serpents".

A venomous snake is a highly evolved organism well-
adjusted to its habitat. For an outside beholder, its strike is
swift and effective, but comprises somewhat limited
options of movement. Unless the observer is an expert
toxicologist, the complexity of the snake venom
composition is completely eluded and not given a deep
thought. In reality, typical snake venom contains dozens of
select components that specifically target any creature the

snake can encounter in its natural milieu. All of them are also optimised to produce the exact desired effects, such as paralysing the prey in a given period of time. This can be compared to a dexterous and advanced attack toolkit, or a scrupulous collection of working exploits attuned to the likely target systems range. Combine it with the economy of action and formidable speed, and you shall penetrate the mystery of the snake.

However, to list the relevant allegoric issues:

- Generally, snakes do not hunt in packs (zoologists say some sea serpents do, however, so it is not impossible in principle).

- Snakes have no outer ear and do not hear sounds travelling through the air well (they are not deaf, however: they have their very own way of hearing).

- They have a rather peculiar vision, often attuned to objects up close while ignoring the 'irrelevant' far away.

Thus, anyone who would want to collaborate with the metaphorical serpents would have to develop distinct communication modes that appreciate their specificity.

In contrast, the power and sweep of the eagle's eye, amalgamated with the ability to reach high altitudes has earned it a well-deserved place in this book's introduction. We used it to illustrate the strategic connotations of the 'bird's-eye view' idiom. At the same time, an eagle has a wide variety of striking options combining its beak, claws and wings. It is also just as swift as any snake could be. What it lacks is the highly specialised venom that our serpents possess. Besides, when objects are covered by thick darkness the eagle's sight strongly deteriorates. Snakes have their own 'technical' method of detecting important objects in the dark – they sense their temperature. A far-sighted and soaring, but not highly focused on minute technical details, strategist within the team of more field-specific experts is akin to eagle amongst the serpents. Whether they realise it or not, they surely need one. The eagle's scope of vision and perspective enable correlation between distant objects or events, and ensure enduring, rather than temporary success.

In fact, an information security auditor team should have two types of a strategist on board. One of them must be directed at the team itself, defining and maintaining its long-term, large-scale development goals, intent, programs and plans. This is typically the role of the dedicated team manager. The other kind should be focused on the strategic aspects of different information security assessments per se. These, as was elaborated earlier and in a great detail, include assembling and disassembling the summary of risks, producing high level conclusions and risk reduction advice, and so forth. This could be the ISMS expert within the group, even though depending on its composition and aims other viable alternatives are possible. If there is a need to formalise these important roles, the first can be called the internal (centred on the auditors), and the second – the external (focused on the auditee) strategist. Again, in a small team that handles a limited number of customers both roles can sometimes be fulfilled by the same person.

However, could the same individual perfectly combine both tactical and strategic functions without losing the offered security assessment services quality and depth? In theory, this is possible. The phenomena of the winged serpent are widely reported in dragon-centric mythology but are, apparently, exceptionally rare to be seen. So, how can we reach the productive union between the eagle and the snake? The 'Boydian approach' towards flexible and adaptive command and control, or *leadership-monitoring-appreciation-error correction flow*, is as directly relevant for the auditors as it can be. To quote Colonel John Boyd himself:

- *'decentralize, in a tactical sense, to encourage lower-level commanders to shape, direct, and take the sudden/sharp actions necessary to quickly exploit opportunities as they present themselves. Centralize, in a strategic sense, to establish aims, match ambitions with means/talent, sketch flexible plans, allocate resources, and shape focus of overall effort'.*

Now you can simply substitute the "*low-level commanders*" with the "*narrowly focused specialists*" to get an accurate, eagle-sighted recommendation.

Science and art of information security evaluation

'Science must become Art.' – Carl von Clausewitz

In medieval times, being able to follow the approved 'traditional' recipe to the last detail was considered a hallmark of a master artist or craftsman. It was aspired to as the pinnacle of advancement. Later, when the Renaissance arrived, some deviation from the prescribed standards finally became acceptable. As time passed by, this slack widened more and more, providing the necessary space for innovation and the unorthodox. The norms were broken, stereotypes discarded, and new principles created from the ashes of the old. Eventually, this process brought us the Enlightenment, then the Industrial Revolution, and then modern science and engineering as we know it. At the same time, valid discoveries of the past were not dismissed and remain in good use, not to mention that we still marvel at artworks by maestros of old. At least in Europe, this entire transformation of scholastics and craft into science, art and contemporary engineering took about a millennium. Notice that the arts were leading, and sciences following.

Forty years ago, the bulk of critical information was still disseminated by personal contact, on paper, over the phone, or via unencrypted radio transmissions. The first message over the ARPANET was sent at 10:30 pm on 29 October, 1969. It was supposed to be 'login', however the system crashed and it turned into "lo". So, the very first remote login over a packet switching network has encountered a severe availability problem, which could also be viewed as a passive security incident of a kind. Back in the nineties, the greater part of hackers, even the most malicious ones, were computer enthusiasts who wanted to prove some point. A phrase commonly ascribed to Kevin Mitnick is "because I can". Nowadays, it is either cyber criminals – casually linked to organised crime with established money laundering channels – foreign government organisations, corporate spies, or sly insiders advancing their personal agendas via illicit means. To effectively counter these rapidly developing threats, information security must fully evolve into proper science and art as we speak. This cannot wait for centuries to happen. Information security auditing, which is more of an art right now, could take the lead.

Unfortunately, rigid approaches to information security assessments that can be clearly described as 'craft and scholastics' are still abundant. And they do have numerous acolytes. Security auditors that strictly follow exact prescriptions – whether coming from standards, textbooks or various forms of professional training – strongly resemble medieval craftsmen. Their colleagues, who fiddle with these prescriptions applying limited creativity and imagination, are their counterparts from the Renaissance times. This would not address modern day information security threats and risks. Especially when it comes to deliberate, planned and timely attacks that tend to come as a total surprise.

When discussing the art of (military) intrusion, MCDP 1 *Warfighting* elaborates that:

- *'There are three basic ways to go about achieving surprise. The first is through deception – to convince the enemy we are going to do something other than what we are really going to do in order to induce him to act in a manner prejudicial to his own interests. The intent is to give the enemy a clear picture of the situation, but the wrong picture. The second way is through ambiguity – to act in such a way that the enemy does not know what to expect. Because he does not know what to expect, he must prepare for numerous possibilities and cannot prepare adequately for any one. The third is through stealth – to deny the enemy any knowledge of impending action. The enemy is not deceived or confused as to our intentions but is completely ignorant of them.'*

A proper information security assessment should be able to counter all three key elements of surprise. The adversaries' options are very much limited by their targets weaknesses. *Deception* can be confronted with thorough reconnaissance and evaluation of security gaps. This produces the right information security picture that no opponents are able to distort. *Ambiguity* can be defeated by decent analysis and prioritisation of risks. Thus, their reduction will be fully adequate. *Stealth* can be refuted with select measures based upon detailed scenarios of attacks. These scenarios should exhaust all valid choices potential assailants might have. However, there is no universal panacea recipe that can successfully stand against the all three.

Instead, the auditors need to adopt a flexible, evolving system or framework of knowledge based upon extensive observations and security research. This is the science half. By having a go at formulating fundamental information security auditing principles and systematising strategic, operational and tactical assessment approaches, we have tried our best to advance it as far as we could. It might be a complete failure, and it is up to the readers to judge – on the grounds of their own practice either as auditors or the audited. This living experience, in fact, constitutes the art side of the subject. The only way to express the art of information security auditing is via effective action and its wholesome results. Incidentally, this is exactly how Carl von Clausewitz distinguished between science and art:

- *'Science when mere knowing; Art, when doing is the object. The choice between these terms seems to be still undecided, and no one seems to know rightly on what grounds it should be decided, and yet the thing is simple. We have already said elsewhere that knowing is something different from doing. The two are so different that they should not easily be mistaken the one for the other.'*

The further astute, apt and detailed definitions of both based upon strength of their actual applicability and functionality is provided within MCDP 1 *Warfighting*:

- *'Various aspects of war fall principally in the realm of science, which is the methodical application of the empirical laws of nature. However, science does not describe the whole phenomenon. An even greater part of the conduct of war falls under the realm of art, which is the employment of creative or intuitive skills. Art includes the creative, situational application of scientific knowledge through judgement and experience, and so the art of war subsumes the science of war. The art of war requires the intuitive ability to grasp the essence of a unique military situation and the creative ability to devise a practical solution. It involves conceiving strategies and tactics and developing plans of action to suit a given situation'.*

This excerpt provides a perfect substrate for the very final substitution exercise to conclude this tome, as we could not agree more.

ITG RESOURCES

IT Governance Ltd sources, creates and delivers products and services to meet the real-world, evolving IT governance needs of today's organisations, directors, managers and practitioners.

The ITG website (*www.itgovernance.co.uk*) is the international one-stop-shop for corporate and IT governance information, advice, guidance, books, tools, training and consultancy. On the website you will find the following pages related to the subject matter of this book:

www.itgovernance.co.uk/infosec.aspx

www.itgovernance.co.uk/iso27001.aspx.

Publishing Services

IT Governance Publishing (ITGP) is the world's leading IT-GRC publishing imprint that is wholly owned by IT Governance Ltd.

With books and tools covering all IT governance, risk and compliance frameworks, we are the publisher of choice for authors and distributors alike, producing unique and practical publications of the highest quality, in the latest formats available, which readers will find invaluable.

www.itgovernancepublishing.co.uk is the website dedicated to ITGP. Other titles published by ITGP that may be of interest include:

- Once more unto the Breach

  www.itgovernance.co.uk/shop/p-985.aspx

- Information Security Breaches: Avoidance and Treatment based on ISO27001

  www.itgovernance.co.uk/shop/p-601.aspx

- The True Cost of Information Security Breaches and Cyber Crime

www.itgovernance.co.uk/shop/p-1338.aspx.

We also offer a range of off-the-shelf toolkits that give comprehensive, customisable documents to help users create the specific documentation they need to properly implement a management system or standard. Written by experienced practitioners and based on the latest best practice, ITGP toolkits can save months of work for organisations working towards compliance with a given standard.

To see the full range of toolkits available please visit:

www.itgovernance.co.uk/shop/c-129-toolkits.aspx.

Books and tools published by IT Governance Publishing (ITGP) are available from all business booksellers and the following websites:

www.itgovernance.eu   *www.itgovernanceusa.com*

www.itgovernance.in   *www.itgovernancesa.co.za*

www.itgovernance.asia.

Training Services

IT Governance offers an extensive portfolio of training courses designed to educate information security, IT governance, risk management and compliance professionals. Our classroom and online training programmes will help you develop the skills required to deliver best practice and compliance to your organisation. They will also enhance your career by providing you with industry standard certifications and increased peer recognition. Our range of courses offer a structured learning path from Foundation to Advanced level in the key topics of information security, IT governance, business continuity and service management.

ISO/IEC 27001:2013 is the international management standard that helps businesses and organisations throughout the world develop a best-in-class Information Security Management System. Knowledge and experience in implementing and maintaining ISO27001 compliance are considered to be essential to building a successful career in information security. We have the world's first programme of certificated ISO27001 education with Foundation, Lead Implementer, Risk Management and Lead Auditor training courses. Each course is designed to provide delegates with relevant knowledge and skills and an industry-recognised qualification awarded by the International Board for IT Governance Qualifications (IBITGQ).

Full details of all IT Governance training courses can be found at *www.itgovernance.co.uk/training.aspx*.

Professional Services and Consultancy

Your mission to plug critical security gaps will be greatly assisted by IT Governance consultants, who have advised hundreds of information security managers in the adoption of ISO27001 Information Security Management Systems (ISMS).

The organisation's assets, security and data systems, not to mention its reputation, are all in your hands. A major security breach could spell disaster. Timely advice and support from IT governance experts will enable you to identify the threats, assess risks and put in place the necessary controls before there's an incident.

At IT Governance, we understand that information, information security and information technology are always business issues, and not just IT ones. Our consultancy services assist you in managing information security strategies in harmony with business goals, conveying the right messages to your colleagues to support decision-making.

For more information about IT Governance Consultancy, see: *www.itgovernance.co.uk/consulting.aspx*.

ITG Resources

Newsletter

IT governance is one of the hottest topics in business today, not least because it is also the fastest moving.

You can stay up to date with the latest developments across the whole spectrum of IT governance subject matter, including; risk management, information security, ITIL and IT service management, project governance, compliance and so much more, by subscribing to ITG's core publications and topic alert emails.

Simply visit our subscription centre and select your preferences: *www.itgovernance.co.uk/newsletter.aspx.*

EU for product safety is Stephen Evans, The Mill Enterprise Hub, Stagreenan, Drogheda, Co. Louth, A92 CD3D, Ireland. (servicecentre@itgovernance.eu)

www.ingramcontent.com/pod-product-compliance
Lightning Source LLC
LaVergne TN
LVHW022259060326
832902LV00020B/3165